THIS JOURNAL BELONGS TO

_____

My Daily Devotional

PRAYER JOURNAL

A 365-DAY
SCRIPTURE
READING PLAN
& DEVOTIONAL
FOR WOMEN

BARBOUR

PUBLISHING

ISBN 978-1-63609-681-0

Portions of the text previously published as *Daily Wisdom for Women 2020 Devotional Collection*, by Barbour Publishing.

Prayer prompts written by Vickie Phelps.

Cover Design: Greg Jackson, Thinkpen Design

Published by Barbour Publishing, Inc., 1810 Barbour Drive, Uhrichsville, Ohio 44683, www.barbourbooks.com

Our mission is to inspire the world with the life-changing message of the Bible.

Member of the
Evangelical Christian
Publishers Association

Printed in China.

WELCOME TO
My Daily Devotional
Prayer Journal

Life holds ongoing changes for everyone, including Christians. As a believer, you're a new creature in Christ. But your story doesn't end there. For if you allow Him, God will continue His work to transform you, making you more and more like Jesus. Through His Word and power, God's Spirit plunges into the very depths of your being, equipping you with a new heart and mind, which changes up your thoughts and attitude, which, in turn, transforms your actions and behavior.

And you play a huge part in your transformation by your obedience and your prayers. Through them and by them, God molds and reshapes you, your situations, and your paths in accordance with His plan.

To help support you amid all the transformations going on within and without, here you'll find 365 scripture-based readings about how to trust, follow, and walk with the unchangeable three—God, Jesus, and the Spirit—as you journey your way through your life, homing in on the new things God is doing in and for you (Isaiah 43:18–19).

As you read each devotion and focus verse, allow them to shed light on God, His Word, and His plan for you, helping you to become the woman God created you to be, beyond what you could ever expect, hope, or imagine.

The Editors

DAY 1

A Blessed Life

*Blessed is the one who does not walk in step with the wicked
or stand in the way that sinners take or sit in the company of
mockers, but whose delight is in the law of the LORD, and who
meditates on his law day and night. That person is like a tree
planted by streams of water, which yields its fruit in season and
whose leaf does not wither—whatever they do prospers.*

PSALM 1:1–3 NIV

. . . .

Want to live out the calendar year in a perpetual state of blessedness? You may be thinking, *That's not even possible!* Yet the truth is, once you've made the decision to become a Christ follower, you've been transformed. . .and blessings—and *so much more*—are yours. The Bible says so! (See 2 Corinthians 9:8 and many other verses throughout scripture.)

If you've accepted Christ as Savior, your life is made new. Gone are your old ways of thinking. . .you're on the path to righteous living! And, what's more, each and every one of the hundreds of promises in scripture are *yours* to claim.

Today, on this first day of the year, make a conscious decision to delight in the Lord. . .to meditate on His law. Don't live so you miss out on the blessings that God's Word promises. Let the theme of your year be one of beautiful transformation. You won't regret it!

Prayer Prompt:

What can you do today to delight yourself in the Lord and continue to live in a state of blessedness? Ask God how to live and delight yourself in Him as you claim His blessings.

....

....

....

....

....

....

....

....

....

....

....

....

....

....

....

....

....

Father God, I claim Your promise of blessing.
If Your Word says it, I believe it!

DAY 2

A Faithful Focus

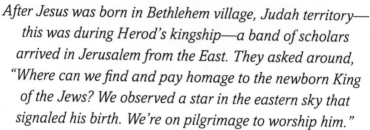

*After Jesus was born in Bethlehem village, Judah territory—
this was during Herod's kingship—a band of scholars
arrived in Jerusalem from the East. They asked around,
"Where can we find and pay homage to the newborn King
of the Jews? We observed a star in the eastern sky that
signaled his birth. We're on pilgrimage to worship him."*
MATTHEW 2:1–2 MSG

. . . .

The Savior of the world was born. . .and the wise men, seeing the star that signaled His arrival, began their "pilgrimage"—their journey—to find and worship Him. These men had been waiting for Jesus. . .anticipating His birth.

The lengthy journey of the wise men was likely arduous and not without uncertainty along the way. But still they persevered in faith and with focus. They traveled on, knowing they would eventually have the honor of being in the very presence of the long-awaited Messiah, where they could shower Him with gifts—gold, frankincense, and myrrh—and praise and adoration (Matthew 2:11).

Like the wise men, our faith journey will not come without trials and tribulation. But we continue on, knowing that if we remain faithful and focused, actively seeking Jesus, He will see to it that we safely reach our final, heavenly destination—where we will spend eternity in praise and adoration of Him!

Prayer Prompt:

What can you do to persevere in the face of uncertainty and difficulty? As you pray, ask God to keep your mind on Jesus today.

....

....

....

....

....

....

....

....

....

....

....

....

....

....

....

....

....

Father God, when the worries of the world threaten to distract me from You, I trust You will help me to maintain a faithful focus. I praise You!

From Despair to Hope

Many are saying of me, There is no help for him in God.
Selah [pause, and calmly think of that]! But You, O Lord,
are a shield for me, my glory, and the lifter of my head.
With my voice I cry to the Lord, and He hears and answers me
out of His holy hill. Selah [pause, and calmly think of that]!

PSALM 3:2–4 AMPC

. . . .

In Psalm 3, we encounter these moving words of David, whose enemies likely longed to see their words—"There is no help for him in God"—come true, hoping for David's total destruction. And knowing the sin that he had committed with Bathsheba, he probably thought their hurtful words had some merit.

David could have easily allowed himself to be swayed by the world's words. But instead of allowing himself to wallow in despair, David recalled God's power, His faithfulness, His protection, and His love. David trusted in God and chose to cling to and focus on His heavenly Father, who "hears" and would no doubt restore David's joy.

As Christ followers, we can trust in our prayer-hearing God just as David did and know without a doubt that God will lift our heads, offering us His protection and salvation from a world that wishes for our downfall. With our trust in God Almighty, we will overcome!

Prayer Prompt:

How can you praise God during the attack of criticism? Pray for those who criticize you and ask God to encourage both of you.

....

....

....

....

....

....

....

....

....

....

....

....

....

....

....

....

*Father God, I praise You for the hope
and joy I can only find in You!*

DAY 4

You Are Called

*One day as Jesus was walking along the shore of the Sea of Galilee,
he saw two brothers—Simon, also called Peter, and Andrew—
throwing a net into the water, for they fished for a living. Jesus
called out to them, "Come, follow me, and I will show you how to
fish for people!" And they left their nets at once and followed him.*
MATTHEW 4:18–20 NLT

. . . .

If you've accepted Christ as the Lord and leader of your life, think back
to what your life was like before you had a relationship with Him. Where
was your focus? Were you ready and willing to drop your plans and follow
God's lead, exchanging your plans for His?

When Jesus called Peter and Andrew, they immediately left their
livelihood—including their nets, their boat, and more—behind, and they
followed Him. The book of Matthew doesn't say they "thought about it,
weighing the pros and cons, and then decided at a later date." No. They
left their nets at once!

When you hear God's call upon your heart, drop everything. *Drop. It.
All. Immediately!* God wants to use you—*yes, you!*—to fulfill His purpose
in this world, which requires a life transformed from service of "self" to
serving others. Surrender all. Say yes to God's plan today, and experience life as you've never imagined!

Prayer Prompt:

How have you heard God's call upon your heart? Allow Him to use
you for His purpose in the world.

....

....

....

....

....

....

....

....

....

....

....

....

....

....

....

....

....

....

Dear Jesus, I surrender all to You. I will follow
You today and all my days to come!

DAY 5

Bringing Light to the Darkness

*"You're here to be light, bringing out the God-colors in the world.
God is not a secret to be kept. We're going public with this, as public as
a city on a hill. If I make you light-bearers, you don't think I'm going
to hide you under a bucket, do you? I'm putting you on a light stand.
Now that I've put you there on a hilltop, on a light stand—shine! Keep
open house; be generous with your lives. By opening up to others, you'll
prompt people to open up with God, this generous Father in heaven."*

MATTHEW 5:14–16 MSG

When you say yes to a relationship with Jesus Christ, something deep inside of you transforms. You now carry within yourself the light of the Holy Spirit . . .and along with this beautiful transformation comes purpose and responsibility:

1. Be a light to others. Shine!
2. Go public with the change God has made in your life. Don't keep it a secret!
3. Be generous with others. Share!

In doing so, you're sure to prompt others to open their hearts to the grace and love of Jesus.

When you know your future is secure because of your relationship with the heavenly Creator, why would you even want to keep it to yourself? When He works in your heart, you'll want to shout His praises from the rooftops for all to hear.

Prayer Prompt:

What are some ways you can let your light shine to others? Ask God to make you a beacon in a dark world.

....

....

....

....

....

....

....

....

....

....

....

....

....

....

....

....

....

....

Father God, I will shine my light for You today!

DAY 6

Unfailing Love

Lord, do not rebuke me in your anger or discipline me in your wrath. Have mercy on me, Lord, for I am faint; heal me, Lord, for my bones are in agony. My soul is in deep anguish. How long, Lord, how long? Turn, Lord, and deliver me; save me because of your unfailing love.

PSALM 6:1–4 NIV

David was deeply anguished. Thoughts of his sinful state likely kept him up at night. His troubles weighed heavily on his soul. His words here in Psalm 6 reveal his absolute dread of God's anger and discipline. In fact, David begs for God's mercy.

And after airing his negative thoughts and feelings, David then acknowledges that God is fully capable of delivering him from his torment. Because God is a God of "unfailing love," David knows, without a doubt, that all will be well if it is God's will for his life. And that's that!

Like David, do thoughts of your sinful past interfere with a good night's sleep? Do your troubles weigh heavily on your spirit? Today is the day to approach the heavenly Father in bold confidence. Let Him know that you trust Him with the outcome. You trust Him to see you through to better days ahead. He will hear you, and He will act. Praise Him!

Prayer Prompt:

Are you weighed down by negative thoughts and feelings? Commit them to God during your prayer time, and trust Him to give you peace.

....

....

....

....

....

....

....

....

....

....

....

....

....

....

....

....

Heavenly Father, I trust You for my comfort. . .for deliverance from my troubles. Thank You for saving me!

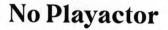

No Playactor

"Be especially careful when you are trying to be good so that you don't make a performance out of it. It might be good theater, but the God who made you won't be applauding. When you do something for someone else, don't call attention to yourself. You've seen them in action, I'm sure—'playactors' I call them— treating prayer meeting and street corner alike as a stage, acting compassionate as long as someone is watching, playing to the crowds. They get applause, true, but that's all they get. When you help someone out, don't think about how it looks. Just do it—quietly and unobtrusively. That is the way your God, who conceived you in love, working behind the scenes, helps you out."

MATTHEW 6:1–4 MSG

. . . .

If you were being completely honest with yourself, would you say there have been times (more often than you'd like to admit) that you've helped others just for the attention—to get noticed for your good deeds? A "look what I did" kind of performance? If so, how does it make you feel?

How much better would it feel to do something good for an audience of one: Jesus? Don't be a "playactor." Rather, work behind the scenes like Jesus. God will notice your good deeds done quietly and in secret, and that's what really matters!

Prayer Prompt:

What are your motives behind your good deeds? Ask Jesus to help you keep your motives pure.

....

....

....

....

....

....

....

....

....

....

....

....

....

....

....

....

....

Father God, help me not do things for the recognition I'll get from others. I want to do good for You and You alone!

Beautiful Lilies

"That is why I tell you not to worry about everyday life—whether you have enough food and drink, or enough clothes to wear. Isn't life more than food, and your body more than clothing? Look at the birds. They don't plant or harvest or store food in barns, for your heavenly Father feeds them. And aren't you far more valuable to him than they are? Can all your worries add a single moment to your life? And why worry about your clothing? Look at the lilies of the field and how they grow. They don't work or make their clothing, yet Solomon in all his glory was not dressed as beautifully as they are. And if God cares so wonderfully for wildflowers that are here today and thrown into the fire tomorrow, he will certainly care for you. Why do you have so little faith?"

MATTHEW 6:25–30 NLT

Do you often worry about everyday things in life—like food and clothing? Or do you instead leave all your worries in the hands of your perfectly capable provider, your heavenly Father?

If you're a worrywart, these verses from the Gospel of Matthew should set your mind to rest and lead you to a place of tranquil transformation. . . from worry to wonder! For the God who cares for the birds and wildflowers also cares for you!

Prayer Prompt:

Are you a worrier? Verbalize your concerns to God, and trust Him to take care of your needs for today and in the days to come.

....

....

....

....

....

....

....

....

....

....

....

....

....

....

....

....

....

Heavenly Father, I trust You—the caretaker of all creation. . .the birds, the beautiful lilies, and me!

DAY 9

Everything Set Right

I'm whistling, laughing, and jumping for joy; I'm singing your song, High God. The day my enemies turned tail and ran, they stumbled on you and fell on their faces. You took over and set everything right; when I needed you, you were there, taking charge.

PSALM 9:1–4 MSG

. . . .

In this psalm we find David singing praises to God, the doer of great things—the one who sets everything to right. David isn't praising half-heartedly, oh no. He's putting his *whole* heart and soul into it. He's "whistling, laughing, and jumping for joy." His *entire being* is directed in praise to almighty God.

We can experience this same kind of bubbling-up joy that David did. Because when hard times come, when nothing is going our way, we can trust our heavenly Father with the outcome. He can—He *will*—transform our troubles. He knows just what we need. And if we give control over to Him, He'll set everything right in His perfect timing.

Ask God to take charge of your life, starting right this very minute. And once He begins to work, remember how He is always there when you need Him. Share with others the great things He has done for you. Telling of God's awesomeness. . .what a wonderful way to praise Him!

Prayer Prompt:

What are you praising God for today? Put your whole heart into praising Him for His amazing goodness to you.

....

....

....

....

....

....

....

....

....

....

....

....

....

....

....

....

Today, I ask You to take complete charge of my life, Lord. No matter what, You are always the one who can set things right. I praise You!

A Strong Foundation

Everyone who hears these words of Mine and acts upon them [obeying them] will be like a sensible. . .man who built his house upon the rock. And the rain fell and the floods came and the winds blew and beat against that house; yet it did not fall, because it had been founded on the rock. And everyone who hears these words of Mine and does not do them will be like a stupid. . .man who built his house upon the sand. And the rain fell and the floods came and the winds blew and beat against that house, and it fell—and great and complete was the fall of it.
MATTHEW 7:24–27 AMPC

Obedience seems like such a stiff, serious, *b-o-r-i-n-g* subject, doesn't it? If you "obey," aren't you really giving up your own will, your own desires, to instead follow the path someone else—in this case, God—has set for you? And can that really lead to a fulfilling life?

These words of Jesus in Matthew 7 confirm that the answer is *yes*— obedience to God *always* leads to a better life, creating a strong, faith-filled foundation to help you stand firm when the storms of life blow and batter against your weary soul. Allow your faithful obedience to transform your life—willingly give up your *imperfect* will for His *perfect* plan. Your house will stand strong!

Prayer Prompt:

Are you having trouble giving up your will for God's will? Ask Him for help to submit to His plans for a fulfilling life.

....

....

....

....

....

....

....

....

....

....

....

....

....

....

....

....

....

....

Father God, help me build my house upon the Rock!

DAY 11

A Sure Faith

A centurion came to [Jesus]. . . . "Lord," he said, "my servant lies at home paralyzed, suffering terribly." Jesus said to him, "Shall I come and heal him?" The centurion replied, "Lord, I do not deserve to have you come under my roof. But just say the word, and my servant will be healed. For I myself am a man under authority, with soldiers under me. I tell this one, 'Go,' and he goes; and that one, 'Come,' and he comes. I say to my servant, 'Do this,' and he does it." When Jesus heard this, he was amazed and said to those following him, "Truly I tell you, I have not found anyone in Israel with such great faith."

MATTHEW 8:5–10 NIV

. . . .

"Just say the word, and my servant will be healed," the centurion said to Jesus (emphasis added). Can you imagine a greater, surer faith than that? Just a *word* was all he asked for. . .nothing more, nothing less.

The centurion didn't ask Jesus for some fancy, elaborate ceremony. He didn't even ask Jesus to come to his house! And Jesus' response? Amazement! In fact, the Bible tells us that Jesus hadn't found a single person in all of Israel who displayed that kind of sure faith.

As a Christ follower, do you have a sure faith? The heavenly Father will assure your uncertain heart today! Just ask!

Prayer Prompt:

What do you need from Jesus today? Ask Him to speak the word that will meet your need.

_____

_____

_____

_____

_____

_____

_____

_____

_____

_____

_____

_____

_____

_____

_____

_____

Father, I thank You for Your Word that gives me blessed assurance!

DAY 12

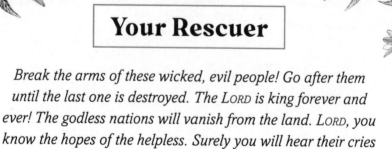

Your Rescuer

Break the arms of these wicked, evil people! Go after them until the last one is destroyed. The LORD is king forever and ever! The godless nations will vanish from the land. LORD, you know the hopes of the helpless. Surely you will hear their cries and comfort them. You will bring justice to the orphans and the oppressed, so mere people can no longer terrify them.
PSALM 10:15–18 NLT

. . . .

Have you ever felt completely and utterly helpless because of the hurt someone has caused you? Just. . .stuck. With nowhere to turn?

Maybe you've been bullied. . .cheated on. . .beaten down. . .by someone you love or by an acquaintance or even a stranger. And maybe you felt like no one had your back. No one was there to pick you up, dust you off, and breathe new life into your weary soul. If this is part of your story, sister, there is hope! As Psalm 10 states: "LORD, you know the hopes of the helpless. Surely you will hear their cries and comfort them."

And this same Lord Jesus promises to deliver you today. For He is your rescuer. . .the justice-bringer. When you know Him as Your Lord and Savior, you never need to feel helpless or hopeless again. Thank Him today for bringing you peace and comfort. . .for offering the ultimate deliverance from hard things: heaven, your glorious and final destination!

Prayer Prompt:

Do you feel hopeless today? Believe the promises of God's Word that He will bring justice and give you hope.

....

....

....

....

....

....

....

....

....

....

....

....

....

....

....

....

....

....

....

Lord Jesus, I look forward to the promise of heaven!

Courageous Faith

Just then a woman who had hemorrhaged for twelve years slipped in from behind and lightly touched his robe. She was thinking to herself, "If I can just put a finger on his robe, I'll get well." Jesus turned—caught her at it. Then he reassured her: "Courage, daughter. You took a risk of faith, and now you're well." The woman was well from then on.

MATTHEW 9:20–22 MSG

This woman mentioned in Matthew 9 had suffered from a health issue for twelve long years. She had likely spent everything she had on doctors who weren't able to heal her or even improve her bleeding issue. We can imagine that she was most certainly desperate, maybe on the verge of beyond hope.

But. . .Jesus. This woman's powerful combination of persistence and courage led her to take action—and in the crowd that followed Jesus, she reached out her arm to Him and touched His robe. And in that moment, she was healed from her bleeding issue.

When we know Jesus, we can *always* have a courageous faith. No matter what we're in need of, all we need to do is reach out to Him. And He will reassure us that all will be fine because He's there to see us through. Praise Him!

Prayer Prompt:

How do you need Jesus to intervene in your life? Ask Him for a persistent courageous faith to meet your need.

....

....

....

....

....

....

....

....

....

....

....

....

....

....

....

....

....

Father God, thank You for the courageous displays of faith
I can read about in Your Word. I'm done playing it safe.
Starting today, I will be courageous in my faith!

DAY 14

Pure and Unchanging

Into the hovels of the poor, into the dark streets where the homeless groan, God speaks: "I've had enough; I'm on my way to heal the ache in the heart of the wretched." God's words are pure words, pure silver words refined seven times in the fires of his word-kiln, pure on earth as well as in heaven.

PSALM 12:5–7 MSG

. . . .

If you've lived any amount of time on this earth, it's certain that another human being—a friend, a family member, a coworker—has let you down because of his or her empty promises. And, just as likely, you've disappointed someone in your life as well. As humans, we're often quick to make a promise and just as quick to fail in the follow-through.

But thankfully, when we've accepted Christ as our Lord and Savior, we can say with confidence, "He will never let us down." He's in the business of promise keeping; His promises are a sure thing. His words are pure.

The truth is:

Humans aren't trustworthy. . . God is.

Humans aren't faithful. . . God is.

Humans are promise breakers. . . God is a promise keeper.

Humans will fail us. . . God won't!

Where men and women fall short, God *always* comes through. His Word is pure and unchanging.

Prayer Prompt:

Has someone broken a promise they made to you? Pray that your faith will rest in God's promises rather than human words.

....

....

....

....

....

....

....

....

....

....

....

....

....

....

....

....

....

Promise-Keeper, my Savior, I trust in You alone. You are all that is pure and right in the world. Thank You for being true to Your Word. You never let me down!

DAY 15

A Lovely Cause for Celebration

Take a good look at me, GOD, my God; I want to look life in the eye, so no enemy can get the best of me or laugh when I fall on my face. I've thrown myself headlong into your arms—I'm celebrating your rescue. I'm singing at the top of my lungs, I'm so full of answered prayers.

PSALM 13:3–6 MSG

. . . .

When you become a Christian and accept Jesus Christ as Lord and leader of your life, it's cause for serious celebration. Out with the old and in with the new, you're a beautifully transformed creation of almighty God!

The old you may have been fearful, insecure, doubtful, depressed, and dismayed. But when you accepted the gift of salvation, you surely felt a significant shift within your spirit. With the power of Jesus Christ in you, you're rescued from the burdens that weigh down the soul. And a growing relationship with the heavenly Father brings about feelings of courage, confidence, belief, joy, and contentment. . .just the things you need to fulfill the wonderful purpose God has for you!

If you've chosen to be a Christ follower, make the choice to celebrate—starting today! Thank Him for the gift of salvation. Sing at the top of your lungs! Praise the Lord for your lovely, transformed life!

Prayer Prompt

Have you praised the Lord for His presence in your life? Starting today, take time to show Him how thankful you are for the new life you have in Christ.

....

....

....

....

....

....

....

....

....

....

....

....

....

....

....

*Father God, thank You for the lovely transformation
You've begun in my life. Because of You, I am
a new creation, and I am so grateful!*

Say Yes!

"Anyone who welcomes you welcomes me, and anyone who welcomes me welcomes the one who sent me. Whoever welcomes a prophet as a prophet will receive a prophet's reward, and whoever welcomes a righteous person as a righteous person will receive a righteous person's reward. And if anyone gives even a cup of cold water to one of these little ones who is my disciple, truly I tell you, that person will certainly not lose their reward."
MATTHEW 10:40–42 NIV

In today's superbusy, run-here-run-there, don't-stop-for-a-minute world, do you ever take the time to pause in the moment and consider the needs of another human being? Or are you stretched so thin that you just can't take a minute to think of anyone other than yourself?

If you find yourself hurried and harried, pause. Right. This. Very. Minute. Quiet your heart. Ask Jesus to calm the chaos in your spirit. Because He *can*. . .and He *will*!

Once your spirit finds the calm it craves, you'll be better able to *really* see the needs of others. Look around! Is there someone who could use your kindness, your hospitality, your generosity? Pinpoint what that person needs—then take action!

In caring for the needs of others, it's as though you're caring for Jesus Himself. Say yes to meeting someone's need today. Say yes to Jesus!

Prayer Prompt:

Are you so focused on yourself that you're blind to the needs of others? Ask Jesus to show you someone else's needs today.

....

....

....

....

....

....

....

....

....

....

....

....

....

....

....

....

....

....

Jesus, thank You for helping me
recognize the needs of others!

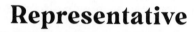

Representative

Lord, who may dwell in your sacred tent? Who may live on your holy mountain? The one whose walk is blameless, who does what is righteous, who speaks the truth from their heart; whose tongue utters no slander, who does no wrong to a neighbor, and casts no slur on others; who despises a vile person but honors those who fear the Lord; who keeps an oath even when it hurts, and does not change their mind; who lends money to the poor without interest; who does not accept a bribe against the innocent. Whoever does these things will never be shaken.

PSALM 15:1–5 NIV

As you go about your day-to-day life, did you know that you are a representative? . . . It's true. The clothes you wear. The speech that comes from your lips. The company you keep. The kindness you show (or don't show) to others. Each of these things says something about you. They tell something to the world about who—and *whose*—you are!

So who do you represent? Do you speak truth, demonstrate kindness, keep promises, and give to others in need? Or could you do better in some areas? Are you a good representative of the King of kings? Today, ask the heavenly Father to help you be a light for Him so others can see His shining transformation within you!

Prayer Prompt:

Who are you representing today? Ask Jesus to make you His ambassador to the world.

....

....

....

....

....

....

....

....

....

....

....

....

....

....

....

....

....

....

....

Father, help me choose to do the right thing all the time. I want to represent You well!

More Jesus

*"Are you tired? Worn out? Burned out on religion?
Come to me. Get away with me and you'll recover your life.
I'll show you how to take a real rest. Walk with me and work
with me—watch how I do it. Learn the unforced rhythms of
grace. I won't lay anything heavy or ill-fitting on you. Keep
company with me and you'll learn to live freely and lightly."*
MATTHEW 11:28–30 MSG

When was the last time you had a real, honest-to-goodness rest? The kind that refreshes you both mentally and physically, that makes you feel completely revitalized and alive?

If that sounds like wishful thinking—if your mind tells you, *Yeah, right! I haven't had a good rest in at least ten years—and there's no end in sight for me!*—take these words from Matthew 11 to heart. Jesus says, "Get away with me. . . . I'll show you how to take a real rest." What a promise!

Instead of more *busy* in your life, get more of *Jesus*. He is just what your weary soul needs. He will pull you from the depths of your day-to-day burnout and give you rest like you've never experienced it before—a rest that leads to free and light living! Praise Him!

Prayer Prompt:

Are you suffering from burnout? Pray for the rest and strength you need. God will supply them.

....

....

....

....

....

....

....

....

....

....

....

....

....

....

....

....

....

Father God, Rest-Giver, comfort my world-weary soul today. I am exhausted! I trust You to show me the way to refreshing rest. Thank You!

Knowing He Will Answer

I am praying to you because I know you will answer, O God. Bend down and listen as I pray. Show me your unfailing love in wonderful ways. By your mighty power you rescue those who seek refuge from their enemies. Guard me as you would guard your own eyes. Hide me in the shadow of your wings.

PSALM 17:6–8 NLT

"Bend down and listen as I pray," says the psalmist, who expresses his expectation that God will answer him. He trusts that the heavenly Father's love for him is so big, so guaranteed, that nothing—absolutely *nothing*—can get in the way of that.

Imagine God bending down from heaven, intently looking you in the eye—you have His full attention. He's focused and waiting to hear what you have to share with Him. Now get this: that's what praying to God is really like. He is *that* focused on you, sister! Talking with Him is like having a conversation with a friend who's the best listener on earth.

So if you've ever questioned whether the Father hears everything that's on your heart, ask Him to assure your spirit, to help you move from uncertain to knowing. Then thank Him for His love, one that is bigger than anything you could ever imagine.

Prayer Prompt:

Have you ever wondered if God hears your prayers? Trust Him to listen to you and answer when you call.

....

....

....

....

....

....

....

....

....

....

....

....

....

....

....

*Heavenly Father, thank You for being the best listener
a girl could ever hope for. Thank You for helping
to grow my trust in Your unfailing love!*

DAY 20

Finding Shelter in the Storms

I love you, LORD; you are my strength. The LORD is my rock, my fortress, and my savior; my God is my rock, in whom I find protection. He is my shield, the power that saves me, and my place of safety. I called on the LORD, who is worthy of praise, and he saved me from my enemies.

PSALM 18:1–3 NLT

How do you typically react when life's storms are raging around you? Imagine receiving a dreaded phone call with someone's news of failing health. Or finding a lifelong friend has unexpectedly turned her back on you. Or discovering a beloved child has made another poor life choice.

Do you cower in fear? Are you drained of all hope, not knowing where to turn for safety and shelter? Or do you look up to your protector—the almighty God—who is a rock, a fortress, a Savior who won't allow you to be enveloped by the pelting rain and gale-force winds?

When you have accepted Jesus as Lord and leader of your life, you have a protector on standby. He's waiting and ready to step in and provide shelter, a safe place where you will find strength and security just when you need it most. Call out to Him, and He will see you through the storm. Hold tightly to Him today!

Prayer Prompt:

What is making you anxious today? Ask God to give you His peace and protection.

....

....

....

....

....

....

....

....

....

....

....

....

....

....

....

....

....

*Father, You are worthy of all my praise. In You I
find the peace and protection my soul craves.*

DAY 21

Beautiful Beginnings

GOD made my life complete when I placed all the pieces before him. When I got my act together, he gave me a fresh start. Now I'm alert to GOD's ways; I don't take God for granted. Every day I review the ways he works; I try not to miss a trick. I feel put back together, and I'm watching my step. GOD rewrote the text of my life when I opened the book of my heart to his eyes.

PSALM 18:20–24 MSG

. . . .

Think about where you are in your life story. . . . Are the chapters before you met Jesus overflowing with one hot mess after another? Bad choices? Jumbled thoughts? Unclear direction? If so, what about *after*?

While life with Jesus certainly isn't all sunshine, rainbows, and unicorns, this new way of living does have its perks. With God in the lead, you always have a guide to help you navigate the messiness of life. You have someone by your side to help you make sense of the madness, to turn your chaos into peace.

Truth is, God's story for you is so much better than anything you could ever write on your own. So don't attempt to write it all by yourself. Make sure you hand over the pen to the heavenly author Himself. He'll see to it that your story of transformation has a beautiful, eternal theme of hope and security.

Prayer Prompt:

Who is writing your story—you or God? Ask Him for direction to write your story for His glory.

....

....

....

....

....

....

....

....

....

....

....

....

....

....

....

....

....

....

....

....

....

Father, thank You for rewriting my life story!

Flawless!

As for God, his way is perfect: The LORD's word is flawless;
he shields all who take refuge in him. For who is God besides
the LORD? And who is the Rock except our God? It is God
who arms me with strength and keeps my way secure.
PSALM 18:30–32 NIV

Dictionary.com defines the word *flawless* as: "having no defects or faults, especially none that diminish the value of something" and "having no discernible blemishes or shortcomings; perfect." Can you name anyone or anything that fits these descriptions? Maybe a lovely red rose in full bloom. Your best friend, who is a stunning beauty. The fragrance of fresh-brewed coffee first thing in the morning. The smell of salty air floating on the warm ocean breeze.

While there are many things in life that bring us sheer delight because of their wonderful qualities, the truth is none of those things is truly perfect or flawless. But you *do* know someone who is the very definition of flawless Himself: the Lord and Savior Jesus Christ. And He alone offers just what you need—security, strength, protection, comfort, and more! He is your shield and your rock. He sets you on the right path with His flawless Word and ways.

Praise Him for drawing your heart near to His, for being the perfection you need today and all your days to come.

Prayer Prompt:

Who or what is your idea of perfection? Let Jesus show you His perfection through His Word and His life.

....

....

....

....

....

....

....

....

....

....

....

....

....

....

....

....

My Redeemer, I thank You for Your flawless ways,
for Your perfect Word that guides my life!

God's Perfect Laws

The law of the LORD is perfect, refreshing the soul.
The statutes of the LORD are trustworthy, making wise the
simple. The precepts of the LORD are right, giving joy to the
heart. The commands of the LORD are radiant, giving light to
the eyes. The fear of the LORD is pure, enduring forever. The
decrees of the LORD are firm, and all of them are righteous.

PSALM 19:7–9 NIV

Laws are created for the good of all people. They are meant to keep us safe, protect our rights, and more. Speed limits are put in place to keep the roads safer for traveling. And we have laws that guarantee basic human freedoms—freedom of speech, religion, and the press.

But no matter how good man-made laws are, they all fall short—which is why many laws are often amended over time. In contrast, the laws of our heavenly Father are "perfect," "trustworthy," and they stand firm forever. His commands are righteous because they stem from His goodness and love.

The bottom line? God is good. And obeying His laws and commands will *always* lead to good things as well. If you're in need of a soul refreshing today, ask Him to give you His wisdom and to lead you all your days. Commit to obeying His laws—and your heart will be filled with joy!

Prayer Prompt:

How do you feel about God's laws? Ask Him to place His laws in your heart so you can live in a way that pleases and honors Him.

....

....

....

....

....

....

....

....

....

....

....

....

....

....

....

....

....

Heavenly Father, thank You for Your perfect, enduring laws. You are so, so good, and I love You!

DAY 24

Nothing but Good Plans

In times of trouble, may the LORD answer your cry. May the name of the God of Jacob keep you safe from all harm. May he send you help from his sanctuary and strengthen you from Jerusalem. May he remember all your gifts and look favorably on your burnt offerings. May he grant your heart's desires and make all your plans succeed. May we shout for joy when we hear of your victory and raise a victory banner in the name of our God. May the LORD answer all your prayers.

PSALM 20:1–5 NLT

. . . .

Do you believe 100 percent, without a doubt, that the heavenly Father will answer *all* your prayers? Not that He will say yes to your every request—but that He will answer with a yes, no, or maybe later?

Whether you're asking God for hope, healing, help, or safety from harm, you can know with certainty that He will do what's best for you— He has nothing but good plans for you, sister! His promise in Jeremiah 29:11 (NIV) says, "For I know the plans I have for you. . .plans to prosper you and not to harm you, plans to give you hope and a future."

So pray with complete confidence to the one who offers protection, strength, hope, and success, and know that an answer is coming your way!

Prayer Prompt:

What is your response when God says no to your request? Pray for faith to trust His answers no matter what.

....

....

....

....

....

....

....

....

....

....

....

....

....

....

....

....

....

....

Heavenly Father, You love me and want only the best for me. Thank You for Your answers to my prayers!

The God of Possible!

Jesus said, "Bring them here." Then he had the people sit on the grass. He took the five loaves and two fish, lifted his face to heaven in prayer, blessed, broke, and gave the bread to the disciples. The disciples then gave the food to the congregation. They all ate their fill. They gathered twelve baskets of leftovers. About five thousand were fed.

MATTHEW 14:18–21 MSG

. . . .

The people who had been listening to Jesus all day were hungry. But instead of doing what seemed to make the most sense at the time—sending them away so they could seek out something to eat—Jesus asked for the five loaves and two fish to be brought to Him.

The famished crowd was impossibly large. Feeding a group of five thousand men, women, and children would have been no small task, even if the supplies had been readily available. But Jesus didn't hesitate to ask for what little food there was. He seemed quite sure of Himself—and remedy the situation, He did! Jesus multiplied the amount of food—enough that each person was able to eat—*and there were leftovers!*

When life throws seemingly impossible situations your way, remember the story of the five loaves and two fish, and know that the same God who fed the five thousand can handle whatever hardship you're facing today. After all, He's the *God of possible!*

Prayer Prompt:

What impossible situation are you facing today? Tell Jesus about your problem, and ask Him to work on your behalf.

Father God, I believe! I know You can help with any situation—even the impossible ones!

Called!

*"The Israelite cry for help has come to me, and I've seen
for myself how cruelly they're being treated by the Egyptians.
It's time for you to go back: I'm sending you to Pharaoh to
bring my people, the People of Israel, out of Egypt." Moses
answered God, "But why me? What makes you think that I could
ever go to Pharaoh and lead the children of Israel out of Egypt?"
"I'll be with you," God said. "And this will be the proof that I am
the one who sent you: When you have brought my people out of
Egypt, you will worship God right here at this very mountain."*

EXODUS 3:9–12 MSG

"Why me?" It's the first question Moses asked when God told him to lead the Israelites out of Egypt. Moses was unsure of his ability to pull off the task; he felt ill equipped to successfully do what God had called him to do.

We Christ followers today are not so different from Moses. Has God ever called you to do something for Him—something that made you hesitate before saying yes?

Lead a small group.

Go on a mission trip.

Serve in your church.

Give more. . .more of your time, talents, or treasures.

If God calls you to do something for His kingdom, He'll make sure you're equipped to complete the task. All you need to do is say yes!

Prayer Prompt:

What is God calling you to do today? Ask Him to equip you for the
job and give you the ability to carry it out.

....

....

....

....

....

....

....

....

....

....

....

....

....

....

....

....

....

....

What would You have me do, Father? My answer is yes!

Lifted Up!

*Here's the story I'll tell my friends when they come
to worship, and punctuate it with Hallelujahs: Shout Hallelujah,
you God-worshipers; give glory, you sons of Jacob; adore him,
you daughters of Israel. He has never let you down, never looked
the other way when you were being kicked around. He has never
wandered off to do his own thing; he has been right there, listening.*

PSALM 22:22–24 MSG

· ·

How do you lift up a friend who's down? Do you send her a small gift—
something you know she'll adore? Do you stop by to give her a hug and
a gentle word of encouragement? Do you take her out to lunch?

There are so many unique ways to lift someone's spirit. . .but truly
none of them has the lasting impact of a sweet reminder that God is there
for her. In fact, He's *always* been there for her. Share your heart along
with your personal faith story, because your story has the ability to leave
a lasting imprint on hearts who are open to hear it. And if the heavenly
Father's presence has been a constant encouragement in your life, you'll
be eager and willing to share it!

So what are you waiting for? Don't hesitate another minute! Share the
good news: God won't take His eyes off you, and He'll *never* let you down!

Prayer Prompt:

Do you know someone who needs a lift today? Encourage them by sharing something Jesus is doing in your life, and give God the glory for the opportunity.

....

....

....

....

....

....

....

....

....

....

....

....

....

....

....

Hallelujah! I praise You, Lord! I will give You the glory!

DAY 28

Erasing Your Fears

*The Lord is my shepherd; I shall not want. He makes me
lie down in green pastures. He leads me beside still waters.
He restores my soul. He leads me in paths of righteousness
for his name's sake. Even though I walk through the valley
of the shadow of death, I will fear no evil, for you are
with me; your rod and your staff, they comfort me.*

PSALM 23:1–4 ESV

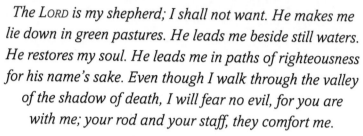

What makes you cringe in fear? Spiders? Snakes? Roller coasters? Tight spaces? Clowns? The dark? Evil? If you're being completely honest, you'll admit you're afraid of *something*. Each of us is afraid of one thing or another. That's the bad news. . . .

Now for the good news! No matter *what* you fear and no matter *how big* your fear, it can be erased—because of Jesus! He will calm your deepest, darkest fears. And because of His loving sacrifice on the cross, even the fear of death can be overcome! What a beautiful promise His Word gives you: "For God so loved the world that he gave his one and only Son, that whoever believes in him shall not perish but have eternal life" (John 3:16 NIV).

Jesus died so that you might live and spend eternity in heaven! If you haven't already, say yes to His gift of fearless living today!

Prayer Prompt:

What causes you to cringe in fear? Ask Jesus to give you peace when you're confronted with the things that make you afraid.

....

....

....

....

....

....

....

....

....

....

....

....

....

....

....

....

....

Lord Jesus, thank You for saving me!
Help me to overcome my fears!

DAY 29

Care and Keeping

The earth is the LORD's and the fullness thereof, the world and those who dwell therein, for he has founded it upon the seas and established it upon the rivers.

PSALM 24:1–2 ESV

· ·

Think about the things you own—your home, your car, your collectibles. Do you hold tightly to those things? Do you work hard to keep them clean and in good condition? Have you taken steps to keep them safe from harm and destruction? Do they give you a sense of pride?

Now think about our world and its ownership. Did you know that God has 100 percent ownership of the earth and everything in it? After all, He made the earth. . .He formed it. . .He filled it with life. He is ruler over all! And everything on this planet has been lent to you and to me. And we are charged with the care and keeping of it.

If you take such amazing care of your own possessions, what better care should you give to the heavenly Creator's workmanship? Today think about some things you might want to change in the ways you live, work, and play on this planet. Then ask God to help you follow through on your actions.

Prayer Prompt:

What can you do to take better care of God's world? Ask God to make you a caretaker of His creation.

_____

_____

_____

_____

_____

_____

_____

_____

_____

_____

_____

_____

_____

_____

_____

_____

_____

Lord Jesus, I thank You for Your creation. I want to take utmost care of the things You've entrusted to me. May my efforts in doing so be a good example to others.

DAY 30

The Faith Perfecter

*And Jesus rebuked the demon, and it came out of him, and the boy
was healed instantly. Then the disciples came to Jesus privately and
said, "Why could we not cast it out?" He said to them, "Because of
your little faith. For truly, I say to you, if you have faith like a grain
of mustard seed, you will say to this mountain, 'Move from here to
there,' and it will move, and nothing will be impossible for you."*

MATTHEW 17:18–21 ESV

If you've been a Christian for a long time, you're quite familiar with Jesus'
parable of the mustard seed. And while you may know that a mustard
seed is quite tiny, you may not know that the length of a mustard seed
can be as little as one millimeter! And Jesus used this *minuscule* seed to
make a *very big* point in His story.

His disciples asked Jesus why they were unable to cast out the demon themselves. Without hesitation, Jesus replied that they didn't have
enough faith—*but* with a mustard-seed-sized faith, they could move
mountains! In fact, He even added, "*Nothing* will be impossible for you"
(emphasis added).

What is the size of your faith? Are you moving mountains, sister?
Or does your faith need some growing? Either way, talk to the one who
holds the world in the palm of His hands—He's the author and perfecter
of your faith (Hebrews 12:2).

Prayer Prompt:

How do you measure your faith? Pray that your faith will grow into mountain-moving proportions.

....

....

....

....

....

....

....

....

....

....

....

....

....

....

....

....

....

Father God, help me move mountains!

DAY 31

Perfectly in Step

Clear my name, GOD; I've kept an honest shop. I've thrown in my lot with you, GOD, and I'm not budging. Examine me, GOD, from head to foot, order your battery of tests. Make sure I'm fit inside and out so I never lose sight of your love, but keep in step with you, never missing a beat.

PSALM 26:1–3 MSG

While he certainly hadn't lived a perfect life, the psalmist David was confident that he had walked in the Lord's truth. He had a genuine trust and ever-growing relationship with his heavenly Father. And so he requested that God examine Him—he wanted to be sure he was spiritually fit. He knew that keeping in step with the Lord's plan would help him to fully experience the love of Christ while "never missing a beat."

So, dear one, what does this mean for you? If you've accepted Jesus Christ as Lord and leader of Your life, you share a bond with Him that can never be broken. Simply trust Him to keep your spiritual "fitness" in check, and you'll never lose sight of His amazing, unconditional love. You can be confident that, no matter what life brings, the Lord will keep you on the right path—staying in step with Him—so you won't waver in your Christian journey.

Prayer Prompt:

If God examined your life, what would He find? Ask Him to show you those things that might need to be removed and what should be added to your life.

_____

_____

_____

_____

_____

_____

_____

_____

_____

_____

_____

_____

_____

_____

_____

_____

Father, examine me; know my heart. I long to keep in step with You today and all my days to come.

Courageously Confident

Though an army besiege me, my heart will not fear; though war break out against me, even then I will be confident.

PSALM 27:3 NIV

. . . .

Some changes can turn your world upside down. It happened to the Israelites. They'd been slaves in Egypt for four hundred years. Then God called Moses to lead them to freedom. Ten plagues later, the Israelites were walking out of Egypt with all the goods they could carry.

But then God's people found themselves trapped between Pharaoh's army and the Red Sea. Driven by fear, they cried to Moses, "Why did you lead us here? It'd be better to be slaves in Egypt than to die here in the wilderness!" Moses answered their complaint, saying, "Do not be afraid. Stand firm and you will see the deliverance the LORD will bring you today. The Egyptians you see today you will never see again. The LORD will fight for you; you need only to be still" (Exodus 14:13–14 NIV). The Red Sea was parted, the Egyptian army destroyed, and God's people began their journey toward the Promised Land with God leading them in front and protecting them from behind.

God is with you. So don't wrestle with change—or Him. Just stand still, courageously confident He's clearing a new path just for you! As you do so, He'll transform your panic to peace.

Prayer Prompt:

What are you questioning God about today? Pray for the direction He wants you to take and trust Him to lead you.

....

....

....

....

....

....

....

....

....

....

....

....

....

....

....

....

....

....

Lord, I'm courageously confident You're with me,
paving a new path ahead, leading me to promised ground.

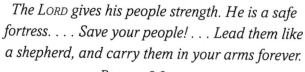

Carried Forever

*The L*ord *gives his people strength. He is a safe*
fortress. . . . Save your people! . . . Lead them like
a shepherd, and carry them in your arms forever.
PSALM 28:8–9 NLT

God had freed then led His people out of Egypt and toward the Promised Land. But while they were traveling through new territory, they once again complained. They were hungry. At least in their slavery, they'd been fed. Now where were they to get food?

In response, God sent quail and something new called *manna* (Exodus 16), which means, "What is it?" A few miles and complaints later, God sated their thirst by providing water from a rock (Exodus 17).

You may be thinking to yourself, *How can these people who've personally witnessed the great power of God be complaining to Him all the time?* Have you never grumbled to God after He'd brought you out of your comfort zone and into a new place?

Instead of lodging complaints, rely on the Rock, Jesus Christ. Know that He, your Bread and Living Water, will continually provide for you. Allow His presence within you to change you from a complainer to a praiser in all situations. There's no need to worry, for your Good Shepherd, the Mighty One, is carrying you in His arms.

Prayer Prompt:

Does life seem out of sorts, making you complain about your state of affairs? Ask Jesus to give you an attitude adjustment.

....

....

....

....

....

....

....

....

....

....

....

....

....

....

....

....

Good Shepherd, when I start to whine, please
change my attitude to one of gratitude,
seeing You as my forever provider.

DAY 34

God Makes the Impossible Possible

The disciples were astounded. "Then who in the world can be saved?"
they asked. Jesus looked at them intently and said, "Humanly
speaking, it is impossible. But with God everything is possible."
MATTHEW 19:25–26 NLT

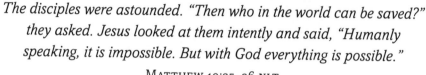

A rich young man asked Jesus what he needed to do to have eternal life. Jesus recited the Ten Commandments. Saying he'd kept all these, the young man asked what he still lacked. Jesus, knowing he loved his "stuff," said, "If you want to be perfect, go, sell your possessions and give to the poor, and you will have treasure in heaven. Then come, follow me" (Matthew 19:21 NIV). So the young man went away sad, having failed to meet Jesus' challenge.

All this prompted the disciples to ask, If this man couldn't make it into heaven, who could? Jesus said, "With God everything is possible."

You may have some challenges before you, ones you're not sure you can meet. Take heart. Jesus is making a new woman out of you and is ready to help you every step of the way. All you've got to do is pray. When you do, He'll make what seems impossible possible!

Prayer Prompt:

Are you facing seemingly impossible challenges? When you pray, ask Jesus to renew your faith in His ability to do the impossible.

....

....

....

....

....

....

....

....

....

....

....

....

....

....

....

Lord, I know there're areas where I fall short of what You'd have me be. Help me have faith, knowing that with You, there's always hope. For You make the impossible possible!

Turned Around by God

You have turned my mourning into joyful dancing. You have taken away my clothes of mourning and clothed me with joy, that I might sing praises to you and not be silent.
PSALM 30:11–12 NLT

· ·

Jesus told us we'd encounter trouble in this life (John 16:33). But along with that trouble, He promised that in Him we'd have peace.

Thus, when you encounter misfortune, when you lose someone you love, your job, your health, your trust in someone you counted on, call on God. Cry out to Him for help (Psalm 30:2). Beg Him to give you His comfort, a new perspective, His love, His balm of healing, His promise of hope, His strength to get through the next moment, hour, day, week. And little by little, or perhaps quite suddenly, you will find God has lifted your head, given you the courage and strength to look up to Him, filled your heart with song, and turned your mourning into joy.

Be assured that your God is a God of transformation. He alone is able to give you exactly what you need when you need it, prompting you to sing your praises to Him.

Prayer Prompt:

What kind of trouble has taken your song away? Ask God to put a song in your heart again and turn your mourning into dancing.

....

....

....

....

....

....

....

....

....

....

....

....

....

....

....

Thank You, Lord, for turning me around, for showing me the Son. With You in my life, I cannot help but dance and sing praises as You continue to bless me beyond all I can expect or imagine.

DAY 36

Heavenly Guardians

"See, I am sending an angel before you to protect you on your journey and lead you safely to the place I have prepared for you. Pay close attention to him, and obey his instructions."

EXODUS 23:20–21 NLT

Two blind men sitting by the side of the road heard that Jesus was going by. They yelled out to Him to have pity on them. The crowd told them to be quiet, yet the men would not. So Jesus stopped and called them to Him. Then He asked them a very important question: "What do you want me to do for you?" (Matthew 20:32 NLT). Jesus already knew the answer. But He wanted the blind men to voice their exact and definite desire in their own words. Their response, "Lord. . .we want to see" (Matthew 20:33 NLT), was their way of declaring their faith that Jesus could heal them. Jesus, feeling sorry for them, touched their eyes. Their sight was instantly restored, and they followed Him.

God has sent not just angels but His Son before you, to protect you on your travels, to help you through your transformations, to enhance your vision, to safely lead you where He wants you to go. Pay close attention to Him. Let Him know your desires. Obey His Word. And you too will see.

Prayer Prompt:

What keeps you from seeing the path you need to follow? Ask Jesus to open your eyes so you can follow wherever He leads.

....

....

....

....

....

....

....

....

....

....

....

....

....

....

....

....

Lord, I'm following close behind You. Lead me to the place You've already prepared for me. I could ask for no better protective and loving guide as I travel Your way.

Triumph

*"If you embrace this kingdom life and don't doubt God,
you'll not only do minor feats. . .but also triumph over
huge obstacles. This mountain, for instance, you'll tell,
'Go jump in the lake,' and it will jump. Absolutely everything,
ranging from small to large, as you make it a part of your
believing prayer, gets included as you lay hold of God."*
MATTHEW 21:21–22 MSG

· ·

With change comes obstacles. Things like fear, apprehensions, and worries, to name just a few. But Jesus tells you that if you have faith that He can do the impossible in and through you, if you trust Him for all things, you'll be able to triumph over anything and everything that comes your way. Those mountainous obstacles rising up before you—ones you find hard to get over, go under, or go through—will become so lightweight they'll disappear from view at your command!

Today look at the obstacles that are keeping you from becoming the woman God already knows you are. Pray, believing that whatever you ask God for, you will receive. Then tell those fears and frets and any other obstacles standing in your way to take a flying leap into the sea, never doubting that with God above, Jesus by your side, and the Spirit within, you *will* triumph!

Prayer Prompt:

What mountain are you facing? As you pray, ask God for faith to see that mountain removed or the clear way around it.

....

....

....

....

....

....

....

....

....

....

....

....

....

....

....

....

....

God, I know You can do the impossible in and through me.
So I'm believing I can and will level all hindrances standing
before me as I become the woman You created me to be.

Abundant Blessings

*What a stack of blessing you have piled up for
those who worship you, ready and waiting for
all who run to you to escape an unkind world.*

PSALM 31:19–20 MSG

. . . .

Jesse told his son David to go see how his brothers were faring in the valley of Elah. They were with Saul, part of the Israelite army, fighting the Philistines. When David got there, he heard Goliath taunting the Israelites. But when Jesse's oldest son, Eliab, saw David, he got angry, telling him to go back to minding their father's sheep. Then he said, "I know about your pride and deceit. You just want to see the battle!" (1 Samuel 17:28 NLT).

Undeterred, David approached King Saul, telling him he'd fight Goliath. Saul said, "Don't be ridiculous! . . . You're only a boy" (1 Samuel 1:33 NLT).

In the end, David, armed with only his faith, a sling, and some stones, walked out on the battlefield and brought down a giant.

Trust that God is always with you, waiting in the wings, ready to pour abundant blessings—courage, perseverance, and so much more—upon you, whenever and wherever they're needed. "Be brave. Be strong. Don't give up. Expect GOD to get here soon" (Psalm 31:24 MSG).

Prayer Prompt:

Which voices are you listening to—discouragement, criticism, fear?
Pray for courage to ignore those voices and face the giant in your life.

....

....

....

....

....

....

....

....

....

....

....

....

....

....

....

....

....

*Help me to be brave and strong in You, Lord. To not give up
or give in to the discouragement of others. I'm trusting in
You to help me fight my battles and supply all I need.*

DAY 39

A Willing Follower

*I [the Lord] will instruct you and teach you in the way you should
go; I will counsel you with My eye upon you. Be not like the horse or
the mule, which lack understanding, which must have their mouths
held firm with bit and bridle, or else they will not come with you.*

PSALM 32:8–9 AMPC

Sometimes a horse will lie down while someone is riding it, refusing to
go backward or forward. Mules can also be obstinate, rejecting any attempts to turn to the right or left, hence the cliché "stubborn as a mule."

Some horses and mules are good examples of how *not* to respond
to God's instructions and teachings. It's clear God doesn't want to have
to drag you down the road He's so carefully laid out for you. He doesn't
want to have to push you from behind. What He *does* want is for you to
go down His path willingly. To trust Him with your life. To understand
He's already gone down that road before you. He's checked everything
out. And it's safe for you to follow the course ahead.

If God is leading you into something new, rely on Him to protect
you, to keep you clear of quicksand and outlaws. And as you do so, He
promises you His love will surround you.

Prayer Prompt:

What kind of road is God asking you to follow? Pray for a willing heart to follow where He leads.

....

....

....

....

....

....

....

....

....

....

....

....

....

....

....

....

....

I want to be a willing follower of Your plan, Lord.
Surround me with Your love as I walk Your way.

Right-Side Up in Jesus

"Do you want to stand out? Then step down. Be a servant. If you puff yourself up, you'll get the wind knocked out of you. But if you're content to simply be yourself, your life will count for plenty."
MATTHEW 23:11–12 MSG

. . . .

Jesus has a way of turning things upside down. In the verses above, He's telling His followers to not be like the scribes and the Pharisees, the religious leaders of the day. They were always looking to take the seats of honor. They wanted to be noticed, to be thought of as above everyone and everything else.

Jesus has a different plan for those who love Him and Abba God. He doesn't want you to follow the old script, the "natural" one that runs inside your head. He wants you to step down. To be a servant. Just like He was. He wants you to not put on an act of holiness, of being better than others. But to be yourself. A woman who loves God with all her heart, soul, strength, and mind. A woman strong in God but humble in heart. A woman who will stand out because she's got the grace to give up her seat to someone who needs it more.

Prayer Prompt:

What kind of impression are you trying to make? Ask Jesus to give you a heart for service to others and remove the desire to be noticed.

Jesus, I want to be just like You. To serve others with a heart of love. To be content to be myself. To love as You love.

DAY 41

God to the Rescue

God's eye is on those who respect him, the ones who are looking for his love. He's ready to come to their rescue in bad times; in lean times he keeps body and soul together.
PSALM 33:18–19 MSG

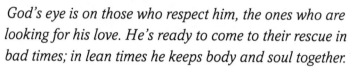

You wake up, pray, get ready for the day, and at some point, see, hear, or read about what's going on in the world. The news isn't good. Before you know it, your happy-go-lucky attitude has gone right out the window and a bit of fear and anxiety has crept in.

Jesus knew this would happen. In fact, He tells you, "When reports come in of wars and rumored wars, keep your head and don't panic. This is routine history; this is no sign of the end" (Matthew 24:6 MSG). He encourages you, saying, "Staying with it—that's what God requires. Stay with it to the end. . . . You'll be saved. All during this time, the good news—the Message of the kingdom—will be preached all over the world" (Matthew 24:13–14 MSG).

So when world news ignites your panic, go to God in prayer. He'll keep you together—body and soul. With the realization that He's all you need, your fear will morph into joy (Psalm 33:20).

Prayer Prompt:

What rumors and reports have you anxious and worried? Ask Jesus to keep you centered on the goal of loving God and loving others.

....

....

....

....

....

....

....

....

....

....

....

....

....

....

....

....

Love me, Lord, with all you've got—that's what I'm depending on [Psalm 33:22 MSG]. Help me focus on Your good news. Bring me to Your place of joy.

DAY 42

Everything Will Be Fine

"Get going. . . . I will send an angel before you.
. . . I will personally go with you."
EXODUS 33:1–2, 14 NLT

God wanted Moses to lead His people to a new place, a land flowing with milk and honey. Yet that new place was one the Egyptian-born Moses had never seen! And he was not to just *go* there himself but to lead God's people there!

Moses knew he was special to God, so he earnestly prayed, "If it is true that you look favorably on me, let me know your ways so I may understand you more fully and continue to enjoy your favor" (Exodus 33:13 NLT). God replied, "I will personally go with you, Moses, and I will give you rest—everything will be fine for you" (Exodus 33:14 NLT).

When God calls you down a new path, know He'll be with you. Instead of focusing on the what-ifs, stressing about the details, trust God's plan for you.

Remember that because God favors you, His angel has already arrived in the place you're bound. So relax. God promises, "Everything will be fine for you" because you walk with Him. And God keeps His promises, just as He "keeps" you.

Prayer Prompt:

When the Lord asks you to make a change, are you willing? Talk to
Him about the change, and trust Him to go with you.

....
....
....
....
....
....
....
....
....
....
....
....
....
....
....
....

*I'm not very fond of change, Lord. But I know You want me to
head down a different road. So, Lord, help me understand
You more so I can rest easy as we walk together.*

DAY 43

Open Doors

If your heart is broken, you'll find GOD right there; if you're kicked in the gut, he'll help you catch your breath. Disciples so often get into trouble; still, GOD is there every time.

PSALM 34:18–19 MSG

You were going along your merry way, walking the path God laid out for you, and all of a sudden, you're thrown for a loop. A loved one dies, a job is lost, your deductible is way more than you can afford, an unexpected illness has set in. Your heart is broken, your world falling apart, and you can't catch your breath much less a break.

In this world, your life can change on a dime. Yet one thing never changes: God. He's right there by your side. He's got the breath of life you need. He's got the love you're aching for.

Your job is to believe in Him and pray. To realize that "GOD's angel sets up a circle of protection around" (Psalm 34:7 MSG) you as you do so. To "worship GOD if you want the best." Why? Because "worship opens doors to all his goodness" (Psalm 34:9 MSG).

If you can't find the words to pray, no worries. God's "ears pick up every moan and groan" (Psalm 34:15 MSG) as the Holy Spirit transforms them into prayer (Romans 8:26–27). Simply go to God. He'll do the rest.

Prayer Prompt:

What has happened to make your world fall apart today? Don't be discouraged. Cry out to the Lord. He's aware of your problem.

....
....
....
....
....
....
....
....
....
....
....
....
....
....
....
....
....
....

Thank You, Lord, for always being there for me. As I pray and worship You, open Your doors of love and blessings.

DAY 44

Stirred Hearts and Hands

Then Moses called. . .every gifted artisan in whose heart the Lord had put wisdom, everyone whose heart was stirred, to come and do the work.
EXODUS 36:2 NKJV

. . . .

God has created you. And as a woman, made in His image, you too are a creator. One whom He's gifted with certain talents, skills, and abilities. And He's stirred your heart, signaling it's time for you to use your transformative powers in this day and age.

Perhaps you're using those talents now. Perhaps you're not. Lacking courage or confidence, you've decided to bury your skills. Or you began to respond to God's call to create then shrank back, discouraged by the remarks of others.

In the parable of the talents, Jesus makes it clear that God has given you certain abilities. And when you are faithful in "investing" that which He's provided, creating for the Creator, He'll praise you, saying, "Well done, my faithful daughter! You've been so faithful handling this little bit, I'll give you even more! Let's celebrate!" (Matthew 25:21).

Today, look at where you're using or burying your talents. Ask God for the confidence to continue or to begin using your gifts, certain that if He's provided them, He'll also provide the opportunities to use them. For His pleasure, appreciation, and approval only.

Prayer Prompt:

What talents or skills have you buried, afraid to use them? Ask God to stir your heart and allow Him to work through you for His glory.

....

....

....

....

....

....

....

....

....

....

....

....

....

....

....

Lord, You've stirred my heart to use my talents to serve You. Now move my hands. Show me what to do and where and when to do it.

An Extension of Jesus

"I was hungry, and you fed me. I was thirsty, and you gave me a drink. I was a stranger, and you invited me into your home. I was naked, and you gave me clothing. I was sick, and you cared for me. I was in prison, and you visited me."
MATTHEW 25:35–36 NLT

It's relatively easy to be kind to your loved ones, to help them when they need it. But how do you fare when it comes to feeding the hungry, quenching the thirsty, hosting the stranger, clothing the naked, tending the sick, and visiting the prisoner?

Jesus wants you to love and care for everyone, no matter what their color, sex, status, politics, wealth, health, or criminal record. For when you do so, you're showing you love and care for Jesus! He says, "I tell you the truth, when you did it to one of the least of these my brothers and sisters, you were doing it to me!" (Matthew 25:40 NLT).

Allow Jesus to help you become an extension of Him, beginning today. As you do so, you'll not only be rewarding others by being Jesus' hands and feet, but you'll be blessed by God, receiving all the riches His kingdom has to offer (Matthew 25:34).

Prayer Prompt:

What can you do to become an extension of Jesus? Pray for direction, asking Him to show you where you can help someone else.

....

....

....

....

....

....

....

....

....

....

....

....

....

....

....

....

....

Jesus, help me become an extension of You and Your love. Show me who to reach out to today.

DAY 46

Following Your Heart

Jesus. . .said to them, "Why do you trouble the woman?
For she has done a beautiful thing to me. . . . Truly, I say
to you, wherever this gospel is proclaimed in the whole world,
what she has done will also be told in memory of her."
MATTHEW 26:10, 13 ESV

At the home of Simon the leper, a nameless woman, transformed by Jesus, makes a name for herself. Here's what happened.

Jesus was sitting down to supper when a woman (who some Gospel writers say was Mary) poured a very expensive flask of perfume on His head. The disciples thought her act was a waste, for the perfume could've been sold and the money given to the poor. But Jesus disagreed, saying the woman acted from her heart, anointing Him for His upcoming burial. And the news of what she had done would be shared with the world.

Somedays you may feel nameless. That what you do in this world seems to have little effect. Yet when you allow God and His Spirit to work in your heart and hold sway over your actions, you too will find yourself doing beautiful things for Jesus, in His name. And your deeds on His behalf will never be forgotten.

Prayer Prompt:

Who are you trying to please—Jesus or the world around you? Ask Jesus to show you what you can do to bring glory to Him.

....
....
....
....
....
....
....
....
....
....
....
....
....
....
....
....

Show me what I can do today to worship You, Jesus.
To honor You as Your Spirit and God's Spirit work in me.
Direct my heart and move my hands to do beautiful things.

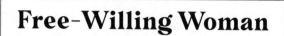

Free-Willing Woman

"If his offering is a burnt sacrifice of the herd, let him offer a male without blemish; he shall offer it of his own free will at the door of the tabernacle of meeting before the LORD."

LEVITICUS 1:3 NKJV

Are you getting all you can out of your relationship with God? Not sure? Well, perhaps it's time to consider a few things, one of which is how freely, how willingly you're offering all that you are—your body, faculties, dreams, spirit, mind, heart, and soul—to Jesus. Are you full of joy as you do so? Or are you whining, moaning, complaining, just following Jesus on the edges, sidling up to the altar, hoping He doesn't even notice you?

God wants you to freely offer yourself to Him, no holds barred. In Romans 12:1 (NLT), the apostle Paul makes it clearer, saying, "I plead with you to give your bodies to God because of all he has done for you. Let them be a living and holy sacrifice—the kind he will find acceptable. This is truly the way to worship him."

Today, before you do anything else, offer yourself to God. Do so willingly, freely, fearlessly. Trust Him to change you for the better. To build you up into the creature He has designed you to be. Then and only then will you be truly transformed.

Prayer Prompt:

Do you worship God willingly or out of obligation? As you pray, ask Him to give you a willing heart to serve Him.

....

....

....

....

....

....

....

....

....

....

....

....

....

....

....

....

....

....

I come to You today, Lord, freely and willingly, offering all of myself to You. Change me as You see fit. In You I trust.

Open Eyes

You're a fountain of cascading light, and you open
our eyes to light. Keep on loving your friends;
do your work in welcoming hearts.
PSALM 36:9–10 MSG

Every once in a while, a situation comes up in which we see our true colors, who we really are. At such times, we may not like what we see. That's what happened to Peter, the disciple who told Jesus he'd never desert Him (Matthew 26:33). But Jesus—who knows all and sees all— knew better. He knew that after He was arrested, Peter would deny being with Jesus or even knowing Him. And Peter did, in fact, deny Jesus—not once but three times! The third time, Jesus' words came back to Peter: "Before the rooster crows, you will deny me three times" (Matthew 26:75 MSG). That's when Peter, full of realization and regret, faced with who he truly was, went out and cried.

Yet later, after this scene and several more, Jesus rose again, had breakfast with His followers, and gave Peter another chance (John 21:15– 17). He instructed Peter to tend His sheep, a task that Peter took up immediately, never losing his faith in or denying Jesus ever again.

As you continue your transformational journey with Jesus, there may be times you'll trip up and discover you're not who you thought you were. Yet Jesus will never leave you. He'll find you once more, continue to love you, and work in your heart.

Prayer Prompt:

How do you handle moral failings and self-disappointment? As you pray, remember that Jesus loves you even when you fail.

....

....

....

....

....

....

....

....

....

....

....

....

....

....

....

....

....

....

....

....

Thank You, Jesus, for continuing
to love me, no matter what.

God's Road Map and Rewards

Don't worry about the wicked or envy those who do wrong. . . .
*Trust in the L*ORD *and do good. . . . Take delight in the L*ORD.
*. . . Commit everything you do to the L*ORD. *Trust him.*
PSALM 37:1, 3–5 NLT

. . . .

Many times, it seems that those who don't follow God, the ne'er-do-wells, are the ones who get all the breaks, make all the money, have all the power. You may find yourself envious of them or, even worse, spending your energy fretting about them because they seemingly have so much more than you.

Yet God wants you to consider the idea, the truth, that the wicked, the braggarts who seem to have it all today, will have nothing tomorrow. They will soon fade away like grass. So don't waste your time worrying about them. Instead, change your course. Follow God's tack, which has its own reward plan. It looks like this:

Trust in God and do good.   Then you'll live safely and prosper.
Take delight in God.   Then He'll give you your heart's desire.
Commit all you do to God.   Then He will act, make you shine.
                                              (Psalm 37:3–5)

Following God's road map outlined above seems like a much better way to expend your energy. For following the path of fretting only leads to a dead end, whereas trusting and delighting in God leads to a life filled with rewards.

Prayer Prompt:

What has you fretting about others and their lifestyle? Ask God to help you focus on His plan for your life, which is eternal.

....
....
....
....
....
....
....
....
....
....
....
....
....
....
....
....
....
....
....
....

Help me keep to Your road map, Lord.

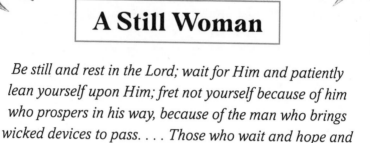

A Still Woman

*Be still and rest in the Lord; wait for Him and patiently
lean yourself upon Him; fret not yourself because of him
who prospers in his way, because of the man who brings
wicked devices to pass. . . . Those who wait and hope and
look for the Lord [in the end] shall inherit the earth.*

PSALM 37:7, 9 AMPC

. . . .

People who liked neither Jesus nor His ideas seemed to be holding the
upper hand. They'd made false accusations against Him, calling for His
death. So Jesus was arrested, beaten, mocked, and crucified. And the
moment He gave up His spirit, the temple's curtain was torn in two, "the
earth shook and the rocks were split" (Matthew 27:51 AMPC). The soldiers watching over Jesus were frightened as they realized, "Truly this
was God's Son!" (Matthew 27:54 AMPC).

Meanwhile, female followers of Jesus, who'd waited on Him and witnessed all this, were "looking on from a distance" (Matthew 27:55 AMPC).
After Jesus' body was laid in a cave, they "kept sitting there opposite the
tomb" (Matthew 27:61 AMPC). These women remained patient and still,
resting in their faith. They kept up their hope as they continued to wait
and look for their Lord.

God wants you to be such a woman. Ask Him to help you be a still,
restful, hopeful, and patient waiter, not worrying over the evil that's done
but looking to the good that overcomes.

Prayer Prompt:

What keeps you from being still and resting patiently on the Lord?
Ask the Lord to bring stillness into your life.

....

....

....

....

....

....

....

....

....

....

....

....

....

....

....

....

....

*Change me into a woman of stillness
as I wait for and hope in You.*

As Promised

*Moses and Aaron went into the Tent of Meeting, and when
they came out they blessed the people, and the glory of the Lord
[the Shekinah cloud] appeared to all the people [as promised].*
LEVITICUS 9:23 AMPC

. . . .

Moses, speaking for the Lord, charged Aaron to remain at the Tent of Meeting (Leviticus 8:35) and later told him what to sacrifice for the people's sins, saying, "This is the thing which the Lord commanded you to do, and the glory of the Lord will appear to you" (Leviticus 9:6 AMPC). After Aaron did as charged, God appeared to the people—just as He'd promised.

When Jesus died, His female followers went to His tomb and met an angel. He told them Jesus was no longer there, that "He has risen, as He said [He would do]" (Matthew 28:6 AMPC). The angel then said, "He is going before you to Galilee" (Matthew 28:7 AMPC), so the women headed there, meeting Jesus on the way. Jesus told them not to be afraid but to "tell My brethren to go into Galilee, and there they will see me" (Matthew 28:10 AMPC). They went and Jesus appeared. As He'd promised.

God has given you a charge, a purpose, a way to serve Him in this generation. He's reshaping you, molding you, to perform that charge. Be pliant to His touch, serve as asked, and you'll receive a reward for your faithfulness. As promised.

Prayer Prompt:

What charge or purpose has God given you to serve Him? Ask Him to shape you and mold you according to His plan.

....

....

....

....

....

....

....

....

....

....

....

....

....

....

....

....

....

Shape me into Your servant, Lord,
knowing You're my reward, as promised.

Ministering Angels

Immediately the [Holy] Spirit [from within] drove Him out into the wilderness (desert), and He stayed in the wilderness (desert) forty days, being tempted [all the while] by Satan; and He was with the wild beasts, and the angels ministered to Him [continually].

MARK 1:12–13 AMPC

. . . .

John baptizes Jesus in the Jordan. And just as He rises up out of the water, the heavens open and the Holy Spirit comes down like a dove upon Him. A voice booms from heaven, saying, "You are My Beloved Son; in You I am well pleased" (Mark 1:11 AMPC). Immediately afterward the Holy Spirit from within compels Jesus to go into the wilderness, alone, for forty days. During that time, as He's tempted by the devil, surrounded by wild beasts, and taken care of by angels, Jesus' trust in His Father never wavers, giving Him the power to defeat the devil's wiles.

God has called you His beloved. Your brother Jesus is by your side. Within you the Holy Spirit resides. Like Jesus, your trust in the God who loves and shapes you will be your greatest strength when you're out of your comfort zone. When you're in a new place, a type of wilderness filled with wild beasts, be assured that God and His angels are there to guard, keep, and comfort you (Psalm 91:11–12), just as they did Jesus.

Prayer Prompt:

How has God called you out of your comfort zone? Ask Him to keep you safe, knowing that His ministering angels are with you.

....

....

....

....

....

....

....

....

....

....

....

....

....

....

....

....

....

....

Thank You, Lord, Jesus, and Spirit for being
with me, for Your angels that protect me.

DAY 53

As the Son Rises

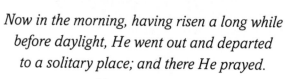

*Now in the morning, having risen a long while
before daylight, He went out and departed
to a solitary place; and there He prayed.*
MARK 1:35 NKJV

After Jesus' baptism, the forty days of temptation, the calling of His disciples, and His walk from Galilee to Capernaum, Jesus heads into the synagogue to teach. Later that afternoon and into the evening, He drives out demons and heals the multitudes. Heaven only knows what time He gets to bed. Yet the next day, Jesus rises before the sun, goes to a deserted place, and prays. There, with Abba God, Jesus receives the strength, power, wisdom, and love He'll need to face the tasks before Him.

How is your daily prayer life? Are you making going to God your first priority? And what happens after you pray? Do you expect anything in your day to change? Are you placing all your hope and expectations in God (Psalm 39:7) and His power or in yourself and your own strength?

Perhaps it's time to change things up, to reenergize your prayer life. Consider setting your alarm five, ten, fifteen, or twenty minutes earlier than usual, giving you time to seek God's face before the husband stirs, the kids clamor for breakfast, or the dog jumps up on your bed.

Today, make it a priority to go to God in prayer, expecting Him to meet all your needs—and more!

Prayer Prompt:

What do you need to do to make prayer time a priority each day?
Ask God for help in setting your priorities in order.

....

....

....

....

....

....

....

....

....

....

....

....

....

....

....

....

*Father, help me make meeting alone with
You my first and most blessed priority.*

A Willing Jesus

Now a leper came to Him, imploring Him, kneeling down to Him and saying to Him, "If You are willing, You can make me clean." Then Jesus, moved with compassion, stretched out His hand and touched him, and said to him, "I am willing; be cleansed."

MARK 1:40–41 NKJV

. . . .

In Jesus' day, lepers were outcasts of society. They were considered to be ceremonially unclean. Yet this leper must have imagined Jesus as someone he could approach. He also must have believed Jesus had the power to make him clean—radically changing his life, allowing him to live among people once more. So the leper approached Jesus. Humbly kneeling before Him, he made this statement of faith: "If You are willing, You can make me clean."

Jesus' heart was deeply stirred at seeing this man's plight. And He not only stated His willingness to make the leper clean but prefaced it by actually stretching out His hand and touching him! Then, "as soon as He had spoken, immediately the leprosy left him, and he was cleansed" (Mark 1:42 NKJV).

No matter where you are, what you've done, how much of an outcast you are, Jesus doesn't just *see* you. He reaches *out* for you. But first you must come to Him, humbly, believing He's willing to help you, that He will effect in you a change—for the better.

Prayer Prompt:

What do you need from Jesus today? No matter what it is, come before Him in prayer and submit to His touch.

....

....

....

....

....

....

....

....

....

....

....

....

....

....

....

....

Jesus, if You are willing, I humbly ask You to. . .

Drawn Up

I waited patiently for the LORD; he inclined to me and heard my cry. He drew me up from the pit of destruction, out of the miry bog, and set my feet upon a rock, making my steps secure. He put a new song in my mouth, a song of praise to our God.

PSALM 40:1–3 ESV

Some changes are easy. They just take a little bit of adjustment on your part. Others can be more than difficult to muddle through. During such times, instead of singing hymns of praise, you might be tempted to sing funeral dirges lamenting your circumstances.

But why waste your time singing the blues? Why not wait patiently for God, for Him to bend His ear, hear your cry? For when He does, He draws you up out of the muck, sets your feet on solid ground, and secures your future steps. In other words, God gives you the safety, security, and guidance you need when you wait for Him to move on your behalf. Then you're bursting with a new song, the one He's prompted you to sing, a song of praise to Him.

No matter what you're going through, remember that although at times you may feel as if you're poor and wanting, the Lord is always ready to meet your needs. He alone is your true Help and Deliverer (Psalm 40:17).

Prayer Prompt

What kind of song do you feel like singing today? If it's the blues, ask the Lord to change it to one of praise to Him.

Thank You, Lord, for coming when I cry,
for drawing me out of trouble and into You.

DAY 56

A Change Up—
for Good

Blessed. . .is he who considers the weak and the poor; the Lord will deliver him in the time of evil and trouble. . . . The Lord will sustain, refresh, and strengthen him on his bed of languishing; all his bed You [O Lord] will turn, change, and transform in his illness.

PSALM 41:1, 3 AMPC

. . . .

God wants to change you up. To have you live a life of love, looking out for the weak and the helpless, the poor. To give someone a helping hand. To love as He loves. When you do, when you're there for others, God will be there for you. But even more than that—He'll "sustain, refresh, and strengthen" you when you need it most. In return, when you're languishing, too tired to even lift your head, spirit, and heart, He'll "turn, change, and transform" you!

God looks out for His daughters, the ones who're moving in the world, stepping out in faith and love, being His Son's hands and feet. He protects, blesses, and delivers them (Psalm 41:2).

As you use your love to transform the lives of others, the ones who need it most, God uses His love to transform you just when you need it most. Whose life can you transform today—for good, for God?

Prayer Prompt:

Are you willing to be changed by God? Ask Him to change you so you might influence change in others.

_____

_____

_____

_____

_____

_____

_____

_____

_____

_____

_____

_____

_____

_____

_____

_____

_____

_____

_____

Lord, I am amazed at what Your love can do! Show me
who You'd like me to reach out to today—for good, for You!

Riding Out the Storm

When Jesus woke up, he rebuked the wind and said to the waves, "Silence! Be still!" Suddenly the wind stopped, and there was a great calm. Then he asked them, "Why are you afraid? Do you still have no faith?"

MARK 4:39–40 NLT

. . . .

At the end of a busy day, Jesus told His disciples to cross over to the other side of the lake with Him. So they boarded the boat and headed out. While Jesus slept in the stern, a great storm rose up and the boat began filling with water. So they woke Him up, saying, "Teacher, don't you care that we're about to drown?" (Mark 4:38). Jesus stood up and said to the wind and waves, "Silence! Be still!" And nature obeyed her King, becoming calm immediately.

Perhaps God has called you to take a certain path. He's pointed out the route. And suddenly, a storm comes up. You feel as if you're going to go under. This is when you need to look to Jesus. To not fear but understand He's still with you. To have faith He'll keep you safe, help you ride out the storm. To not lose hope but stay calm, filled with the assurance that no matter what happens, you *will* recover, you *will* succeed, and all *will be* better than before.

Prayer Prompt:

Are you caught in a storm with waves and wind that threaten to overwhelm you? Ask Jesus to calm the storm and give you peace.

....

....

....

....

....

....

....

....

....

....

....

....

....

....

....

....

....

....

You, Jesus, are the calmer of storms. Help me stay cool, to know that with You in my boat, I cannot help but reach the shore safely!

DAY 58

Soul Speak

Why are you cast down, O my inner self? And why should you moan over me and be disquieted within me? Hope in God and wait expectantly for Him, for I shall yet praise Him, my Help and my God.
PSALM 42:5 AMPC

. . . .

Where do you go for help and hope when discouraged? How do you keep your inner self lifted up, expecting good to come?

The author of Psalm 42 spoke to his inner self, his soul, telling it not to be discouraged, sad, or in turmoil. He told himself to hope in God, be patient in waiting for His help, knowing he would praise the God who loves him.

About a thousand years later, both a synagogue leader and an unclean woman expressed the same hope and faith in God as did the psalmist. The religious leader knew that if Jesus laid His hands on his dying daughter, she'd be healed and live (Mark 5:23). The woman who'd been bleeding for twelve years knew Jesus could heal her, and so she said to herself with certainty, "If I only touch His garments, I shall be restored to health" (Mark 5:28 AMPC).

No matter what you're going through, hang on to your expectant hope and faith in God. Speak to your soul, knowing His transformational love is being poured out upon you by day, leading you to songs of praise each night (Psalm 42:8).

Prayer Prompt:

What thoughts are you speaking to yourself? As you pray, speak out the promises in God's Word, knowing He can perform them.

....

....

....

....

....

....

....

....

....

....

....

....

....

....

....

....

....

....

Pour out Your love upon me today, Lord,
leading me to songs of praise tonight.

God Gets the Glory

So shall you heartily accept My commandments and
conform your life and conduct to them. . . . I am the Lord. . .
Who brought you out of the land of Egypt to be your God.
LEVITICUS 22:31–33 AMPC

. . . .

God took the Israelites through some major changes, delivering them from slavery in Egypt and into the freedom of the Promised Land. In a way, He's done the same thing for you. Through Jesus, God has brought you out of the slavery of sin and into the freedom of a relationship with Him. But the story doesn't end there. Your transformation is not yet over. God is still working on, in, and with you, making you more and more like His beloved Son—with the help of the Holy Spirit.

Your role is to let God continue to do His work. To not boast about your achievements, but to recognize that where you are and who you've become hasn't been accomplished in your power but in God's.

The psalmist got it right when he wrote that it wasn't the Israelites' swords or strength that allowed them to conquer the Promised Land but God's "right hand and strong arm" (Psalm 44:3 NLT). May you too recognize in whom your triumph lies.

Prayer Prompt:

If you're fighting a battle, are you relying on yourself or on God's strength? Ask God to step into the battle and fight for you.

....

....

....

....

....

....

....

....

....

....

....

....

....

....

....

....

You are the one who gives us victory. . . . O God, we give glory to You all day long and constantly praise Your name [Psalm 44:8 NLT].

DAY 60

Fields of Caring

When ye reap the harvest of your land, thou shalt not make clean riddance of the corners of thy field when thou reapest, neither shalt thou gather any gleaning of thy harvest: thou shalt leave them unto the poor, and to the stranger: I am the LORD your God.

LEVITICUS 23:22 KJV

When Moses is handing down God's law to the Israelites, He's setting down laws that will form and, at the same time, transform the Israelites into a new people. Some of the laws address purification and health, others the proper worship of God, others still the ways in which the members of the community are to interact.

Today's passage concerns how one treats her own possessions—in this case, the harvests of her fields. The command is to refrain from clutching to yourself every bit of what belongs to you in the harvest and, instead, leaving something there for the poor, the hungry wanderer.

The command is meant to inspire the work of shaping our hearts to develop a heart that's willing to sacrifice at least some small part of its own to the needs of another. In this moment in the law, God appears to want hearts, nurturing hearts, that will grasp the greater worthiness of sharing the leftovers rather than hoarding them.

God invites you to transform your heart into a field of caring.

Prayer Prompt:

What are you willing to sacrifice to help someone else? Pray for a heart that cares for those less fortunate.

Lord, help me develop a heart that's happier when I let go of what I have, instead of grasping for more. Amen.

DAY 61

Moved to Action

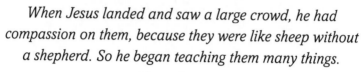

When Jesus landed and saw a large crowd, he had
compassion on them, because they were like sheep without
a shepherd. So he began teaching them many things.
MARK 6:34 NIV

The apostles had been commissioned by Jesus and sent out to heal the sick, cast out demons, and preach repentance. Now having come back, they reported to Him the things they had said and done. Since there were crowds around, Jesus invited the apostles to go to a secluded place, a quiet place, and get some rest. However, that rest was not to come. The crowds beat Jesus and the apostles to the secluded spot. The crowd overwhelmed them in number—five thousand strong—and they overwhelmed the heart of Jesus, because "they were like sheep without a shepherd."

This compassion of Jesus is noteworthy. He has His own concerns; He wants to rest with His friends. But then He is suddenly transformed. Something within Him turns to these many people, people who are starving in spirit and starving in body. And Jesus, His heart full of compassion, feeds their spirits, "teaching them many things." Then, He teaches them in body, multiplying loaves and the fish to satisfy their stomachs.

You may feel compassion on occasion, but do you allow your compassion to change and transform you? Do you allow your compassion to propel you into action, as Jesus did?

Prayer Prompt:

What can you do to become a more compassionate person? Ask the Lord to give you a compassionate heart and opportunities to practice compassion.

....

....

....

....

....

....

....

....

....

....

....

....

....

....

....

....

....

Lord, let my heart be moved when I first see people in need. Amen.

What's That Up Ahead?

The bride, a princess, looks glorious in her golden gown.
In her beautiful robes, she is led to the king, accompanied
by her bridesmaids. What a joyful and enthusiastic
procession as they enter the king's palace!
PSALM 45:13–15 NLT

The wedding day of a young woman is a day of great joy and anticipation, as well as one of change and transformation. In the psalm, there is excitement as the bride and her companions enter the palace. There's also a splendid showcasing; the bride is beautifully dressed when she is led to the king. This change in life is a glorious one, worthy of praise.

Psalm 45 also celebrates the wedding as a passage from one family to another. The psalmist counsels the bride: "Forget your people and your family far away" (v. 10 NLT). This is a forward-looking, not a backward-looking, change. Sons, one day, will take the place of fathers.

Psalm 45 celebrates the joys and anticipations of weddings and the changes that come along with marriage, but it also invites you to think about the other ways in which you are transformed over time, whether it be owing to professions, relocations, or simply aging. You can reflect on the joys of these changes and the positive anticipations that can come with them. You can look for the beauty in them. How often are you made over new through life changes?

Prayer Prompt:

What kind of life changes are you going through? As you pray, listen and watch for God's direction in those changes.

....

....

....

....

....

....

....

....

....

....

....

....

....

....

....

....

....

Lord, let me look for Your glory
in each season of life. Amen.

Welcome to the New Self

"Whoever wants to be my disciple must deny themselves and take up their cross and follow me."

MARK 8:34 NIV

- -

This saying of Jesus comes after a striking interaction between Jesus and Peter. When Jesus asks the disciples who they think He is, Peter declares, "You are the Messiah" (Mark 8:29 NIV). But just subsequent to that, Jesus predicts that He will suffer and die. When Peter rebukes Jesus for saying this, Jesus rebukes him in turn: "Get behind me, Satan! . . . You do not have in mind the concerns of God, but merely human concerns" (Mark 8:33 NIV).

At that point, Jesus instructs the crowd on what being a follower of His entails. Clearly, following Him involves transformation. For, in the first place, one must deny herself, and this denial of self is immediately replaced by another self, which is now carrying a cross and following Jesus. The taking up of the cross is not to be equated with the ordinary hardships of life. No, the taking up of the cross is in imitation of Jesus, whose cross is not being carried for His sake but for our sakes. When we take up our crosses, then, we take them up in order to engage in loving actions toward others. This is how our transformation is brought about, when attempting to turn from ourselves to follow Christ.

Prayer Prompt:

What cross is Christ asking you to carry? When you pray, ask Him to give you the courage to take up the cross He has for you.

....

....

....

....

....

....

....

....

....

....

....

....

....

....

....

....

....

Lord, help me turn from the things of this world and follow Your heart. Amen.

DAY 64

Belonging

The nobles of the nations assemble as the people of the
God of Abraham, for the kings of the earth belong to God.
PSALM 47:9 NIV

. . . .

It is one thing to belong to humankind, to be a being among human beings on the earth. It is quite another thing to belong to God. To be a human being on earth is to be a fortuitous thing. Where you grew up and in what kind of family are things that happen outside of your control.

But the Israelites had a different perspective. From the time of their father Abraham through the time of Moses, the lawgiver, they belonged to almighty God and to the covenant. Because of that belonging, they rose above other nations on earth. And when they were at their best, they knew that belonging to God was their outstanding feature, the thing that elevated them and changed them from being just another nation, merely other human beings. And so, as they do in Psalm 47, they praised the God who had lifted them up. They praised Him.

How much does your belonging to God enter into your life? Do you see your faith in God as the transformative thing that it can be? It's the thing that shapes you into a creature who can give praise. May you not shy away from belonging to God, for therein lies your spiritual transformation.

Prayer Prompt:

To whom do you belong? Pray that your life will reflect that you belong to Almighty God.

....

....

....

....

....

....

....

....

....

....

....

....

....

....

....

....

....

....

Lord, let me always remember that whatever
I become, I always belong to You. Amen.

DAY 65

Measure of Greatness

*Sitting down, Jesus called the Twelve and said, "Anyone who
wants to be first must be the very last, and the servant of all."
He took a little child whom he placed among them. . . . "Whoever
welcomes one of these little children in my name welcomes me."*

MARK 9:35–37 NIV

Jesus had only just been prophesying yet again that He would suffer and
die, but the disciples, not knowing what to make of that, were discussing
among themselves who was the greatest. Jesus took this opportunity to
teach them a couple of things.

First, Jesus teaches them what it means to be great. *His* measure
of greatness is service. The one who is greatest or first is the one who
serves everyone else. Jesus has just told them that He is going to suffer
and die—not for anything that He did wrong, but for us. Then, He takes
a child into their midst and tells them whoever receives this child receives
Him and God the Father, the one who sent Him. In taking the child into
His arms, Jesus is indicating who is to be served.

Service is the measure of greatness, but not service to the rich and
powerful. No, it's service to the weakest, the most in need, those who
are crying out.

Prayer Prompt:

What is your definition of greatness and how does it compare to God's definition? Ask Jesus to show you how to be in His service.

Lord, show me what kind of change I must make to be a servant like You. Amen.

Service on the Journey

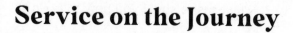

*According to the commandment of the LORD they were
numbered by the hand of Moses, each according to
his service and according to his task; thus were they
numbered by him, as the LORD commanded Moses.*
NUMBERS 4:49 NKJV

The book of Numbers contains a recounting of the Israelite movement from Mount Sinai to the Promised Land. As the title suggests, it is a story replete with numbers, largely from census taking. Since the Israelite journey encompasses the entire community, there are very special elements to it. Among these are the transportation of the tabernacle, the altar, and the various sacred items used in worship. The Levites are, as is known, the priestly portion of the people, and so it falls to their clans to serve by transporting the holy things.

In Exodus and Leviticus, the Israelites were very much involved in their relationship with God. Now they are involved in more earthly and practical considerations. Now they are involved in their first journey as a new people, a people who live under a law. Now there are things to do and a right and a wrong way to do them. Now they are no longer wandering, but in a truly transformative journey to a new land, with God among them as they travel.

Prayer Prompt:

Whose voice guides you on your journey as a woman of God? Pray for ears that hear God's voice above the other voices around you.

....

....

....

....

....

....

....

....

....

....

....

....

....

....

....

Lord, in my journey in the world, help me to keep You front and center. Prod me to keep a solid count on all my blessings. Amen.

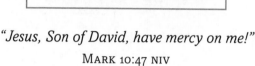

Double Vision

"Jesus, Son of David, have mercy on me!"
MARK 10:47 NIV

. . . .

Bartimaeus, the blind man, must have appeared quite insignificant there on the roadside, begging as Jesus happened along. After all, people are actually rebuking him and trying to keep him away. At the same time, Jesus by this point in His mission must have loomed very large, seemingly someone not to be concerned with small fry. So the operative word in this encounter is *mercy.*

Bartimaeus is a man who needs mercy, and he knows it. Hence, he asks for it right from the outset. He doesn't say immediately that he wants to see. He cries out for mercy from the Son of kings. And Jesus hears him, despite the attempted screening by His disciples, and He stops to help. He shows Bartimaeus mercy at that moment. Having gotten that much relief, the blind man tells Jesus that he wants to see. But to be sure, he already does see; he sees with the sight of faith. And Jesus, in granting the man's physical desire, fills his spiritual cup of faith to the brim. Then the man sees two fabulous things—the world and that the world belongs to Jesus.

So Bartimaeus doesn't go off into the world on his own; he goes and follows Jesus into the world.

Prayer Prompt:

What is your heart's cry today? Ask Jesus for mercy in your life situations.

....

....

....

....

....

....

....

....

....

....

....

....

....

....

....

....

....

....

....

Lord, change me so that I can see more and more that You are the true guide. Amen.

Beastly Riches

People, despite their wealth, do not endure; they are like the beasts that perish. This is the fate of those who trust in themselves, and of their followers, who approve their sayings. They are like sheep and are destined to die; death will be their shepherd.

PSALM 49:12–14 NIV

The question of true faith is inseparable from how we live out our days. Without doubt, there are everyday cares that seem to be unavoidable. Then there is a temptation to insure oneself against the chance occurrences of the future by building up an endless store of riches, though we do not build up a similar foundation of uprightness.

And it is in giving in to that temptation to build up our earthly treasures that human beings get overtaken by something that reduces them to something less than they are, something "like the beasts that perish." In giving in, people make the foolish mistake of thinking God will be impressed by their store of wealth, at whatever cost it may be achieved. They trust in their wealth, but not in God.

There may be human beings who are impressed by earthly treasures, but not God. And so it is that we must transform ourselves to get over our misguided awe of "people who have wealth but lack understanding" (Psalm 49:20 NIV).

Prayer Prompt:

What are you impressed by—wealth, power, possessions? Ask God to focus your eyes on what impresses Him.

....

....

....

....

....

....

....

....

....

....

....

....

....

....

....

....

Dear Lord, I don't want to be like a sheep, flocking to follow the wealthy and their ways. Help me trust in and follow You alone. Amen.

The Choice

"But those farmhands saw their chance. They rubbed their hands together in greed and said, 'This is the heir! Let's kill him and have it all for ourselves.'"

MARK 12:7 MSG

This moment in Jesus' parable of the tenants is the culmination of a choice that had been made by these farmers, a choice that they made from the beginning, from the time that they began to rent the vineyard. While they could have recognized the beauty of the vineyard and the good that accrued to them on account of it being made available to them by the owner for their livelihood, well-being, and enjoyment, they instead chose to view it as somehow theirs and theirs alone; they chose to wrest it from its owner. This is the choice that traces its roots back to the Garden in Genesis: Do we accept the world as a world given to us by God, or do we accept it as something other than that, as ours and ours alone?

In line with that, just as with the tenants, from time to time, God calls us to account. What have we been doing with our lives and talents? Are we open to that call? Are we prepared to hand over or share something of what we have produced?

Prayer Prompt:

How do you view God's blessing—as a gift or something you earned and solely possess? Pray for the right attitude toward what God has given you.

....

....

....

....

....

....

....

....

....

....

....

....

....

....

....

Dear God, help me to reflect on and adjust my choices where necessary; help me to be accountable in new and better ways than I have been. Amen.

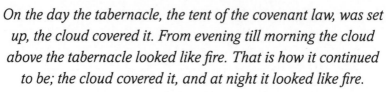

Follow the Leader

On the day the tabernacle, the tent of the covenant law, was set up, the cloud covered it. From evening till morning the cloud above the tabernacle looked like fire. That is how it continued to be; the cloud covered it, and at night it looked like fire.

NUMBERS 9:15–16 NIV

Where are we headed? Who will lead us? When are we to move and go forward? And how far do we go? When are we to rest? And for how long do we rest?

Those are questions of the journey, questions that faced the Israelites on their march away from Egypt and from Sinai. But the Israelites are slowly but surely revealing themselves as a people of God. He is ever with them, and He is their God. God determined the answers to all the questions posed here. That cloud and that fire in union with the tent of the covenant governed their travel days and their days of rest. "At the LORD's command they encamped, and at the LORD's command they set out" (Numbers 9:23 NIV). The cloud and fire are things of beauty, representing a whole people living intimately with their Maker. They are God's people and He is their God.

Today consider how intimately you are living with your Maker.

Prayer Prompt:

Where are you headed and who is leading you? Ask God to show you when He wants you to move and in what direction.

....

....

....

....

....

....

....

....

....

....

....

....

....

....

....

....

Lord, reign in my heart like the cloud over the tent;
take me wherever it is that You want me to go.

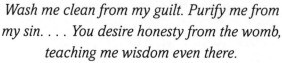

Heart Cleaning

Wash me clean from my guilt. Purify me from
my sin. . . . You desire honesty from the womb,
teaching me wisdom even there.

PSALM 51:2, 6 NLT

• •

After Nathan reveals David's transgression (committing adultery with Bathsheba and all that followed) to him, there's this wrenching plea for forgiveness and expression of repentance. In the first moment, David discloses that it's finally against God that he's sinned. So he asks God to cleanse him; to hide His face from David's sin; to revive David's bones, crushed by his sin, so that he might rejoice and hear joy and gladness. This cleansing will be one with truth that comes in the womb, truth that God desires, and one with the wisdom which God teaches him.

In Psalm 51, David comes to light as a sinner who has faith in a God of unfailing love. So even as he is uncovered as a sinner, he doesn't shrink from making his appeal. He doesn't shrink from the possibility that he can be changed and brought to a better place. However late it may be, David has now become fully aware of his wrongs, and he offers himself with openness and willingness to God, appealing to God's mercy and kindness for forgiveness.

This is the first transformation, the transformation from a proud agent of sin to a humbled and repentant servant of the Lord.

Prayer Prompt:

What sins do you need to repent of? Pray and ask God to forgive you and transform your life into one that is pleasing to Him.

....

....

....

....

....

....

....

....

....

....

....

....

....

....

....

....

Lord, help me to see my transgressions when they escape me; help me to cross the road to You for forgiveness.

So Humble the Heart

Create in me a clean heart, O God. Renew a loyal spirit within me. . . . The sacrifice you desire is a broken spirit. You will not reject a broken and repentant heart, O God.

PSALM 51:10, 17 NLT

. . . .

In this part of his lamentation, the psalmist David asks God to create a clean heart within him and renew the loyalty of his spirit. One gets the strong sense of David's former closeness to God and how much he desires to recover that intimacy. He faces up to the absence of purity of heart that led him to destroy Uriah and turn his face away from God. Now he seeks to return to the spirit that once found him dancing for joy before the ark of the covenant; now he yearns for a pure heart, a willing spirit, and a voice to sing new praises to the Lord.

But David knows well that the faithful live with a broken spirit, a humbled heart. In the wake of his transgression, he knows he has been overtaken by an enemy, at some juncture, stronger than he; and he has been humbled by that enemy. He knows well that the sacrifice of pride—the giving up of a boastful, stubborn spirit—is a sacrifice more pleasing to God than any burnt offering. Certainly, God will not despise this offering of humility and contrition.

Prayer Prompt:

What is the condition of your heart? Ask God to give you a broken spirit and a repentant heart before Him.

....

....

....

....

....

....

....

....

....

....

....

....

....

....

....

....

Lord, help me surrender my pride and value humility over my own strength. Amen.

Strength in Loving Forgiveness

"Now may the Lord's strength be displayed, just as you have declared: 'The LORD is slow to anger, abounding in love and forgiving sin and rebellion. . . . In accordance with your great love, forgive the sin of these people, just as you have pardoned them from the time they left Egypt until now."

NUMBERS 14:17–19 NIV

Here we find Moses interceding before God for the rebellious Israelites. Having received bad reports about the Promised Land, the Israelites begin to complain bitterly to Moses and Aaron. The Lord is so exasperated by the people that He's ready to destroy them and create anew. Moses implores God not to destroy but to forgive the Israelites. He portrays as the Lord's strength His slowness to anger and His capacity to love and forgive. Moses asks God to forgive the Israelites in "accordance with [God's] great love." Yet while the Lord does not destroy the rebellious Israelites, He declares the grumbling people will not set sight on the Promised Land: "No one who has treated me with contempt will ever see it" (Numbers 14:23 NIV).

When things are going poorly in our lives and a bright future seems doubtful, how often do we blame God for what has gone awry? How often do we fail to ask God for the strength and fortitude we need to envision a brighter future both in the world and within ourselves?

Prayer Prompt:

What are you facing that is causing you frustration in life? Ask God to forgive your complaining and help you to trust Him.

Lord, transform my heart when it weakens
in the face of life's troubles. Amen.

Who Knew?

*Immediately the rooster crowed the second time. Suddenly,
Jesus' words flashed through Peter's mind: "Before the
rooster crows twice, you will deny three times that you
even know me." And he broke down and wept.*

MARK 14:72 NLT

Sometimes we think good things about ourselves; we think highly of
ourselves. We want to be someone genuinely good. We want very badly
to do the right thing. Peter was a person like that. When Jesus is telling
him what he is actually going to do, Peter says, "Even if I have to die with
you, I will never disown you." He wasn't alone in that claim, but he was
the leader and the most vocal. And again, he was expressing a desire that
we all have going into the challenges of life. How many of us, especially
in our younger days, would not have spoken as vigorously and positively
about our intentions? What are those speeches, except expressions of
our best wishes and deepest hopes for ourselves and our future?

So, there is Peter boasting before the Lord about what he's going to
do. And then there's Peter in the courtyard, strike one, strike two, strike
three. And then comes that awful awakening by the rooster. And then
the tears: *How could I have failed so miserably! And You knew, Jesus, You
knew all along and loved me still.*

Prayer Prompt:

What self-important thing have you been declaring in your life? Ask Jesus to show you what He wants to perform in you.

....

....

....

....

....

....

....

....

....

....

....

....

....

....

....

....

....

....

Lord Jesus, help me to know myself better, to see myself clearly, more like the way You see me.

First Pride, Then the Fall

"He has brought you and all your fellow Levites near himself,
but now you are trying to get the priesthood too. It is against the
Lord that you and all your followers have banded together."
NUMBERS 16:10–11 NIV

One of the sad but harsh realities that any community of God may face is the emergence of pride and jealousy among members of a congregation, including its leaders. In Numbers 16, we come upon such a dispute, one that pits certain leaders of the Levites, namely, Korah, Dathan, and Abiram, against Moses and Aaron. Korah publicly accuses Moses and Aaron of prideful exaltations of themselves above the rest of the community. Moses and Aaron are indeed the chief priests of the Israelites, but Korah aspires to that role. His jealousy of Moses particularly is manifest in his accusations.

Moses did not aspire to be the leader of the Israelites, nor did he desire to be the spokesman for God. God assigned him to his position and made Aaron the one who would do the speaking. Moses tests Korah by allowing him to do priestly things, such as the lighting of the censers, and then waiting to see how God would respond. God punishes Korah's pride severely, to say the least. Transformation of oneself should never come through the jealous grasping for honor and power.

Prayer Prompt:

What do you aspire to be in your church and what are your motives?
Ask Jesus to give you the right motives and place you in the position
that pleases Him.

....

....

....

....

....

....

....

....

....

....

....

....

....

....

....

....

Dear Lord, help me to accept who I am and
to grow in the church in accordance with
Your will rather than my desire. Amen.

Deep Sighs

I call to God; GOD will help me. At dusk, dawn, and noon I
sigh deep sighs—he hears, he rescues. . . . Pile your troubles
on GOD's shoulders—he'll carry your load, he'll help you out.
PSALM 55:16–17, 22 MSG

. . . .

Psalm 55 finds the psalmist, David, in terrible straits. He is assailed from
within by terrible thoughts and worries. He is threatened by the very voice
of his enemies. He is afraid of dying violently. If he could, he would fly far
away. Although he complains about having many enemies, in the middle
of his lament, he reveals that it is a former friend who is the source of his
anguish—a best friend. This person attacks friends and violates covenants;
there is oily duplicity in his speech, his words warring with his heart.

Yet, with all of his anguish, what does the psalmist do? What does he
counsel his hearers to do? He draws closer to God, calling out to Him,
crying aloud to Him. And he calls out to God continually, morning, noon,
and night. And clearly, God is at his side, caring for him, easing his distress.

As did the psalmist, take all your troubles and pile them on God. He
can carry whatever load you have to give Him.

Prayer Prompt:

What thoughts or worries are threatening your peace of mind? Ask Jesus, the Prince of Peace to carry that load and bring you peace.

....

....

....

....

....

....

....

....

....

....

....

....

....

....

....

....

....

Lord, when I am beset by worries and am so,
so careworn, open my heart to turn to You
for strength and guidance. Amen.

The Awesome Change

But he said to them, "Do not be alarmed. You seek
Jesus of Nazareth, who was crucified. He is risen!
He is not here." . . . So they went out quickly and fled
from the tomb, for they trembled and were amazed.

MARK 16:6, 8 NKJV

How awful, how very full of awe, those women must have felt to find a messenger from God sitting at the tomb! Sitting at the tomb to report a thing that was hardly to be believed, although Jesus had prophesied it. . . and more than once. And now here they were, with instructions to go tell the others, the others who had run away. Who would believe their report? Who would believe this news, when they themselves could hardly believe it? Who would be the first to accept that everything had changed, that everything in the whole wide world had changed and changed forever?

One can hardly fathom what life must have been like early in the day of the resurrected Lord. Here we live now, more than two thousand years on, and it is something that we almost take for granted. But can we consider what must have been an incredibly transformative experience of those women at the tomb and those disciples holed up in their room—to learn that Jesus had risen and the whole world was made over new?

Prayer Prompt:

What change do you need to experience in your life? Ask the resurrected Jesus to transform your life so it pleases Him.

....
....
....
....
....
....
....
....
....
....
....
....
....
....
....
....
....

Lord, bring my faith to that empty tomb, and change me the way those women were changed. Amen.

DAY 78

Silent Change

But the angel said to him, "Do not be afraid, Zacharias,
for your prayer is heard; and your wife Elizabeth will bear
you a son, and you shall call his name John." . . . And
Zacharias said to the angel, "How shall I know this? For I
am an old man, and my wife is well advanced in years."
LUKE 1:13, 18 NKJV

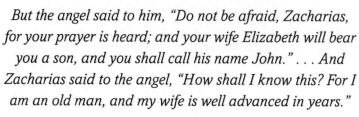

This priest was an old man when he was chosen for temple duty. For him, that duty was probably the most auspicious thing that was bound to happen to him. So Zacharias was understandably startled when the messenger from God appeared. And he was understandably dubious when the angel announced that his aging wife would bear a child. But Zacharias had a role to play in salvation history. He had been chosen by God, as had his wife and prospective son. So that Zacharias could play his part well, the Lord struck him dumb. The old man emerged from the inner temple in silence, a silence that he maintained until his son was born. And all the time that he was silent, his wife's belly swelled, and her barren shame was taken away.

How does silence change this man? Perhaps, in that silence, he learned to accept his place in salvation history. He learned that God does the choosing, and God had chosen him to play one small part in a grand movement to bring "light to those who sit in darkness and the shadow of death" (Luke 1:79 NKJV).

Prayer Prompt:

Being unable to speak changed Zacharias. What would it take to change you? Pray for courage to accept whatever change may come.

....

....

....

....

....

....

....

....

....

....

....

....

....

....

....

....

....

....

Lord, help me to say yes on the day that You call,
however life-changing the call may be. Amen.

DAY 79

The Way Forward

"Why did you beat your donkey those three times?"
the angel of the LORD demanded. "Look, I have come to
block your way because you are stubbornly resisting me."
NUMBERS 22:32 NLT

. . . .

The way was blocked. The way was not only blocked, there was an angel of the Lord impeding the way forward. The donkey could see the way was blocked, but Balaam could not. The donkey tried to communicate to Balaam that the way was blocked, listing to one side and then to the other. Finally, he simply lay down beneath Balaam. He had always borne his master faithfully, but now the donkey suffered blows for not moving forward where the angel of the Lord stood waiting for them, blocking the way. The Lord loosened the donkey's tongue so he could challenge Balaam and remind Balaam of his faithful service. Then He opened Balaam's eyes so he could see the way was blocked and by whom. Balaam comes to see his sinful blindness. But the Lord does not give up on Balaam; the Lord wants Balaam to be His instrument.

How often is the way forward blocked in your life, and you cannot see it? How often is someone trying to help you, but you cannot hear her or you cannot sense her prodding? How often is God trying to use you as an instrument, but you're getting in God's way?

Prayer Prompt:

What's blocking your way forward? Ask the Lord to let you see His way and direct you where He is leading.

_____

_____

_____

_____

_____

_____

_____

_____

_____

_____

_____

_____

_____

_____

_____

_____

_____

_____

Lord, open my eyes, my ears, and my touch to Your guidance. Amen.

Children of Hope

John [the son of Elizabeth and Zechariah] grew up and became
strong in spirit. . . . [Joseph] took with him Mary, to whom
he was engaged, who was now expecting a child. And while
they were there, the time came for her baby to be born.

LUKE 1:80; 2:5–6 NLT

Consider the people in these two families. Elizabeth and Zechariah late in life have a child born to them, announced by a messenger of God. Mary and Joseph have a child born to them, announced by a messenger of God. It is as if these parents were all called out of time by God to act in the roles of a great drama.

And then, of course, there are these two children, Jesus and John—two children whose lives were determined for them from all eternity. For them the world was not the world as we know it. For them the world belonged to God, pure and simple. And while Jesus is the Son of God, John in his special role belonged to God from the beginning as well, his life from the beginning shaped to be the herald of the Savior. These were children of tomorrow and hope, endless hope, the herald and the Savior.

You too belong to God, from the beginning, to be shaped by Him to serve Him. You too are His child, His beloved daughter.

Prayer Prompt:

How are you being shaped to serve God? Ask Him to soften your heart to receive the shaping you need to serve Him.

Lord, shape me to serve You in endless hope. Amen.

Keep Me Safe

I did nothing to deserve this, GOD, crossed no one, wronged no one.
All the same, they're after me, determined to get me. Wake up and
see for yourself! You're GOD, GOD-of-Angel-Armies, Israel's God!

PSALM 59:4 MSG

. . . .

When Saul is removed from the kingship by God through Samuel and David is elevated, Saul is bewildered about why he is deposed. It is impossibly hard for him to accept the reign of David. So he sends henchmen after David.

David prays to the Lord to keep him safe from the jealous attacks of Saul. David knows both that he has not done anything wrong (this time) and that Saul too is anointed by God. David only wants God to shield him from misguided attacks. Though he is in power, he asks the God he loves for protection.

The assaults you may face will probably never rise to the seriousness of the ones David faced. Yet you may be inundated by all sorts of cares and pressures, stresses and worries that certainly drive you to the wall. Then it is that you find yourself realizing the extent of your weakness and turning quickly to God for strength. And the God who commands the armies of angels is somehow, astoundingly, merciful to you.

Prayer Prompt:

Who has wronged you without cause? Pray for them and for yourself that you won't be pulled into despair. Ask God to care for you.

....

....

....

....

....

....

....

....

....

....

....

....

....

....

....

....

Dear Lord, in my weakness let me rely on Your strength. Protect me from the cares that assault me needlessly; soothe away my worries. Amen.

DAY 82

My Father's House

His mother said, "Young man, why have you done this to us?
Your father and I have been half out of our minds looking for
you." He said, "Why were you looking for me? Didn't you know
that I had to be here, dealing with the things of my Father?"
LUKE 2:48–49 MSG

. . . .

It's nice to live in a close-knit community, one in which people are perpetually looking out for the good of the whole. So it was that Jesus' parents believed He was among the traveling band of family and friends exiting Jerusalem. Poor Mary and Joseph! You can imagine their dismay and their fright upon finding out Jesus had disappeared. They go back to Jerusalem and search for Him for three whole days! And where do they find Him? Precisely where He belongs.

However, though He was impressing the teachers with His answers, His folks were not quite so impressed. Jesus has a ready answer to His mother's question, though, a twofold one. First, "Didn't you know" suggests that Jesus thinks Mary and Joseph should know who He is and what He's about. Second, Jesus declares that He is not about worldly business. He is there for the business of His Father's house, the business of salvation.

And perhaps that is exactly where we all belong and exactly the business we should all be concerned with.

Prayer Prompt:

Whose business are you involved in—God's or the world's? Ask Jesus to show you what's important for you to be involved in.

....

....

....

....

....

....

....

....

....

....

....

....

....

....

....

....

....

*Lord, help me see with Jesus my true concern
and interest—eternal life with You. Amen.*

My Banner and My Shield

For those who fear you, you have raised a banner to be unfurled against the bow. Save us and help us with your right hand, that those you love may be delivered.

PSALM 60:4–5 NIV

Who possesses a healthy regard for the Lord? Who has a firm hold on the divine shield in times of trouble? For times of trouble will surely come. The land will be shaken, fractured, and torn open. Indeed, the very ground under our feet will quake; the times will be desperate. But God has shown Himself to us. He has bequeathed to us His laws, ways, and awesome power. And the one who has built up in herself a strong regard for those things, for her, God will raise the banner against the bow. And again, she who has reflected well on her gifts from God will be shielded by Him in desperate times.

In the world itself there will be shows of power, demonstrations and strikes, petitions and drives of all sorts. But those are all nothing in comparison with the strength that comes from an alliance with God. For God loves you with a love far greater and far beyond the love of any human being. And God knows your needs. So the psalmist sings to Him to "save us and help us with your right hand."

Prayer Prompt:

What troubles you about your surroundings? Pray that your trust will always be in the God who saves in times of trouble.

....

....

....

....

....

....

....

....

....

....

....

....

....

....

....

....

Dear God, help us place our trust in You in times of trouble and desperation. Amen.

Who Has the Power?

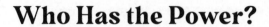

The devil led him up to a high place and showed him
in an instant all the kingdoms of the world. And he said
to him. . . "If you worship me, it will all be yours."
LUKE 4:5–7 NIV

- -

Jesus had been in the desert, fasting for forty days and perhaps reflecting on His life and mission. He was hungry. But what was He hungry for? Bread? Man does not live on bread alone. Was He hungry for affirmation? Did He want the Father to send angels to save Him?

Jesus was a human being. What are humans hungry for? Power. How thrilling it must have been to see all the kingdoms of the earth in an instant, to ponder the thought of reigning over it all! But the prospect was not so thrilling perhaps to this human being, at least not at the price that was being asked. Jesus, is, of course, equal to the challenge: "It is written, 'Worship the Lord your God and serve him only'" (Luke 4:8 NIV).

The challenge that Jesus faced in the desert is a challenge we all face. It's the challenge of choosing between worlds. Do we choose the world ruled by God, or do we change allegiances to choose a world ruled by humankind and a devilish master? Without God, that latter world becomes an inescapable desert.

Prayer Prompt:

What are you hungry for? Ask Jesus to give you the desires that result in eternal life rather than temporary pleasure.

....

....

....

....

....

....

....

....

....

....

....

....

....

....

....

....

*Jesus, help me put away my worldly desire for power
and wealth and the things of this world. Amen.*

Change through Loss

*They left Kadesh and camped at Mount Hor, on the border
of Edom. At the Lord's command Aaron the priest went up
Mount Hor, where he died on the first day of the fifth month
of the fortieth year after the Israelites came out of Egypt.*

NUMBERS 33:37–38 NIV

Forty years had gone by since the Israelites had been delivered from
Egypt. Led by Moses and Aaron, so many times had they camped and set
off, camped and set off again. Now on the doorstep of their destination,
Canaan, Aaron was gone.

Pressed as the Israelites were to follow the Lord's command and
cross the Jordan in Canaan, they could hardly help but stop and reflect
on what had happened over those forty years with Aaron at the side of
Moses. So many things had changed, most especially them. And Moses,
surely he had changed. There was no more going to the Lord and telling
Him he didn't know how to speak before the people.

The journey across the desert with Aaron at his side had been a trial
period for Moses, and now he was the sole leader of the Israelites. He
hardly had a chance to mourn the death of his brother, with the struggle
with the Canaanites immediately at hand. After so much strife, Moses
had learned to obey and walk on.

Prayer Prompt:

Have you experienced a loss that causes you to worry about tomorrow? Ask the Lord to give you strength and courage for the journey and walk on.

....

....

....

....

....

....

....

....

....

....

....

....

....

....

....

....

Dear Lord, in times of loss, fill your faithful ones with understanding and courage to keep going. Amen.

DAY 86

Follow

*"Follow me," Jesus said to him, and Levi got up, left everything and
followed him. Then Levi held a great banquet for Jesus at his house,
and a large crowd of tax collectors and others were eating with them.*

LUKE 5:27–29 NIV

. . . .

What an incredible feeling it must have been for Levi to have been called
by Jesus. After so many years of being shunned by the authorities, now
there was a leader, a new leader, who sought after him and called him.
That was surely an occasion for a great celebration with his new teacher.
Whereas the Pharisees looked upon the feasting as a comedown of sorts
for Jesus, Levi looked on it more properly as an elevation for him and
his fellows.

Jesus was announcing to everyone in sight that these were the people
for whom He had come. Somehow the old authorities did not deem these
people worthy of being called to repentance. But Jesus embraced them
rather than shunning them. He saw their need for a restored relationship
with their God.

And Levi heard the call. He left everything and followed. One can
hardly imagine the kind of charisma that Jesus must have had to evoke
such a response. But moved by that powerful call, Levi changed from a
collector to a follower, a servant of the Lord.

Prayer Prompt:

What is Jesus asking you to leave behind so you can follow Him? Pray that His call will cause you to answer without hesitation.

....

....

....

....

....

....

....

....

....

....

....

....

....

....

....

....

....

Dear Jesus, help me follow You wherever You lead me, no matter what I must leave behind. Amen.

Bearing Burdens

"May the Lord, the God of your ancestors, increase you a thousand times and bless you as he has promised! But how can I bear your problems and your burdens and your disputes all by myself? Choose some wise, understanding and respected men from each of your tribes, and I will set them over you."

Deuteronomy 1:11–13 niv

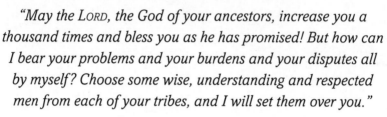

At the beginning of Deuteronomy, we hear that "the Lord your God has increased your numbers so that today you are as numerous as the stars in the sky" (v. 10 niv). That report from Moses, which echoes God's covenant with Abraham, has now, in its fruition, brought about a new need. That need is, of course, a need for help in ministering to the Israelite nation.

By himself, Moses can no longer deal with the various problems and disputes that arise among the people. But he has a plan. He takes the "leading men" of the tribes and appoints them as judges. These judges are to settle disputes of all kinds, some between and among Israelites, others between Israelites and outsiders, to judge with impartiality and fearlessness.

Once again, the situation of the nation is transformed. Governance from within the nation begins to emerge. But it's always within the framework of understanding that wisdom and justice come first from God.

Prayer Prompt:

What kind of burdens do you need help with? Ask God to show you where help can be found to ease those burdens.

....

....

....

....

....

....

....

....

....

....

....

....

....

....

....

Dear God, help me reach out to others for help when the burdens of life become too great to bear alone. Help me remember to reach out to You. Amen.

Praise God

Because your love is better than life, my lips will glorify you.
I will praise you as long as I live, and in your name I will
lift up my hands. I will be fully satisfied as with the richest
of foods; with singing lips my mouth will praise you.

PSALM 63:3–5 NIV

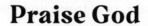

Here we have the psalmist very clearly in the presence of God. His longing for God is like a great thirst in his soul. He longs to take in his God, like being filled with life-giving water, the way water gives life to dry ground.

Life is good. But the love of the Lord is better than life. For it is the love of the Lord that gives meaning to life. Without that love, the soul would be like a desert. So it is that the Lord is worthy of all glorification and all praise.

With the love of the Lord, the soul is filled and satisfied as with the finest food. It is filled with the kind of joy that brings a song to the lips spontaneously, a song of praise that never ceases.

How often are you drawn to look around and see the love of God in its various forms? How often are you moved like the psalmist to sing the praises of God, whose love is better than life?

Prayer Prompt:

What prompts you to see God's love? Ask Him to open your eyes to His love, and praise Him for His presence in your life.

_____

_____

_____

_____

_____

_____

_____

_____

_____

_____

_____

_____

_____

_____

_____

_____

Dear God, please draw me closer to You. Help me to feel Your love as better than life, prompting me to praise.

Mercy on Us All

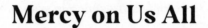

"Be merciful, just as your Father also is merciful. Judge not, and you shall not be judged. . . . For with the same measure that you use, it will be measured back to you."
LUKE 6:36–38 NKJV

. . . .

In the course of ordinary life, we are all called to make certain judgments. That is inescapable, and obviously, Jesus knows that. While we need to listen when He tells us not to judge, we need to hear it with the reminder that "with the measure you use, it will be measured back to you." In saying this, Jesus appears to be pointing to something that He sees in us human beings. He sees people who are all too prone to judge someone using a yardstick that they do not use when considering their own choices and decisions. In consideration of their own cases, there are extraneous circumstances and convenient excuses that fend off the harsh judgments that they quickly make in considering the actions and choices of someone else. Or in the cases where they are convicted of wrongdoing of some sort or other, people do not want the justice that they so readily want someone else to face and suffer. No, for themselves, they want mercy.

Jesus teaches us: don't judge when you don't have to be judging; be forgiving; be merciful. Just as God is merciful to you.

Prayer Prompt:

By what measure do you judge others? Ask Jesus to give you a
forgiving spirit and the ability to show mercy to others.

....

....

....

....

....

....

....

....

....

....

....

....

....

....

....

....

....

*Jesus, help me love others and not to
judge them. Help me be merciful. Amen.*

Faith That Heals

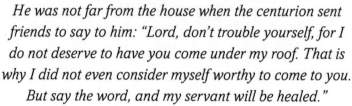

He was not far from the house when the centurion sent friends to say to him: "Lord, don't trouble yourself, for I do not deserve to have you come under my roof. That is why I did not even consider myself worthy to come to you. But say the word, and my servant will be healed."

LUKE 7:6–7 NIV

Here we have a very strong instance of the transformative power of Jesus. The centurion is not himself part of the Jewish community to which Jesus belongs. Yet he is friendly to that community and has heard of Jesus. He believes that Jesus can help him, that Jesus can heal his servant. Moreover, the centurion appears to have a grasp on the fact that Jesus is someone who possesses a higher authority, an authority in the face of which he is unworthy. Even Jesus Himself is impressed by that, as He remarks to the crowd around Him, "I tell you, I have not found such great faith even in Israel" (Luke 7:9 NIV). Jesus sees for Himself the way in which His presence and power are beginning to permeate the world.

Those of us who want transformation would do well to consider the authority that Jesus has in our lives. Each of us may ask, *What is the extent of Jesus' authority in my life? Am I willing to let Jesus just "say the word"?*

Prayer Prompt:

How submissive are you to Jesus? Pray for a submissive spirit to His authority in your life.

....

....

....

....

....

....

....

....

....

....

....

....

....

....

....

....

....

....

Dear Lord, help me change by placing myself
more and more under Your authority. Amen.

DAY 91

Don't Forget!

They tell what God has brought about and ponder what he has done.
Let the righteous one rejoice in the LORD and take refuge in him!
PSALM 64:9–10 ESV

. . . .

If you've lived through a rough season in life—whether days or decades—you might have wondered, *What is God doing?* Israel probably wondered the same thing while trekking to the Promised Land. That rough season lasted forty years. Forty years of making camp then pulling up stakes. Forty years of following pillars of cloud and fire. Forty years of clinging to a promise when surrounded by a wilderness of not knowing.

But, Moses reminded them, for forty years the Lord had never let them go hungry, never let their clothes wear out, never let their feet swell. He had never left their side. God was bringing His people through hardship to a better land. Once in this better land, though, Israel was in danger of forgetting the One who had done the doing. Surrounded by blessing, they might take the credit. Moses' advice was "Remember the LORD your God" (Deuteronomy 8:18 ESV).

In the middle of a rough season? Don't forget the Doer. God is working around and through you "to do you good in the end" (Deuteronomy 8:16 ESV). On the other side of a rough season? Don't forget the Doer. Think on and praise God for all He has done—and is yet to do.

Prayer Prompt:

Do you have questions about what God is doing in your life? Ask Him to remind you of all He has already done for you.

_____

_____

_____

_____

_____

_____

_____

_____

_____

_____

_____

_____

_____

_____

_____

_____

*Lord, even when I can't understand
what You're doing, I'll remember You.*

Love on Display

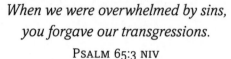

When we were overwhelmed by sins,
you forgave our transgressions.

PSALM 65:3 NIV

· ·

Simon the Pharisee invited Jesus to dinner, though no sooner had Jesus settled at the table than an uninvited guest arrived. Deeply aware of her sin, the woman wept openly and began washing and anointing the feet of the man she sought. At the sight, the Pharisee's mind churned—clearly this Jesus fellow wasn't all He claimed, or else why would He let this *sinner* touch Him? But Jesus had a reply to Simon's unspoken judgment. "Her many sins have been forgiven—as her great love has shown. But whoever has been forgiven little loves little" (Luke 7:47 NIV). The woman knew her sin was much; she also had faith that Jesus could forgive much more. Her response was an unabashed, unstinting display of love.

That can be your response too. As you realize the depth of your sin and that God's forgiveness is deeper still, you can willingly pour out all that is precious to you for Him. You can make your lives a bold display of your love for the one who forgives and makes you new. You can hear Jesus' words every day: "Your faith has saved you; go in peace" (Luke 7:50 NIV).

Prayer Prompt:

What do you need to confess before Jesus? Come to Him boldly, asking His forgiveness, and allow Him to make you new.

_____

_____

_____

_____

_____

_____

_____

_____

_____

_____

_____

_____

_____

_____

Lord, I kneel today seeking forgiveness. I've sinned, and right now the sin weighs heavily on me. But You are able to remove that sin and replace it with Your forgiveness, Your peace. Thank You!

Wait for It. . .

*"A sower went out to sow his seed. . . . And some fell
into good soil and grew and yielded a hundredfold."*
LUKE 8:5, 8 ESV

. . . .

Along the path, on the rock, among the thorns—this was how Jesus described the Word that did not take root in listeners' hearts. There's also a fourth category: into good soil. He said, "As for that in the good soil, they are those who, hearing the word, hold it fast in an honest and good heart, and bear fruit with patience" (Luke 8:15 ESV).

When we hear God's Word and believe, it grows down deep into our hearts, and through Him we begin to yield a crop. Yet don't miss Jesus' words on how we bear fruit—*with patience*. The New International Version translates the end of verse 15: "and by persevering produce a crop." The Message says: "sticking with it until there's a harvest." But let's face it, in a fast-paced, instant-download culture, aren't we more likely to become *impatient* waiting for that bounty of fruit? While some fruit we do see immediately, often the working of God in our lives takes time. As we continue to obey, though—as we persevere and stick with it—we *will* see a harvest!

Prayer Prompt:

What kind of soil is in your heart? Ask God to till your heart to receive His Word so it can take root and grow.

....

....

....

....

....

....

....

....

....

....

....

....

....

....

....

....

God, I want to be fruitful. Help me hold Your Word
fast in my heart and not give up before I yield
an abundance of good works for You.

Quite a Transformation

Come and see what God has done: he is awesome
in his deeds toward the children of man.
PSALM 66:5 ESV

- -

What a sight it must have been! Here was a demon-possessed man named Legion who lived among the tombs, wore no clothes, and would often break the chains that bound him and flee to the desert. That is, until Jesus came ashore. Jesus commanded the demons to leave the man and enter a herd of pigs, which then ran into the lake and were drowned. When word spread, curious spectators arrived to see a man transformed! Once tormented by demons, he now sat at Jesus' feet, "clothed and in his right mind" (Luke 8:35 ESV). So astonishing was the change, the people feared. But while the people asked Jesus to go away from them, the man begged to go with Him. Jesus responded, "Return to your home, and declare how much God has done for you" (Luke 8:39 ESV).

Jesus calls us to do the same. Chances are we don't have a story to tell like Legion, but God has touched our lives in equally miraculous ways. He takes souls dominated by sin and sets them free, casting that sin into the sea. He takes hearts driven into the desert and gives them a home at His feet. With whom can you share how much God has done?

Prayer Prompt:

Who needs to hear what God has done for you? Ask the Lord to show you those you can share with.

....

....

....

....

....

....

....

....

....

....

....

....

....

....

....

....

....

....

....

Lord, You've transformed me, are still transforming me, in so many ways—now I'll go and declare it!

"Only Believe"

While he was still speaking, someone from the ruler's house came and said, "Your daughter is dead; do not trouble the Teacher any more." But Jesus on hearing this answered him, "Do not fear; only believe."

LUKE 8:49–50 ESV

Jairus's young daughter was dying, so he approached Jesus for help. But their journey to the girl came to a halt when a woman in the crowd touched the hem of Jesus' garment and was healed. Jesus hadn't yet finished speaking to the woman when a messenger arrived with the sad news that Jairus's daughter had died. Although Jesus told them not to fear, they wept. Later, after Jesus told them that the child was only asleep, they laughed. *Obviously, she's dead,* they must have thought. *It's too late.* But it wasn't.

We may know God's commands and promises—that we shouldn't fear, that He's with us, that through Him *anything* is possible—but sometimes the circumstances in our lives make us want to laugh or cry. *It's no use,* we might think. Or, *Yeah right, that* [whatever "that" is in our lives] *will never happen!*

When you lack faith in God's power to do even the impossible, remember this: the one who rode into Jerusalem to conquer death on the cross says not to fear, that He's with you, and that through Him *anything* is possible.

Prayer Prompt:

What situation in your life seems impossible to fix? As you pray, remember God's promises in His Word that He can do all things whatsoever you ask.

Lord, my situation seems impossible, but You are the God who can raise the dead. Help me to simply believe.

And Then Some

*And taking the five loaves and the two fish, he looked
up to heaven and said a blessing over them.*
LUKE 9:16 ESV

. . . .

Do you ever feel as if you're running low, that there's just not enough in
a particular area of your life? The cupboards are bare. The bank account
reaches single digits. Your internal battery has next to no juice. You're not
getting any younger. Your problems outnumber your solutions.

Jesus' disciples knew the feeling. A crowd had gathered to hear Jesus teach, but evening was fast approaching. Thousands of people were
about to get hungry. Instead of sending the throng away to fend for itself,
as the disciples had suggested, Jesus told the Twelve to feed the people.
But there wasn't enough to go around, they argued. "We have only five
loaves of bread and two fish. . . . Or are you expecting us to go and buy
enough food for this whole crowd?" (Luke 9:13 NLT). Focused solely on
what they lacked, the disciples were correct: there wasn't enough. They
needed to look to God to provide—and He provided. Those five loaves
and two fish became a feast with some to spare.

Whether you're short on supplies, funds, energy, time, ideas. . .look
to God. He is able to turn a little into a lot.

Prayer Prompt:

What are you running low on? Turn to God in prayer for the answers and the supply that you need.

....

....

....

....

....

....

....

....

....

....

....

....

....

....

....

....

....

God, I'm running low, so I'm looking to You. You alone can provide. You alone can transform weakness into strength, make something out of nothing—and then some.

My Cross

*Then he said to the crowd, "If any of you wants to
be my follower, you must give up your own way,
take up your cross daily, and follow me."*

LUKE 9:23 NLT

The Bible says that as believers we are new creations (2 Corinthians 5:17). Out with the old, in with the new. We cannot profess faith in Jesus and continue on as we did before, because He transforms us from day one and into eternity.

That's why when Christ spoke to the crowds eager to follow Him, He did not soften His message. He did not sugarcoat what it meant to be called by His name then or now. "If you want to be known as a Christian," He said, "you must say no to 'you' and follow Me." Jesus' instruction to "take up your cross" wasn't a crowd-boosting catchphrase. His listeners knew what the cross symbolized, and an agonizing death was anything but appealing. And it would only become less appealing when, later, Jesus lived out His words—denying Himself, taking up a cross, and following where His Father led.

So why would anyone want to be His follower? God's promise stands: "If you try to hang on to your life, you will lose it. But if you give up your life for my sake, you will save it" (Luke 9:24 NLT).

Prayer Prompt:

What keeps you from taking up your cross? Ask Jesus to give you the strength to let go of your desires and follow Him.

....

....

....

....

....

....

....

....

....

....

....

....

....

....

....

....

....

....

....

....

Lord, teach me how to leave myself behind as I shoulder
that cross and follow You. For in You, my loss is really gain.

DAY 98

He Shall

God shall arise, his enemies shall be scattered; and those who
hate him shall flee before him! . . . But the righteous shall be glad;
they shall exult before God; they shall be jubilant with joy!
PSALM 68:1, 3 ESV

. . . .

Look around, and you might conclude that those who are against God
have the upper hand. Wickedness thrives, while God's ways are dragged through the mud. You may wonder why God doesn't defend His
good name. In your heart, you may even be like James and John who,
after some Samaritan villagers rejected Jesus, said, "Lord, do you
want us to tell fire to come down from heaven and consume them?"
(Luke 9:54 ESV). But Jesus didn't turn to His disciples and say, "Yes!" He
rebuked them.

Once saved, your job on earth is not to avenge. What's more, you don't
have to fret over the state of your world today or any number of tomor-
rows. You're to show the love and mercy of your Savior to a generation
of people who are against God and dying apart from Him. You're to rest
in the promise that, at the right time and with perfect justice, God shall
arise. He will take care of those who ultimately reject Him just as surely
as He will care for those who receive righteousness through His Son.

Prayer Prompt:

What troubles you about the people in the world around you? Ask God to take away any feelings of vengeance and lead you to those who need Him.

....

....

....

....

....

....

....

....

....

....

....

....

....

....

....

....

....

....

God, I was Your enemy, but now I am Your child. Lead me to where I can share Your salvation with others.

What Are You Waiting For?

"Woe to you, Chorazin! Woe to you, Bethsaida! For if the mighty works done in you had been done in Tyre and Sidon, they would have repented long ago."
LUKE 10:13 ESV

. . . .

When God brings a sin to your attention, how do you respond? Do you hem and haw a bit before admitting the wrong and asking for forgiveness? Do you drag your feet before making changes?

Dealing with sin in our lives isn't easy, but as God forms us from the inside to be more like Christ, repenting of bad behavior and living in obedience is vital. We shouldn't close our ears to the things God calls us to do and be like the unrepentant cities that Jesus spoke about. And why would we not *want* to repent? Think on what Moses told Israel: "All these blessings shall come upon you and overtake you, if you obey the voice of the LORD your God. Blessed shall you be in the city, and blessed shall you be in the field. . . . Blessed shall you be when you come in, and blessed shall you be when you go out" (Deuteronomy 28:2–3, 6 ESV). Our loving heavenly Father reaches to us with blessing in place of woe. He offers forgiveness if only we'll repent.

Is God whispering to your heart? Don't wait.

Prayer Prompt:

What do you need to confess to God? As you pray, listen for God speaking to your heart and respond to Him.

_Father, You've been revealing a sin in my life,
and I've been ignoring it. Please forgive
me and help me start fresh._

DAY 100

Borne

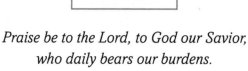

Praise be to the Lord, to God our Savior,
who daily bears our burdens.
PSALM 68:19 NIV

. . . .

Burdens. They weigh us down. What do you envision when you think about the thing that burdens you? Maybe a chock-full schedule, a difficult marriage, a chronic illness, or a trying job. Yet no matter who we are or what we're experiencing, our greatest burden is sin. Sin not only weighs us down but can crush us beneath its weight. Sin separates us from God and exacts a steep penalty—death. But there's good news! On a day long ago, Christ bore our greatest burden. He shouldered the consequences of our sin on the cross.

And the impact of Christ's death ripples through the centuries to change us today. Before Christ we were dead in sin; now because of Him we live. Jesus exchanges a heavy yoke for a light one, promising to walk with us, side by side. So the next time you think about the thing that burdens you, instead of envisioning yourself alone to carry that burden, picture your Savior lifting the load and supporting you to boot. As the psalmist wrote, "Blessed be the Lord, who daily bears *us* up; God is our salvation" (Psalm 68:19 ESV, emphasis added). The one who did not bend beneath sin's weight but rose again is carrying your burden—and you.

Prayer Prompt:

What are you trying to carry all by yourself? Ask the Lord to help you carry those burdens.

....

....

....

....

....

....

....

....

....

....

....

....

....

....

....

....

....

....

Lord, thank You for life in You! When I'm lugging burdens alone, tap my shoulder; remind me that You are here.

Your Choice

But the Lord answered her, "Martha, Martha, you are anxious and troubled about many things, but one thing is necessary. Mary has chosen the good portion, which will not be taken away from her."

LUKE 10:41–42 ESV

. . . .

Every human being on earth has a choice. Either believe in God, loving and obeying Him, or don't. Moses outlined that choice for God's people on the plains of Moab. He said, "Today I have given you the choice between life and death, between blessings and curses. . . . Oh, that you would choose life, so that you and your descendants might live!" (Deuteronomy 30:19 NLT).

Over a thousand years later, Jesus addressed another choice for believers on a visit to His friends Mary, Martha, and Lazarus. While Martha hurried around serving her guests, Mary hunkered down at Jesus' feet. But in response to Martha's request—"Tell her to help!"—Jesus replied, "Martha, Martha. . ." He knew what would help Martha more than an extra pair of hands. Mary's choice to worship her Lord and to soak up His teaching was "the good portion," an investment in her soul.

Moses longed for Israel to choose life. Can you hear the longing in Jesus' words also? Oh, that we would choose the good portion and see what a difference it makes!

Prayer Prompt:

What are you choosing today? Spend some time at the feet of Jesus as you pray.

....

....

....

....

....

....

....

....

....

....

....

....

....

....

....

....

....

Lord, You deserve my full attention. And as I spend time with You, You work in me. So I choose life. I choose You every day.

Proof Positive

"Behold, something greater than Jonah is here."
LUKE 11:32 ESV

. . . .

"I just need a sign!" You're not alone if you've ever wanted a sign to help you believe.

People in Jesus' day requested signs, some people with good motives, others not. To a group of bad-motive sign seekers, Jesus said, "The mood of this age is all wrong. Everybody's looking for proof, but you're looking for the wrong kind. All you're looking for is something to titillate your curiosity, satisfy your lust for miracles. But the only proof you're going to get is the Jonah-proof given to the Ninevites, which looks like no proof at all" (Luke 11:29 MSG). The crowd asked for a sign, and Jesus pointed to the scriptures. Jonah spent three days in the belly of a fish and was spewed out to preach God's message to Nineveh. With only Jonah as proof, the Ninevites believed God.

But Jesus went further: "What Jonah was to Nineveh, the Son of Man is to this age" (Luke 11:30 MSG)—and He was something greater. Christ spent three days in a tomb and was raised from the dead to shout God's love to the world. Jesus' generation had all the proof necessary. So do we.

God's Word records the grandest sign of all. It begins with a cross and ends with an empty grave.

Prayer Prompt:

What kind of sign are you seeking today? Ask God to open your eyes to the signs He has already given you in His Word.

....

....

....

....

....

....

....

....

....

....

....

....

....

....

....

....

....

God, when I need a sign, direct my eyes to Your Word.
It's powerful, transforming my uncertainty into belief.

From the Inside Out

And the Lord said to him, "Now you Pharisees cleanse the
outside of the cup and of the dish, but inside you are full of
greed and wickedness. You fools! Did not he who made the
outside make the inside also? But give as alms those things
that are within, and behold, everything is clean for you."

LUKE 11:39–41 ESV

With the Pharisees, what you saw wasn't what you got. This group of religious elites was skilled at putting up a facade. Outwardly, the Pharisees fulfilled the law but inwardly lacked a godly heart. Jesus compared their actions to cleaning the outside of a cup but leaving the inside untouched. They sure looked giving but were actually greedy. Jesus had a few words of warning and advice for them: "What sorrow awaits you Pharisees! For you are careful to tithe even the tiniest income from your herb gardens, but you ignore justice and the love of God. You should tithe, yes, but do not neglect the more important things" (Luke 11:42 NLT).

God, who created the whole person, cares about the inside too. In fact, God prioritizes the inside. He first changes the heart, and out of it flows the good. So rather than getting caught up in appearances, check your attitude. Give from inner stores of goodness, and you'll be clean inside and out.

Prayer Prompt:

What condition is your heart in? Pray like the psalmist David did:
"Create in me a clean heart, O God."

_____

_____

_____

_____

_____

_____

_____

_____

_____

_____

_____

_____

_____

_____

_____

_____

_____

*God, I'm not fooling You. Change me so that my
outside is a true reflection of the good within.*

Unhidden

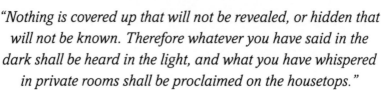

"Nothing is covered up that will not be revealed, or hidden that will not be known. Therefore whatever you have said in the dark shall be heard in the light, and what you have whispered in private rooms shall be proclaimed on the housetops."

LUKE 12:2–3 ESV

God is a mystery. Right? There's so much we don't understand about God and what He does. But while we cannot know everything, God chooses to reveal His truth—He wants to reveal it! When Jesus came to earth, He did not come seeking to make God's truth known to only a few. His mission, and now ours, included announcing the truth to the whole world.

Spending time in God's Word is one way believers learn divine truth. As we read, the Holy Spirit interprets for us. Through scripture, we grow in our understanding of God and His ways, and we learn how to pattern our lives after truth.

Part of God's instructions to Joshua after Moses' death was to read scripture. The Lord said: "Keep this Book of the Law always on your lips; meditate on it day and night" (Joshua 1:8 NIV). It was by keeping God's words close that Joshua would obey and be successful. That goes for you too; Jesus would later tell believers to abide in the Word, because by abiding you will know truth and be set free (John 8:31–32).

Prayer Prompt:

What have you been meditating on? Ask the Lord to give you a hunger for His truth.

....

....

....

....

....

....

....

....

....

....

....

....

....

....

....

....

....

....

....

Lord, show me Your truth so I can
proclaim it on the housetops.

Worriless

Fear not, little flock; for it is your Father's
good pleasure to give you the kingdom.
LUKE 12:32 KJV

. . . .

Your heart is beating fast. Your mind won't settle. Your breaths barely reach your lungs. You're anxious, worried about this or that. Truth is, there's a lot you can choose to be anxious about—family, work, money, health, war, weather, the future. . . But this is also true: you can't change anything with anxious thoughts. Even before there was cyberbullying, nuclear weapons, and pages-long to-do lists, Jesus anticipated your tendency to worry. He told His disciples, "And which of you by being anxious can add a single hour to his span of life? If then you are not able to do as small a thing as that, why are you anxious about the rest?" (Luke 12:25–26 ESV).

Since worry achieves nothing but more worry, what should you do instead? "Seek the Kingdom of God above all else, and he will give you everything you need" (Luke 12:31 NLT). Your God—the one who fills the bellies of the birds and clothes the lilies like royalty—knows your needs, and He is capable and faithful to satisfy them. More than that, it is His *pleasure* to care for you. So turn every anxious thought into a chance to focus on your Father. With eyes fixed on Him, the kingdom itself is yours.

Prayer Prompt:

What is causing you to be anxious today? As you pray, give that anxiety to God. Ask Him to bring peace into your life.

Father, use this anxiety to draw me toward You. I can be calm because You care.

A Verbal Sacrifice

I will praise the name of God with a song; I will magnify him with thanksgiving. This will please the Lord more than an ox or a bull with horns and hoofs.

Psalm 69:30–31 esv

Growing up, how hard did you work to please your parents or the people who raised you? What was on your mental list of things to do? Make good grades, excel at sports, do your chores, mind your manners? When we think of pleasing the ones we love, our minds often go to *actions*. And why not? Actions speak louder than words, we're told.

As children of God, we want to please our heavenly Father too. What is on our mental list of things to do for Him? Read the Bible, volunteer at church, give weekly tithes, follow God's rules? Good things, every one, because through them we grow in God and express a heart devoted to Him. But consider what the psalmist said: "I will praise the name of God with a song, and will magnify Him with thanksgiving. This also shall please the Lord better than an ox or bull" (Psalm 69:30–31 nkjv). In Old Testament times, animal sacrifices pleased the Lord, yet the "actions" that would please Him more than oxen and bulls were words.

Take time to praise—and please!—God today.

Prayer Prompt:

What are you offering to God today? As you pray, spend some time in praise to God, sing a song to Him, magnify His name.

....

....

....

....

....

....

....

....

....

....

....

....

....

....

....

....

....

God, my words seem so inadequate to praise
You, the Most High, but may even my small
offering become a pleasing aroma.

Ask First

Then the men of Israel took some of their provisions;
but they did not ask counsel of the LORD.

JOSHUA 9:14 NKJV

. . . .

Jericho and Ai had fallen, but the Gibeonites weren't cowering; the Bible says they "acted with cunning" (Joshua 9:4 ESV). The plan was simple: gather worn-out sacks, wineskins, sandals, and clothes, along with some stale bread, and go appeal to Joshua as inhabitants of a faraway country. The Gibeonite spokesmen asked for mercy and presented their props as proof: "Here is our bread. It was still warm when we took it from our houses as our food for the journey on the day we set out to come to you, but now, behold, it is dry and crumbly. These wineskins were new when we filled them, and behold, they have burst" (Joshua 9:12–13 ESV). All that was missing was a plaintive violin solo. Israel fell for it anyway. But why? Because they did not seek God's advice. God commanded Israel to destroy the inhabitants of the land, and Israel ended up pledging peace to Gibeon. That one decision would have consequences, but what's remarkable is the fact that in the days that followed, God would work around their blunder. His people's lack of obedience would not derail His plan.

God has the power to redeem your mistakes too. Yet isn't it better to ask His counsel in the first place?

Prayer Prompt:

What kind of decisions are you facing? Pray and ask God for His direction before you make the final choice.

_____
_____
_____
_____
_____
_____
_____
_____
_____
_____
_____
_____
_____
_____
_____
_____
_____
_____

God, You offer wisdom freely.
Remind me to seek before I act.

A Little Longer

*"But he answered and said to him, 'Sir, let it alone this year
also, until I dig around it and fertilize it. And if it bears
fruit, well. But if not, after that you can cut it down.' "*
LUKE 13:8–9 NKJV

. . . .

An ordinary day had just begun as the man surveyed his garden. Yes! Over there, in that open spot, was the perfect place for a fig tree. He summoned his gardener, who planted the tree. But day after day the man checked the tree only to find—nothing! No figs ever graced the branches. Three years went by without any fruit, and finally the man grew tired of that barren fig tree. "Cut it down," he ordered. "It's just taking up space in the garden" (Luke 13:7 NLT). The gardener, however, was not ready to write off the figless fig tree. He said, "Sir, give it one more chance. Leave it another year" (Luke 13:8 NLT). With extra care, maybe the tree would bear fruit.

Aren't you glad that our Lord is like the gardener? If our lives resemble the barren fig tree, Jesus does not shout, "Cut it down!" He intercedes for us. He is patient toward us. He puts in the extra work to make us fruitful. Let's not resist His hand when He digs up the soil and pours His Word into our hearts.

Prayer Prompt:

What kind of fruit are you bearing or is your life barren? Ask the Lord to dig around your roots and fertilize your life.

....

....

....

....

....

....

....

....

....

....

....

....

....

....

....

....

....

Lord, I was dormant many years. Thank You for grace. Thank You for Your tender care.

Strive!

*"Strive to enter through the narrow door. For many,
I tell you, will seek to enter and will not be able."*

LUKE 13:23–24 ESV

Grace alone. By faith, not by works. At the core of the gospel is the truth that we cannot earn a place in heaven. Only Christ's righteousness can make us right with God. And when we believe in Him, eternal life is ours. So what are we to make of Jesus' response in Luke 13? *"Strive* to enter"? Salvation, although freely offered, isn't a free pass. Jesus called it the narrow door for a reason: choosing Christ costs us, and not everyone is willing to pay. Truly accepting goes beyond agreeing to facts; we must turn from sin and bow not to ourselves but to our Lord, even when our flesh and the world shout to do the opposite. Still Jesus tells us, "Make every effort to enter through the narrow door. . . . Once the owner of the house gets up and closes the door, you will stand outside knocking and pleading, 'Sir, open the door for us.' But he will answer, 'I don't know you' " (Luke 13:24–25 NIV). *Now* is the time to choose Christ and follow Him, to go through that narrow door and hear Jesus say, "I know you—come in!"

Prayer Prompt:

What are you striving for? Who are you striving to please? Spend
time talking to God about the goals and direction of your life.

....

....

....

....

....

....

....

....

....

....

....

....

....

....

....

....

....

*Lord and Savior, I choose to model my life after
Yours. Thank You for opening Your door to me.*

Be Humble

"All those who exalt themselves will be humbled,
and those who humble themselves will be exalted."
LUKE 14:11 NIV

Humility isn't trending these days. So much in our culture promotes a "Look at me!" lifestyle that humbling oneself seems unnatural. Turns out humility wasn't too popular in biblical times either, because Jesus broke into a dinner conversation to tell the guests a parable:

> *"When you are invited to a wedding feast, don't sit in the seat of honor. What if someone who is more distinguished than you has also been invited? The host will come and say, 'Give this person your seat.' Then you will be embarrassed, and you will have to take whatever seat is left at the foot of the table! Instead, take the lowest place at the foot of the table. Then when your host sees you, he will come and say, 'Friend, we have a better place for you!'"*
> LUKE 14:8–10 NLT

Jesus did as He preached. He was, in fact, an expert at humility. He traded a kingly crown for a thorny one—for our sake. Yet He was exalted and now sits on His throne in heaven.

We could all use a lesson in humility from the expert. And as we learn how to humble ourselves, we can rest assured that we too will be exalted.

Prayer Prompt:

What part does humility play in your life? Ask Jesus to place you where He wants you to be, exalted by Him, not by others or yourself.

....

....

....

....

....

....

....

....

....

....

....

....

....

....

....

....

....

*Lord, show me where I can be more humble
so that I'm exalted by You, not me.*

Pass the Salt, Please

"Salt is good, but if it loses its saltiness, how can it be made salty again? It is fit neither for the soil nor for the manure pile; it is thrown out. Whoever has ears to hear, let them hear."

LUKE 14:34–35 NIV

Rubbed into a hunk of meat or fish, salt allows it to remain in unrefrigerated air and not spoil. That homely mineral keeps the bad stuff at bay. Just as salt preserves foodstuffs, Christians, who Jesus called the "salt of the earth" (Matthew 5:13), are to act as a preservative in society, slowing the decay that sin inevitably causes.

"Salt is good," Jesus said. But salt that isn't salty? Not so much. It's not even useful for the manure pile.

In a rotting world, we as believers need to be salt—*and* to maintain our saltiness! To do this, we're to have salt in ourselves (Mark 9:50). But the source of that pure salt isn't us; it's God. His Word and the Spirit rubbed into our hearts not only stop the decay but reverse the damage, making us new and seasoning our interactions with Him and others.

So no skimping on the purest of salt. Add whole cupfuls of scripture and prayer to your day, and let the world see what salt can do.

Prayer Prompt:

What kind of seasoning is being sprinkled into your life? Ask the Lord to season you with His Word and Spirit.

....

....

....

....

....

....

....

....

....

....

....

....

....

....

....

....

....

....

I can't be salt without You, Lord. Keep me salty so others will notice and seek You.

Kingdom Come

Give the king Your judgments, O God,
and Your righteousness to the king's Son.
PSALM 72:1 NKJV

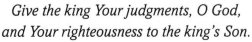

Psalm 72 is a coronation psalm asking God's favor for the reign of Solomon, who became king of Israel following his father, David. Although no New Testament writers use the psalm to describe Jesus, Psalm 72 also anticipates a future time when the King of kings will reign. Here are just a few glimpses of what His kingdom will be like:

> *He will bring justice to the poor of the people; He will save the children of the needy, and will break in pieces the oppressor. . . .*
> *He shall come down like rain upon the grass before mowing, like showers that water the earth. In His days the righteous shall flourish, and abundance of peace, until the moon is no more. He shall have dominion also from sea to sea, and from the River to the ends of the earth. . . . Yes, all kings shall fall down before Him; all nations shall serve Him.*

PSALM 72:4, 6–8, 11 NKJV

If life today discourages you, train your eyes on Jesus. One day, maybe this very day, He will return, and when He moves in, He'll renovate this old world. He'll reign over every inch and every being, and with His reign there will be justice, blessing, and peace.

Prayer Prompt:

How are you preparing for Jesus and His kingdom? Ask Him to keep you kingdom-ready for His return.

....

....

....

....

....

....

....

....

....

....

....

....

....

....

....

....

....

Lord, You already reign in my heart—
I can't wait for You to reign here on earth!

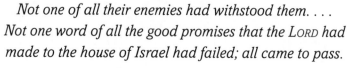

Trust Him

Not one of all their enemies had withstood them. . . .
Not one word of all the good promises that the LORD had
made to the house of Israel had failed; all came to pass.
JOSHUA 21:44–45 ESV

- -

Can I trust God? Has that thought ever crossed your mind? When looking for an answer, don't overlook the Word. It's a sixty-six-book chronicle of God's faithfulness—from the beginning of time to the end times—that you can hold in one hand.

Take Israel's entering and claiming the Promised Land. God promised that Abraham's descendants would possess the land—and what God promised, God fulfilled. Every word came about. Every enemy fell. God saw to it.

You have the record of how God kept His promise in the book of Joshua. True, your eyes might glaze over as you read the lists of allotments and inheritances, but the detail goes to show the intimacy of the Lord in His children's lives, the meticulous attention He gives to the ones He loves.

God hasn't changed since then and never will (Hebrews 13:8). Although you may not be a nomad conquering a vast territory, God is just as involved, just as powerful, just as faithful in your life as He was in the life of Joshua's Israelites.

Prayer Prompt:

What promise do you need to claim today? As you pray, claim God's promises and trust Him to keep His promises.

....

....

....

....

....

....

....

....

....

....

....

....

....

....

....

....

....

....

God, You are faithful from generation to generation,
age to age, time without end. Whatever You've done in
my life and whatever You're going to do, I can trust You.

Money Matters

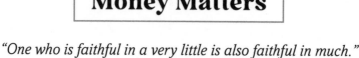

"One who is faithful in a very little is also faithful in much."
LUKE 16:10 ESV

. . . .

The *m*-word. *Money.* Does a day go by without some thought to the greenbacks in your wallet? While money may make the world go 'round, Christ calls Christians to have a different perspective. This, in a nutshell, is what He taught the disciples:

Point #1: "If you have not been trustworthy in handling worldly wealth, who will trust you with true riches?" (Luke 16:11 NIV). Money isn't about the here and now but the hereafter. Use it for eternal purposes by investing in souls before stocks.

Point #2: "If you have not been trustworthy with someone else's property, who will give you property of your own?" (Luke 16:12 NIV). Money isn't yours but His. Manage the Master's finances well while He's away.

Point #3: "No one can serve two masters. Either you will hate the one and love the other, or you will be devoted to the one and despise the other. You cannot serve both God and money" (Luke 16:13 NIV). Money isn't your god—God is! Live for and worship Him alone.

Regardless of your budgeting skills, spending habits, or bank balance, God *can* change your mind-set about money. You *can* be faithful whether in small things or big.

Prayer Prompt:

What is your relationship with money? Ask God how you can be a
better money manager.

....

....

....

....

....

....

....

....

....

....

....

....

....

....

....

....

....

....

*I'm not always a good steward, God. Would You give me
Your mind for money? In all I do, I want to please You.*

"I Don't Know!"

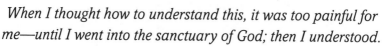

When I thought how to understand this, it was too painful for
me—until I went into the sanctuary of God; then I understood.
PSALM 73:16–17 NKJV

No amount of research or number of advancements would change the situation. We could all be as wise as Solomon, and we would never run out of tough questions—from broad, age-old quandaries like "Why do bad things happen to good people?" to personal, in-the-moment cries of our hearts.

The writer of Psalm 73 wrestled with some questions of his own. He observed the wicked, their opulence and pride, yet they had nary a trouble in sight. He said, "Look at these wicked people—enjoying a life of ease while their riches multiply," then asked, "Did I keep my heart pure for nothing? Did I keep myself innocent for no reason?" (Psalm 73:12–13 NLT). But any attempts at understanding led to more frustration. "What a difficult task it is!" he concluded. Not until he turned to God did he find his answer: "*Then* I went into your sanctuary, O God, and I finally understood the destiny of the wicked" (Psalm 73:16–17 NLT, emphasis added). What relief! God took a troubled mind and settled it with His wisdom.

Are you wrestling with a tough question? Hear this: when you try and try and still don't know the answers, go to the omniscient one, the one who *does* know.

Prayer Prompt:

What questions do you have for God? When you pray, talk to God about those questions on your mind.

_____

_____

_____

_____

_____

_____

_____

_____

_____

_____

_____

_____

_____

_____

_____

_____

_____

_____

_____

_____

God, You know everything. Please help me understand.

DAY 116

Heaven Minded

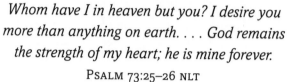

Whom have I in heaven but you? I desire you more than anything on earth. . . . God remains the strength of my heart; he is mine forever.
PSALM 73:25–26 NLT

. . . .

The alarm rings, dings, or sings. You get out of bed, get ready for the day. You work, eat, play. Then you do it again tomorrow. You go through the routine of living—day by day, year after year, life stage to life stage. With the world humming along as usual, how easy it is to forget that suddenly it won't.

Jesus warned His second coming would happen out of the blue. To describe the scenario, He used illustrations from the past: "When the Son of Man returns, it will be like it was in Noah's day. In those days, the people enjoyed banquets and parties and weddings right up to the time Noah entered his boat and the flood came and destroyed them all" (Luke 17:26–27 NLT). Then He compared His arrival to Lot's day when people were occupied with "eating and drinking, buying and selling, farming and building" (Luke 17:28 NLT), unaware of their and Sodom's imminent destruction.

God doesn't ask you to stop living. Merely, as you go about your daily routine, never lose sight of the one who's above all.

Prayer Prompt:

How does your routine affect your spiritual life? Pray that Christ will keep you alert to His coming and keep you ever ready.

....

....

....

....

....

....

....

....

....

....

....

....

....

....

....

....

....

God, nothing in heaven or on earth outshines
You. May I never be so preoccupied with
this life that I forget the next one.

O Mighty Woman

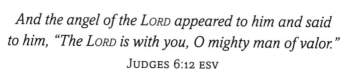

*And the angel of the L*ORD *appeared to him and said
to him, "The L*ORD *is with you, O mighty man of valor."*
JUDGES 6:12 ESV

Preposterous—that's what the greeting must have seemed to Gideon. There he was threshing wheat in a winepress, keeping the crop hidden from the Midianites, and *whoosh*, the angel of the Lord appeared and called him "mighty man of valor." Then the angel told Gideon to go rescue Israel. What?! Gideon couldn't believe it. He replied, "Please, Lord, how can I save Israel? Behold, my clan is the weakest in Manasseh, and I am the least in my father's house" (Judges 6:15 ESV). Gideon was a little guy among little guys. Surely God didn't mean for *him* to deliver a nation. But the Lord was figuring on something that Gideon wasn't in that moment. "I will be with you," He said (Judges 6:16 ESV).

At times, God's plans and purposes for you may seem, well, preposterous. Yet God often calls you to do incredible things, because He also calls you to depend on Him. Jesus told the disciples, "Truly, I say to you, whoever does not receive the kingdom of God like a child shall not enter it" (Luke 18:17 ESV). Entrance into the kingdom requires utter dependence on God. Just think what He can do through you until then.

Prayer Prompt:

What is God asking you to do? Talk to Him about His plans for you, and confess that you need His help.

....

....

....

....

....

....

....

....

....

....

....

....

....

....

....

....

....

....

Lord, I'm far from a mighty woman without You,
but I'm not without You. I'm totally depending on You.

Godly Conduits

*While each man held his position around the camp,
all the Midianites ran, crying out as they fled.*

JUDGES 7:21 NIV

Gideon's army was encamped and ready for battle, but the troops didn't quite pass muster. The problem? There were *too many* soldiers. So the Lord whittled the army down to size—a grand total of three hundred men versus an enemy that looked "like locusts in abundance" with enough camels to outnumber the sand on a beach (Judges 7:12 ESV). What might seem senseless to us made a lot of sense to God, though. God didn't need a powerful army. He had every ounce of power necessary within Himself, and He was going to prove it.

Contrast this with an incident that occurred before the Israelites headed off to fight. God instructed Gideon to destroy an altar dedicated to Baal. When the men in town discovered the ruins, they threatened Gideon. But Gideon said, "Will you contend for Baal? . . . If he is a god, let him contend for himself" (Judges 6:31 ESV). Baal could no more act than the rocks that once comprised his altar. The false god was as powerless as God Almighty was powerful.

God sometimes chooses to display His power in people. A few hundred men stood still while the Lord brought a vast army to its knees. Have faith that your God works as mightily even now.

Prayer Prompt:

How is God choosing to act in your life? Are you willing to stand still while He works? As you pray, ask God to make His power known to you.

God, I stand in awe of how powerful You are!

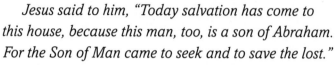

A New Résumé

*Jesus said to him, "Today salvation has come to
this house, because this man, too, is a son of Abraham.
For the Son of Man came to seek and to save the lost."*

LUKE 19:9–10 NIV

. . . .

Zacchaeus: chief tax collector; wealthy; disloyal to the Jews. Nothing in Zacchaeus's résumé suggested what he was about to do. Jesus was passing through Jericho, and Zacchaeus was curious. But he was also short. The gathered crowds blocked his view. Not to be dismayed, Zacchaeus climbed a convenient sycamore tree, using a branch as an overhead-row seat. Yet the spectacle of this grown man, who probably strutted down the streets of Jericho and was now up in a tree, is not where the story ends. Zacchaeus would receive Jesus joyfully, repent of his old ways, and make restitution. Zacchaeus's new résumé read "son of Abraham; saved by the Lord."

Jesus came to seek and save sinners—people like Zacchaeus, like us. While the crowds grumbled and thought of Zacchaeus as beyond redemption, Jesus knew better. *No one* is barred from salvation, because *nothing* is impossible for God. He can radically change even the worst sinners (1 Timothy 1:15).

Yes, Jesus came to seek and save sinners, to change lives. How will He revise your résumé?

Prayer Prompt:

Are you looking at someone's past and doubting they can change? Jesus came to seek and save even that person. Ask Him to change how you see this person.

....

....

....

....

....

....

....

....

....

....

....

....

....

....

....

....

Lord, give me eyes to see as You see. You look through the sin to the soul, to the difference You can make there. Rewrite my life as I seek You.

DAY 120

Let the Whole World Rejoice

He answered, "I tell you, if these were silent,
the very stones would cry out."
LUKE 19:40 ESV

. . . .

Jesus—sitting atop a colt, cloaks spread out on the road in front of Him—entered Jerusalem. As He journeyed toward the Mount of Olives, all at once the air reverberated with sound. Luke recorded the event this way: "The whole multitude of his disciples began to rejoice and praise God with a loud voice. . .saying, 'Blessed is the King who comes in the name of the Lord! Peace in heaven and glory in the highest!' " (Luke 19:37–38 ESV). These words echo Luke's earlier account of Jesus' birth, when "suddenly. . .a multitude of the heavenly host" filled the sky and proclaimed, "Glory to God in the highest, and on earth peace, goodwill toward men!" (Luke 2:13–14 NKJV). A child had been born (Isaiah 9:6). The Messiah had arrived. First the angels and later the disciples responded with praise.

Ever the spoilsports, though, some Pharisees objected to the hubbub. "Rebuke them!" they demanded. But the worship was not only appropriate, it was inevitable. Should the crowd cease praising Him, Jesus said, creation would take up the refrain. God would make worshippers out of the rocks. Just as He makes worshippers out of all who believe in Him.

Prayer Prompt:

Who or what has taken your place in worshipping God? Cry out to God in prayer and worship Him.

_____

_____

_____

_____

_____

_____

_____

_____

_____

_____

_____

_____

_____

_____

_____

_____

_____

_____

Praise to You, God! You are so worthy that even the stones and fields and seas worship You. How glad I am to join in!

Foundation Keeper

*"When the earth quakes and its people live in turmoil,
I am the one who keeps its foundations firm."*
PSALM 75:3 NLT

Do parts of life ever feel like a moving target? Maybe you're focusing your aim in a certain direction when some change in circumstance causes upheaval, refocus, and re-aim. And if that upheaval is a result of some kind of trauma—an accident, a natural disaster, a financial setback, an illness, a scandal—it can feel like the whole world has turned upside down.

Our Father God knows these times will come for us all. Jesus even told His disciples to *expect* tough times, saying, "Here on earth you will have many trials and sorrows" (John 16:33 NLT). In the same breath (and verse), He added a hope-filled promise: "But take heart, because I have overcome the world."

The shifting sands of this world will move, but if Jesus is the foundation of your faith and hope, your world cannot be rocked so hard that you will not prevail. The more you learn about Him and become like Him, the better you can stand on a solid foundation, relying on His immovable nature to see you through. For as God said clearly in Malachi 3:6 (NLT), "I am the LORD, and I do not change."

Prayer Prompt:

What's shaking your world right now? As you pray, turn it over to God. He is the victor in all circumstances.

....

....

....

....

....

....

....

....

....

....

....

....

....

....

....

....

Father, keep me rooted firmly in You as my immovable foundation. Keep me in Your Word. Keep me in constant communication through prayer. Amen.

Know Your Purpose

"You will become pregnant and give birth to a son, and his hair must never be cut. For he will be dedicated to God as a Nazirite from birth. He will begin to rescue Israel from the Philistines."

JUDGES 13:5 NLT

Baby Samson came with an instruction manual *and* a prophecy:

1. Don't cut his hair.
2. Dedicate him to God as a Nazirite.
3. Someday he will begin to rescue Israel from the Philistines.

This infant grew to be an amazingly strong man with superhero-like qualities who, despite his own shortcomings and sin (read Judges 13–16 for his full story), ultimately fulfilled his prebirth prophecy.

Do you ever wish that an angel had not only given your parents an instruction manual but proclaimed your purpose before your birth? If you've ever struggled with meaning—what you're meant to do on earth—you're not alone.

Although you may sometimes feel small and insignificant and unable to do anything really worthwhile in this messed-up world, know this: when God designed your life, He didn't roll the dice and arbitrarily place you. No, He crafted your unique position—the years you live, the family you belong to, the career you pursue, the friends you choose, your passions and abilities—to give you the opportunity to make an everlasting impact on the world. Big, earth-changing revivals or small, personal kindnesses alike—you can make a difference.

Prayer Prompt:

What do you feel God has planned for you to do? If you are unsure, ask Him to show you where He wants you to make an impact.

....

....

....

....

....

....

....

....

....

....

....

....

....

....

....

....

....

God, please show me how to make an everlasting impact today. Use me, Father. Amen.

Two Small Coins

"I tell you the truth," Jesus said, "this poor widow has given more than all the rest of them. For they have given a tiny part of their surplus, but she, poor as she is, has given everything she has."
Luke 21:3–4 nlt

• •

Financial giving seems like a pretty simple transaction. Some person or organization has a need, and others give to fill that need. It's opening up a wallet and removing bills. It's swiping a card or tapping an app. On rare occasions, it's trying to remember the proper way to write a check. Not much different than any other time currency changes hands, right?

Wrong. Jesus doesn't just want our cold, hard cash. He wants our hearts to be involved in the giving. A generous spirit that honors God, Jesus says, gives sacrificially. It's about stretching ourselves to give out of gratefulness for what God has provided, whether we have much or little.

When it comes down to it, God owns it all anyway. We are merely the caretakers of His resources. So the next time an opportunity to give arises, ask the supplier what He wants you to do. He can and will use you in a mighty way!

Prayer Prompt:

How do you feel about giving money or giving of yourself? Ask the Lord to give you a generous spirit and show you what and where to give.

....
....
....
....
....
....
....
....
....
....
....
....
....
....

Generous supplier of my needs, forgive me when I act like my money is solely mine to hoard and squander. I want the resources You've blessed me with to be used to further Your kingdom. Show me how and where. Amen.

Disappearing Act

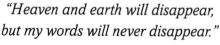

*"Heaven and earth will disappear,
but my words will never disappear."*

LUKE 21:33 NLT

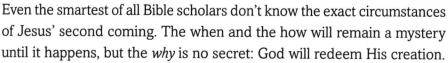

Even the smartest of all Bible scholars don't know the exact circumstances of Jesus' second coming. The when and the how will remain a mystery until it happens, but the *why* is no secret: God will redeem His creation.

Part of that redemption means the present heaven and earth will be replaced with a new heaven and a new earth, which the apostle John wrote about in Revelation 21. Jesus mentioned a similar disappearing act to His followers in Luke 21, probably causing some angst in the crowd. Yes, the evaporation of heaven and earth *seems* troubling, but Jesus followed that preface by saying *His words will never disappear.* That means God's Holy Word and all the promises within it are more real and eternal today than the ground beneath your feet.

When friends walk out, when a job goes up in smoke, when a loved one dies, when it feels as though heaven and earth are disappearing now, God's power, compassion, grace, love, authority, and dominion over all speak through His Word. Dig in, and hold on to the true source of hope.

Prayer Prompt:

How often do you read God's Word? Ask God to give you a hunger for His Word that will never disappear.

....

....

....

....

....

....

....

....

....

....

....

....

....

....

....

....

Never-ending God, I read in Isaiah 40:8 (NIV) that "the grass withers and the flowers fall, but the word of our God endures forever." Create in me a hunger to devour Your Word, and give me a fertile heart to receive it to grow good things.

DAY 125

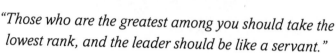

Servant Leaders

*"Those who are the greatest among you should take the
lowest rank, and the leader should be like a servant."*
LUKE 22:26 NLT

. . . .

When Jesus' disciples started arguing about who among them was the greatest, the Messiah must've sighed and shook His head. It's one thing for His sermons to go in one ear and out the other, but He'd been practicing what He was preaching, and they *still* didn't get it! His teaching truly was radically upside down to them. Nowhere else on earth did the disciples see powerful leaders who were humble servants.

By being a servant—choosing to honor others above Himself—Jesus demonstrated just one aspect of the upside-down nature of God's kingdom. The first will be last and the last will be first (Matthew 19:30). To have new life in Christ, one must give up one's life (Matthew 16:24–25). Return hate with love (Romans 12:19–21). True wealth results from giving generously (Luke 6:38).

Not one aspect of Jesus' teaching is easy; each rubs against the grain of our selfish desires. But they are surprisingly simple. And the rewards of doing as Jesus said (and as He does) are immeasurable—both as a peaceful present and as a joyful future.

Prayer Prompt:

What is the difference between a servant's heart and a self-serving heart? Which do you have? Ask God to give you a heart to serve others.

....

....

....

....

....

....

....

....

....

....

....

....

....

....

....

....

Jesus, fix my vision to see and fully understand Your right-side-up kingdom. When my sinful heart wants to flip upside down with the world, renew me and strengthen me. I will serve. I will love. I will give. Amen.

DAY 126

The Hidden Path

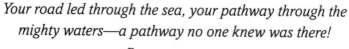

Your road led through the sea, your pathway through the
mighty waters—a pathway no one knew was there!
PSALM 77:19 NLT

. . . .

For some people, it's unnerving to not see the path ahead. Airplane travel is a real challenge for passengers who can't deal with not seeing out the front of the cabin. They're the ones who prefer to drive or call forever dibs on shotgun. They need to see where they're going.

The Israelites found themselves unable to see an escape on the shore of the Red Sea. With Pharaoh's army hot on their heels, not only couldn't they see a way ahead, but there *literally* was no road ahead. But God's pathway was there, and He revealed it in a mighty miracle by parting the waters and giving His people a bone-dry avenue of escape.

So when you find yourself on the shore with seemingly no path to take or at a crossroads with multiple ways ahead, stop and look at your surroundings. Ask God to guide you. Take the time to dig your way into scripture. Seek godly advice from mature Christians. Then rest assured the Lord will set you on His perfect pathway, even (or especially) if that means parting waters or moving mountains.

Prayer Prompt:

What kind of feelings do you experience when you can't see the path ahead? Pray for God's direction and then trust His plan for you.

....

....

....

....

....

....

....

....

....

....

....

....

....

....

....

....

Way-maker God, thank You for bringing me this far.
I need Your help to find the next step in the
journey. Make Your way evident and obvious
so I am confident in my steps. Amen.

Keep Your Guard Up

About an hour later, someone else spoke up, really adamant:
"He's got to have been with him! He's got 'Galilean' written all over
him." Peter said, "Man, I don't know what you're talking about."
At that very moment, the last word hardly off his lips, a rooster crowed.
LUKE 22:59–60 MSG

The rooster's crow may have been the worst "aha" moment of Peter's life. After being so amped up for the cause of Christ that he told Jesus he was ready to go with Him "to prison and to death" (Luke 22:33 ESV), the very next day Peter denied even *knowing* Jesus.

Oh "how the mighty have fallen" (2 Samuel 1:27 ESV).

We, like Peter, are vulnerable to temptation—especially during times of great stress. Hard lines we've set for ourselves get blurry as we struggle through difficulties. But, when in the Garden of Gethsemane, Jesus gave us an example of what to do to resist:

1. Pray (Mark 14:35).
2. Seek support of others (Mark 14:33, 37, 40, 41).
3. Focus on God's purpose for you (Mark 14:36).

Peter's story doesn't end at the rooster crow. He found redemption and forgiveness through Jesus and went on to do mighty works in forming the early church. Don't let your failures define you either. God can and will use a willing and humble heart for great things.

Prayer Prompt:

What failures have you allowed to define you? Pray for courage to resist allowing this to happen again.

....

....

....

....

....

....

....

....

....

....

....

....

....

....

....

....

....

....

Jesus, create in me a pure heart that resists temptation.
I'm living for You and You only! Amen.

The Small, Right, Kind Thing

[Joseph of Arimathea] went to Pilate and asked for the body of Jesus.
Then he took it down and wrapped it in a linen shroud and laid
him in a tomb cut in stone, where no one had ever yet been laid.

LUKE 23:52–53 ESV

. . . .

Joseph of Arimathea never felt right about how the other members of the Jewish high council plotted against Jesus. Later, when the council handed Jesus over to Pilate, Joseph knew it meant a death sentence for the seemingly rebellious rabbi. Although Joseph felt certain it was wrong, he was also powerless to stop it. And what good would it do if *he* ended up on a cross next to Jesus?

This world is full of injustice—from bullying on the playground to sexism to favoritism to racism. Often we can and should take a stand against it, but there are times that we can't. But that doesn't mean we shouldn't do *anything*.

Take a lesson from Joseph of Arimathea. He couldn't do the big thing (saving Jesus' life), but he *could* do the small, right, kind thing by giving Jesus' body a proper burial and place to rest. God used Joseph as part of His perfect plan of salvation. And in that light, it was no small thing!

Prayer Prompt:

What are some small, right things you can do for the kingdom? Ask God to show you a simple action you can take today.

....

....

....

....

....

....

....

....

....

....

....

....

....

....

....

....

....

....

God, when I am not able to do the big thing, give me eyes to see the small, right, kind thing. And use that small thing to result in big things for You! Amen.

Not a Ghost

*"Why are you troubled, and why do doubts rise in your minds?
Look at my hands and my feet. It is I myself! Touch me and see;
a ghost does not have flesh and bones, as you see I have."*

LUKE 24:38–40 NIV

. . . .

When Jesus came back to life in the tomb, perhaps His first physical sensations were the gaping nail holes in His hands and feet, verifying all that had happened three days prior. He'd been crucified, and the Holy Spirit's power had brought Him back to life!

So when the newly risen Lord's friends reacted to Him with eyes wide with terror, Jesus gave them the simplest and most compelling evidence He could: "Look, touch—I'm real. I'm not a ghost!" Still, Luke wrote, it wasn't until Jesus "opened their minds so they could understand the Scriptures" and His title role in them that the disciples started to grasp their new reality (24:45–48 NIV).

Following Christ sometimes means you don't have all the *why* and *how* answers to your questions. Scripture tells you that living a life of faith requires setting aside your human desire to understand the whole picture (see 2 Corinthians 5:7; Hebrews 11). But while Jesus, in His newly risen body, isn't here with you today, He *will* give you clarity and insight through His Word if you continually seek Him there.

Prayer Prompt:

What can you do to "touch" the risen Lord? Ask the Lord to open your understanding as you read His Word.

_____

_____

_____

_____

_____

_____

_____

_____

_____

_____

_____

_____

_____

_____

_____

_____

_____

_____

*Jesus, give me a hunger for Your Word and clarity
from its living, powerful message. Amen.*

Reborn into God's Family

*To all who did receive him, who believed in his name, he gave
the right to become children of God, who were born, not of blood
nor of the will of the flesh nor of the will of man, but of God.*

JOHN 1:12–13 ESV

· ·

The nine months leading up to the birth of a baby are filled with excitement, expectation, anticipation, and a whole lot of joy in a family. From nursery prep to acquiring baby gear, planning a shower, and stocking up on diapers and wipes, there's hope and promise in every moment. *Who will this tiny person be? What will she become? Who will he take after? Where will her strengths and passions lie?*

As much as your family may have looked forward to your physical birth, God's anticipation for your rebirth into His family is even greater. His call to you began when He first thought of you. He claimed you for *His* family and marked you for rebirth. He loved as you came into the world an infant and grew first physically, then spiritually as you began to understand His love and loved Him in return.

Then came that glorious day when you took the step of faith and publicly declared that Jesus is the Son of God and Lord of your life. You became a Father/daughter duo for eternity. Can you hear the applause of heaven (Luke 15:10)?

Prayer Prompt:

Can you name the date that you accepted Jesus into your life? As you pray, give Him thanks for accepting you into His family.

....
....
....
....
....
....
....
....
....
....
....
....
....
....
....
....
....
....

You are my good Father. I am Your
grateful child. I love You! Amen.

DAY 131

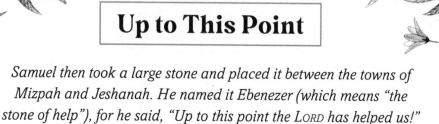

Up to This Point

Samuel then took a large stone and placed it between the towns of Mizpah and Jeshanah. He named it Ebenezer (which means "the stone of help"), for he said, "Up to this point the LORD has helped us!"

1 SAMUEL 7:12 NLT

. . . .

Some seasons of life are just plain hard. In these tough times, it's easy to let doubts seep in and faith to waver. *Why is God letting this happen? Does He even care? Where is He?*

In trying times, follow the prophet Samuel's example and set up an Ebenezer. An Ebenezer can be anything that reminds you that up until now, God has helped you, and He will be faithful in continuing to help! Maybe that means writing an entry in your calendar app or a journal, recording the date when you felt God's presence or saw His provision in a difficult situation. Maybe it's planting a tree or placing a rock in a garden. Maybe it's crafting a bracelet or necklace charm with a date etched on it—a possible conversation starter to talk to others about when God has helped you.

God's help is ever present. And you become more aware of that help when you're looking for it. Today, remember and thank God for the things He has done, is doing, and will do.

Prayer Prompt:

What can you set up an Ebenezer reminder for? Spend time thanking God for that time in your life.

....

....

....

....

....

....

....

....

....

....

....

....

....

....

....

....

....

God, I'm not worthy of Your help, yet You offer it freely and generously. I praise You for each milestone of Your provision in my life. Amen.

Asking for What God Wants

But the people wouldn't listen to Samuel. "No!" they said.
"We will have a king to rule us! Then we'll be just like all the other
nations. Our king will rule us and lead us and fight our battles."
1 SAMUEL 8:19–20 MSG

Have you ever tried reasoning with a two-year-old? Listing eight compelling reasons why he or she shouldn't dump a shoebox of LEGO blocks into the toilet will get you nowhere.

The Jews were as irrational as two-year-olds when they wanted a king. Samuel gave them a laundry list of the consequences of having a king (1 Samuel 8:10–18), yet their demand grew louder.

God is a generous Father who will give good gifts when asked (Matthew 7:11), but He is also a Father who knows what will benefit you and what will harm you. A toddler may want a box of matches with all his heart, but no loving father will hand them to her.

So how do you work in harmony with God's generosity? By living in His will and asking for good gifts that are in line with His kingdom: gifts to love others, share the good news, feed the hungry, care for the sick. Ask for the opportunity, tools, and the means to carry out these things, and God's generosity will overflow.

Prayer Prompt:

What are you asking for that may not be in line with God's plan?
As you pray, ask Him to show you His will and give you a compliant
heart.

....

....

....

....

....

....

....

....

....

....

....

....

....

....

....

....

Generous Father, show me Your will so I know I am
offering up requests that bring You joy to answer. Amen.

You Will Be Changed

*"The Spirit of the LORD will come powerfully upon you,
and you will prophesy with them; and you will be changed
into a different person. Once these signs are fulfilled,
do whatever your hand finds to do, for God is with you."*
1 SAMUEL 10:6–7 NIV

We often associate heart transformation with the New Testament—from John the Baptist blazing the trail to repentance (Matthew 3) to Paul's assurance that we are made into new creatures in Christ (2 Corinthians 5:17). But throughout history, God has delighted in radical transformation.

Consider the account of Samuel's anointing Saul as king. First God gave Saul a new heart (1 Samuel 10:9). Then, generations before the Holy Spirit arrived at Pentecost (Acts 2), the Spirit came powerfully on Saul and changed him—into a different person (1 Samuel 10:10)!

This same transformation is available to you today, sister! Is your heart heavy with worry, jealousy, self-loathing, or hatred? If so, release your heart to God, who has a new one ready just for you. All you need to do is pray, asking God to take away your old heart. He's merely waiting for you to sign the release forms required for the spiritual transplant.

Prayer Prompt:

What condition is your heart in? Do you need a spiritual transplant?
Ask the Lord for a transformation in your life.

....

....

....

....

....

....

....

....

....

....

....

....

....

....

....

....

....

God, I release my stained heart to You. Please replace it
with Your pure heart and change me in a radical way.
I can't do this on my own. For only You can make
lasting, real, holy, perfect change in me. Amen.

Always a Best Man

"He must become greater and greater,
and I must become less and less."
JOHN 3:30 NLT

. . . .

Jesus' cousin John dunked converts in the Jordan River in preparation for Jesus' arrival. This ministry had resulted in John's own followers as well as rumors that *he* was actually the long-awaited Messiah.

John must've been tempted to use his reputation for personal gain. Whether it was offers of financial bribes for salvation or invitations to prestigious parties, scripture tells us John the Baptist remained humble and committed to the singular calling on his life. He even told his followers that he considered the joy he felt at the arrival of Jesus to be like that of a best man on his best friend's wedding day (John 3:29).

What was John's secret to such humility? God had given him a heart for the Messiah—an uncanny understanding of the hope Christ's salvation would bring to the world. John was tapped into the power of God, and nothing would distract his focus.

What about you? What singular calling has God placed on your life? Ask Him to make that calling clear and to show you how amid your ministry—and life—Jesus will become greater and you less.

Prayer Prompt:

What has God given you a heart for? Ask Him to show you where He needs to increase in your life—and where you need to decrease.

....

....

....

....

....

....

....

....

....

....

....

....

....

....

....

....

....

Father, may the love of Jesus overtake my thoughts, actions, and speech in everything so that my circle no longer sees me—but a beautiful reflection of You.

A Satisfying Meal

Jesus said to them, "My food is to do the will of him who sent me and to accomplish his work."

JOHN 4:34 ESV

. . . .

Have you ever been so focused on a project that tasks like drinking water, sleeping, or even eating get pushed to the very bottom of your to-do list? If you're passionate and excited about what you're doing, time has a way of slip-sliding past.

The disciples had been with Jesus long enough by now to know that when it came to loving others, He was always in that deep-focus mode. So they'd gotten into the habit of gently reminding Him, "Rabbi, eat" (John 4:31 ESV).

Although Jesus absolutely needed to nourish His human body, He also understood the fulfillment that comes from doing God's will—the kind of satisfaction that leaves your soul full after a filling, spiritual feast. Maybe you've experienced that fulfillment too—in leading someone to Christ, doing someone a kindness, or using your God-given talents to further His kingdom.

God has uniquely positioned you at His banquet table with a deeply satisfying feast laid before you. If you don't recognize what or where your soul food is, ask Him to show you. Then be on the lookout for the opportunity to dive in, heart first.

Prayer Prompt:

How are you feeding your soul? Seek the Lord for spiritual food as you pray.

....

....

....

....

....

....

....

....

....

....

....

....

....

....

....

....

Father, I long for that deep satisfaction that I only find in working for You. My napkin is laid in my lap. I'm ready for the first course. Amen.

The Heart's Judge

*"The L*ORD *doesn't see things the way you see them. People judge
by outward appearance, but the L*ORD *looks at the heart."*
1 SAMUEL 16:7 NLT

. . . .

Samuel had served God in many roles: judge, priest, prophet, counselor,
and anointer of kings.

So when God sent Samuel to Bethlehem to find King Saul's replacement among Jesse's sons, Samuel thought he had a pretty good idea who
was God's "type." He hadn't spent his entire life in service of the Lord
without learning anything.

To Samuel, Jesse's firstborn son, Eliab—tall, strong, and handsome—
seemed to be the obvious choice. But before Samuel could crack open
the anointing oil, God warned him against judging on appearance alone.

God knows it's human nature—even for someone as devout as
Samuel—to judge by how someone looks. But appearance doesn't reveal the true self or a person's actual value. God judges on heart and
character. And because only He can see what's on the inside, only He
can judge fairly.

If you're like most women, your daily outer-beauty routine is almost
second nature. But how about your *inner*-beauty routine? Are you putting
in enough time to cultivate the true beauty God looks for?

Prayer Prompt:

What do you do to take care of your inner woman? Ask God to beautify your inner woman and remove those things that shouldn't be there.

....

....

....

....

....

....

....

....

....

....

....

....

....

....

God, examine my heart and give me a full report.
If there are ugly motives or hidden sins in the
recesses of my heart, help me clear them out.
Then fill me with Your pure and holy love. Amen.

Eliab's Jealousy

When David's oldest brother, Eliab, heard David talking to the men, he was angry. "What are you doing around here anyway?" he demanded. "What about those few sheep you're supposed to be taking care of? I know about your pride and deceit. You just want to see the battle!"

1 SAMUEL 17:28 NLT

. . . .

Eliab didn't like David's youthful zeal for going to battle for the Lord. The older brother viewed David as just a child, one who needed to go home to do his little job of tending the needs of his flock.

Newbie, on-fire Christians can be so annoying with their excitement and passion. They need to take a breath and settle down.

Ever felt this way, longtime woman of faith?

Instead of squelching the fire in a new Christian's heart, what if you used her enthusiasm to propel you on to deeper faith and greater work for God's kingdom? If Eliab had been successful in sending David home, the shepherd boy and soon-to-be king would not have defeated Goliath, leaving the Israelites to continue suffering at the hands of the Philistines.

What sparks do you see around you that you can fan into flames? What will you do to keep the cares of the world from dampening or putting them out?

Prayer Prompt:

What can you do to encourage a new Christian? Ask God to give you a new heart for Him and His work just like a newborn Christian.

....

....

....

....

....

....

....

....

....

....

....

....

....

....

God, add fuel to my fire and restore my passion for You and for Your work. Give me a pure heart that willingly comes alongside others who are ignited with love and excitement for You. Amen.

DAY 138

Turn Us, God

Turn us again to yourself, O God of Heaven's Armies.
Make your face shine down upon us. Only then will we be saved.
PSALM 80:7 NLT

. . . .

Compared to many other species, we humans have mediocre peripheral vision—what we can see that's outside the center of our gaze. The closer something is to the center of our gaze, the sharper and more clearly we can see it. The farther to the left and right, our vision becomes blurrier. (A typical visual field is about 170 degrees around—slightly less than halfway around your head.)*

The psalmist understood the importance of keeping God at the center of one's gaze. So he asked the Lord to turn the focus of the Israelites back to Him and away from the distractions of other gods and idols. For it's not enough to have a slightly blurry God in the periphery. He must be in the sharpest vision plane; and other good but nonessential parts of life must be in the periphery.

As you think about these things, remember that God doesn't move; it's you who turns away. Today, ask God to turn you back to Him. And as He comes into focus, note His eyes full of love for you.

*www.eyehealthweb.com/peripheral-vision/

Prayer Prompt:

What are your eyes focused on? As you pray, ask God to move into the center of your vision and become the main focus in your life.

....

....

....

....

....

....

....

....

....

....

....

....

....

....

....

....

Father, once again I've been distracted by the temptations of this world and You've become blurry. Forgive me and turn me back to You. I long to see Your face shine down on me. Amen.

Expect a Miracle

When Jesus looked up and saw a great crowd coming toward him,
he said to Philip, "Where shall we buy bread for these people to eat?"
He asked this only to test him, for he already had in mind what he
was going to do. Philip answered him, "It would take more than half
a year's wages to buy enough bread for each one to have a bite!"

JOHN 6:5–7 NIV

. . . .

When Jesus asked Philip how they could feed the thousands of people coming to hear Him speak, Philip was at a loss. Jesus had no money, and neither did His disciples. But Jesus knew the miracle that was coming, and it had the power to change Philip's faith forever.

There are times in every Christian's life when Jesus presents him or her with a challenge—something that seems impossible—but it's really an opportunity for God's power to shine, making the impossible possible.

What question do you hear Jesus asking? "How can we keep the homeless warm this winter?" Or, "How can we show love to children in the foster care system?"

If Jesus has put a need on your heart, He already has a way to move forward. If you're willing to be used for good and it's in God's will, He'll make it happen—on an enough-food-to-feed-more-than-five-thousand-people-with-just-five-loaves-and-two-fish scale!

Prayer Prompt:

What miracle do you want to see happen? When you pray, ask God to give you the faith to believe for the miracle He can work.

....

....

....

....

....

....

....

....

....

....

....

....

....

....

....

....

....

....

Jesus, I expect a miracle. Use me to bring it about. Amen.

Our Greater Purpose

"For I have come down from heaven, not to do my own will but the will of him who sent me."
JOHN 6:38 ESV

. . . .

One trait of an exceptional boss is that she clearly communicates expectations and instructions for her employees. When a leader sets a goal and launches the trajectory toward that goal, it provides purpose and focus that point each person toward the same result, pushing each other toward the finish line.

Our heavenly Father is an exceptional, supernatural boss. He's all about building His kingdom. To that end He sent His Son to earth with a singular focus: to make a way to bring His children into grace.

Jesus understood God's plan in a personal way that gave Him a mission unlike any other human in the past or in the future. Doing God's will meant that Jesus' actions and decisions had a greater purpose than His own human desires and temptations. For us, that means that we don't have to make an educated guess about what God's will is. God's written instruction for our lives comes down to four simple letters: L-O-V-E.

Take comfort in the fact that you're working for all of creation's greatest boss. Follow His instruction, carry out His will, and live a life of greater purpose.

Prayer Prompt:

What do you think is God's will for your life? When you pray, remember that He knows what's best for you and will enable you to follow His will.

....

....

....

....

....

....

....

....

....

....

....

....

....

....

....

....

God, thank You for the gift of Your Word. Forgive me for taking it for granted. Give me a Christlike desire to lay aside my own will and do only Yours. Amen.

Our Advocate and Rescuer

"May the Lord therefore judge which of us is right and punish the guilty one. He is my advocate, and he will rescue me from your power!"

1 Samuel 24:15 NLT

. . . .

David had every right to take revenge on King Saul. For Saul had publicly declared his plans to kill David *and* had enlisted the help of three thousand of his elite troops to hunt David down in the wilderness. So when Saul happened to take a pit stop in the very cave where David was hiding, David knew it was his best chance to strike.

But he didn't. All he did was cut a piece from Saul's robe. And even that made him feel guilty (1 Samuel 24:5).

We might be tempted to think David a better man than Saul, but the truth is that both kings were sinful, fallen humans who each messed up big-time in his own way. The difference was that David had a personal relationship with the Lord—a God he trusted to rescue him in times of distress.

What wrongs have been done to you that you need to let go of? What hope of revenge do you hold in your heart? Ask Jesus to remove it; then replace it with the peace of knowing He will champion you.

Prayer Prompt:

What injustices or grudges do you harbor in your life? Ask God to forgive you and remove them from your heart.

....

....

....

....

....

....

....

....

....

....

....

....

....

....

....

....

....

....

....

....

Advocate God, when I am feeling the icy fingers of revenge creep into my heart, stand for me. Rescue me and put my feet on solid ground. Amen.

The Courage to Speak Up (or Not)

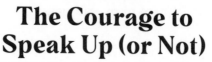

*There was a lot of grumbling about him among the crowds.
Some argued, "He's a good man," but others said, "He's
nothing but a fraud who deceives the people." But no one had
the courage to speak favorably about him in public, for they
were afraid of getting in trouble with the Jewish leaders.*

JOHN 7:12–13 NLT

. . . .

Judea was abuzz with rumor that Jesus was there in secret, trying to stay out of public view (John 7:10).

Some people said quietly among themselves, "He's a good man, and we need more like Him."

Others proclaimed more loudly so the Jewish leaders could hear, "He's a fraud and a liar and he's pulling the wool over all our eyes!"

Have you ever known what's right but were too afraid to speak up? Whether it's fear of public ridicule or the possibility of losing a position, a friendship, or something else, there are lots of reasons to remain silent. Speaking up takes courage. But it also takes wisdom to know when and when not to speak. So before setting up your soapbox:

1. Pray and ask God what He wants you to do.

2. Seek counsel in scripture and from godly friends/family.

3. In all things, love.

Prayer Prompt:

What do you need to speak up for in your life? Ask God for the courage to speak and to know when it's time to do so.

....

....

....

....

....

....

....

....

....

....

....

....

....

....

....

....

....

....

....

....

....

Father, when I need to stand up for what's right, give me the courage and the words to use. And when I need to remain silent, give me peace as I keep my mouth shut.

Hard Questions

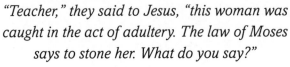

*"Teacher," they said to Jesus, "this woman was
caught in the act of adultery. The law of Moses
says to stone her. What do you say?"*
JOHN 8:4–5 NLT

. . . .

The teachers of the law and the Pharisees didn't care one bit about the woman they'd dragged before Jesus. She was simply a way to test and trap Him (John 8:6). They held up the Old Testament law that says adultery warrants death by stoning, daring Jesus to disagree. With white knuckles firmly grasping rocks, what they *really* wanted to do was hurl the stones at Jesus, the man some people were beginning to murmur was the Messiah.

But Jesus wasn't tricked by their trap. He didn't seem riled by the question or unsettled by the mob, and He didn't retaliate by calling out their hypocrisy or naming specific sins and vices of each one. Instead, He turned the focus from their legalism of keeping the ancient law to His law of compassionate love by reminding them no one has the right to judge another's guilt.

As a Christian, there may be times when you're assaulted by questions from hard hearts who are hoping to make your faith in God look foolish. Don't fall into the trap of angry retaliation. Instead, take a breath and choose the path of compassionate love of Jesus.

Prayer Prompt:

Who or what do you feel is attacking your faith? As you pray,
ask Jesus for His peace to keep you calm in those times.

....

....

....

....

....

....

....

....

....

....

....

....

....

....

....

....

....

....

....

*Jesus, when I feel my faith being attacked, give me
the strength to pause and react in love. Amen.*

Jesus the Great Emancipator

*Jesus replied, "I tell you the truth, everyone who sins is a slave of sin.
A slave is not a permanent member of the family, but a son is part
of the family forever. So if the Son sets you free, you are truly free."*
JOHN 8:34–36 NLT

. . . .

Jesus' Jewish followers were confused. *They* didn't need to be set free.
It was their ancestors who had been slaves—not them. That was behind
them now, so how would the truth set them free? Free from what?

One word, three letters: S-I-N.

Sin's grip on our minds, hearts, and bodies is stronger than any link
of chain used by the cruelest slave master. It begins with a temptation
that leads to a decision to act in a way that separates us from God and
results in death. Try as we might, we cannot wish, bargain, buy, or fight
our way out of sin's slavery.

But just as Jesus' followers begin to understand their own sin-slave
status, He gives them an important reminder: slaves aren't born into sin
the way a son or daughter is born into a family. Slavery is not permanent
if an emancipator comes. And Jesus is that great emancipator, the one
who, because of His death on the cross, frees sin's most captive slave.

Prayer Prompt:

What temptation is keeping you a slave? Ask Jesus to set you free.

....

....

....

....

....

....

....

....

....

....

....

....

....

....

....

....

....

....

....

....

*Jesus, unlock these chains of sin and set me free.
I want to change my status from sin's
slave to God's daughter. Amen.*

The Hard Whys

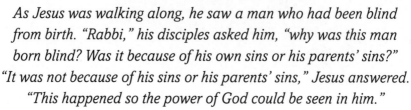

As Jesus was walking along, he saw a man who had been blind from birth. "Rabbi," his disciples asked him, "why was this man born blind? Was it because of his own sins or his parents' sins?" "It was not because of his sins or his parents' sins," Jesus answered. "This happened so the power of God could be seen in him."

JOHN 9:1–3 NLT

. . . .

Why was a baby born blind only to grow up to beg along the side of the road? Jesus' disciples wondered. *A punishment for his sin?*

Jesus' response must've surprised them. This man had been born blind so that God's power would be displayed in his healing. After Jesus healed his blindness, the now-seeing man repeatedly told the story of a Jewish rabbi named Jesus who'd restored his sight with mud, saliva, and a wash in the Pool of Siloam. His testimony allowed more people— including his neighbors and a group of Pharisees investigating Jesus— to hear about and see God's power firsthand.

What hard whys are in your life right now? Maybe the *why* is less important than the *how*. How is God displaying His power to you and to others around you? And how is your testimony of Him being a kind, merciful, and powerful God pointing others to Him?

Prayer Prompt:

What are you questioning God about today? Spend time in prayer, asking Him to show you how it can bring glory to Him.

_____

_____

_____

_____

_____

_____

_____

_____

_____

_____

_____

_____

_____

_____

_____

_____

_____

_____

Healer God, today I'm trusting that You are working everything in my life—the easy and the difficult—for Your glory. Show me how to testify of Your power, God. Amen.

It's Clear

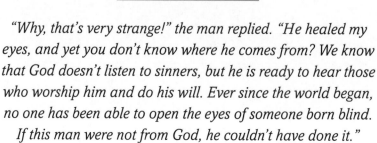

*"Why, that's very strange!" the man replied. "He healed my
eyes, and yet you don't know where he comes from? We know
that God doesn't listen to sinners, but he is ready to hear those
who worship him and do his will. Ever since the world began,
no one has been able to open the eyes of someone born blind.
If this man were not from God, he couldn't have done it."*

JOHN 9:30–33 NLT

The man Jesus healed from blindness already knew the rabbi who put
mud and saliva on his face was no ordinary rabbi. When the Pharisees
summoned the healed man to answer questions, looking to find evidence
in Jesus' wrongdoing, he couldn't believe his highly refined ears.

Were these religious leaders so blind they couldn't see that Jesus was
doing God's work? What was clear to him was obscured by the Pharisees'
hard hearts.

When you've personally experienced the life-changing power of God,
you see His presence and power in daily life. Prayer, scripture reading,
and listening to God only add to your awareness of Him.

Who do you know who could be encouraged by your story of God's
work in your life? Remember that although it's not your job to change
hard hearts—only the Holy Spirit can do that—your personal, relatable
stories can go a long way in beginning to soften a heart.

Prayer Prompt:

Who can you share your personal story with today? Ask God to lead you to the one who needs to hear about God's goodness in your life.

....

....

....

....

....

....

....

....

....

....

....

....

....

....

....

....

....

....

*Father, use me to encourage someone
going through a difficult time. Amen.*

Michal's Misstep

As the ark of the LORD was entering the City of David,
Michal daughter of Saul watched from a window.
And when she saw King David leaping and dancing
before the LORD, she despised him in her heart.

2 SAMUEL 6:16 NIV

Scripture doesn't tell us exactly what Michal's problem was, but it's likely this contempt for her husband, David, didn't start when she looked out her window and saw his passionate, animated worship before the Lord.

Perhaps she thought it was undignified for a king to display such emotion. Or maybe she thought celebration was a trivial pursuit as there were more pressing matters in the kingdom. Whatever the reason, Michal's ongoing bitterness and resentment escalated into a fight (2 Samuel 6:20–23) that did real damage to their relationship, resulting in their childless marriage.

Bitterness and resentment are insidious emotions that may simmer on the back burner of a relationship for some time before coming to a boil. But bitterness has no power to change circumstances, and resentment only makes a bad situation worse. Left unchecked, they can destroy a relationship. Although you may not have control over what happens to you, you *do* control how you respond. When you feel those simmering emotions, reset, ask God for clarity, and deal with your feelings.

Prayer Prompt:

What has made you bitter toward someone else? Ask God for
forgiveness and then ask Him to take away your bitterness toward
that person.

....

....

....

....

....

....

....

....

....

....

....

....

....

....

....

*God, I cannot live with this bitterness
in my heart. Cleanse me and give me
a new heart full of love and patience.*

A God Who Bends Down

Bend down, O LORD, and hear my prayer;
answer me, for I need your help.
PSALM 86:1 NLT

Preschool teachers spend much of their days down on the level of their students. Kneeling to tie a shoe, sitting on tiny chairs at miniature tables, and bending to hear a soft voice or offer a hug. Sometimes they lower themselves for practical reasons, but other times they get down simply to show these little people that they are important, valued, and loved.

The writer of Psalms asked God to bend down, to listen to his prayer for help—a brazen request to the almighty Creator of the sky and sea! But God heard that request, just as He hears your requests today. Jesus proved once and for all that the Lord is a God who gets down on the level of His children. He came to earth fully God and fully human, bending low to pull us out of the pit of sin. Jesus knows bending down—low enough to sacrifice His life on the cross.

Yes, God will bend down to look you in the eye, to hear your whispered need, but He won't stay bent over. He'll pick you up in His strong arms and take you to where you can weather the storms of life.

Prayer Prompt:

Do you need God to bend down and lend you an ear today? As you pray, share with Him the deepest secrets of your heart. He listens.

....

....

....

....

....

....

....

....

....

....

....

....

....

....

....

Father, I need You. Please bend down so I can see You and feel Your presence here as I whisper my fears into Your ear. You alone can rescue me. Amen.

DAY 149

Long Fuse

*You, O God, are both tender and kind, not easily angered,
immense in love, and you never, never quit.*
PSALM 86:15 MSG

- -

We all know someone who has a short fuse. The one who, at the smallest traffic delay or offense, loses her temper. Or turns red if she has to wait at the store checkout or gets a glare from a fellow shopper. She's the one others have to watch their words around for fear of setting her off.

Thankfully, the Bible says God has a long fuse—that He's slow to get angry (Exodus 34:6; Numbers 14:18; Nehemiah 9:17; Psalm 103:8; Joel 2:13; Jonah 4:2; Nahum 1:3). Yet does the fact that God has lots of patience mean we should give ourselves a pass when it comes to sin? Certainly not!

God's desire is for our salvation through Jesus Christ and adopting as many children into His family who'll accept His gift of grace. He knows we aren't perfect—but His love is.

Ask God to show you where you might need to repent, remembering He's not angry. He's just waiting in compassion and mercy to give you the full life He's designed for you.

Prayer Prompt:

What gives you a short fuse? As you pray, ask God to help you be less angry and to show mercy to others just as He shows mercy to you.

....

....

....

....

....

....

....

....

....

....

....

....

....

....

God, You've every right to get frustrated with me when I mess up, but Your patient mercy and love is greater than Your anger. Clean my hands and face and purify my heart, Father. I don't want any sin to stand between us. Amen.

DAY 150

If Only

When Mary arrived and saw Jesus, she fell at his feet and said,
"Lord, if only you had been here, my brother would not have died."
JOHN 11:32 NLT

Nobody wants to live with regrets, but we all suffer from a case of the "could haves," "should haves," and "would haves" every now and then. Decisions and plans would be a lot easier to make if we could know what's going to happen.

In John 11, Jesus finds Mary overflowing with regret when He arrives after her brother, Lazarus, died. "Lord, if only you had been here, my brother would not have died," she sobbed at Jesus' feet.

But Jesus knew something Mary hadn't yet realized: there are no "if onlys" in God's kingdom. No regrets. No "should haves," "could haves," or "would haves." What the suffering Mary and her sister, Martha, were going through was temporary. And in a matter of minutes, the Son of God would be glorified, bringing eternal joy to a mourning family once He raised Lazarus from the dead.

Do you have any regrets you're currently struggling through? Lay those "if onlys" at the feet of Jesus. He knows what's next, and He can take any situation (even death!) and use it for His glory—and your joy.

Prayer Prompt:

What regrets taunt you and torment you? When you pray, ask Jesus to help you with those regrets and to bring you peace.

Regrets, Jesus, I have a few. Forgive me and help me forgive myself. Please use these missteps to Your glory—to further Your kingdom here and for eternity. Amen.

Extravagant Gratitude

Then Mary took about a pint of pure nard,
an expensive perfume; she poured it on Jesus'
feet and wiped his feet with her hair.
JOHN 12:3 NIV

. . . .

As Christians, we spend a lot of time counting the cost of Jesus' sacrifice on the cross. It's the cornerstone of our faith, so we rightly should remember His death and resurrection. But while it's true that there's nothing we can do to repay Jesus, that doesn't mean we can't show extravagant gratitude for all He has done—even to the point of our seeming ridiculous to others.

For Mary, extravagant gratitude meant spending what perhaps was her life's savings to purchase a jar of the most expensive perfume she could find. Imagine Mary's excitement to present Jesus with such a loving gift. With each ounce she poured upon His feet and wiped with her hair, she celebrated the love He had already poured out on her family through His teaching, encouraging, challenging, and most of all saving her brother, Lazarus, from the grave. Such extravagant love from the rabbi deserved the most extravagant gratitude she could muster.

What does extravagant gratitude look like in your life? Don't let naysayers keep you from displaying your thankfulness (see John 12:4–5). Jesus Christ is worthy and deserving of all your praise!

Prayer Prompt:

What can you do to express extravagant gratitude to Christ? Ask Jesus to give you the courage to express that gratitude in the face of criticism.

....

....

....

....

....

....

....

....

....

....

....

....

....

....

....

Jesus, I know there is nothing I can do to repay You.
Please accept my offering of extravagant gratitude,
and may it be a blessing to You. Amen.

Whatever the King Chooses

The king's officials answered him, "Your servants
are ready to do whatever our lord the king chooses."

2 SAMUEL 15:15 NIV

God is in the transformation business. He longs to take what we give Him and morph it into something even greater. In order to grow and develop, however, we have to give up our right to stay the same. We have to be willing to say, "Not my will, but Yours be done, Lord." When our hearts are tipped toward His, when we're flexible and ready to see Him move in our lives, He can work. Unfortunately, many times we stiffen up and refuse to bend. It's time to ready our hearts, to prepare ourselves for His best.

Take a look at today's scripture verse. How wonderful it must have been for the king to hear the words "Your servants are ready to do whatever you choose." Wow! God is waiting to hear those words from you even now. When you bow the knee and submit to His will, you are saying, "Lord, whatever You choose. I'm in."

Prayer Prompt:

What can you give God today that He can transform into something greater? When you pray, submit to Him and listen to His plan for you.

....

....

....

....

....

....

....

....

....

....

....

....

....

....

Lord, whatever You long to do in my life,
whatever plans You have for my future, I submit!
I let go of stubbornness and pride. I'm ready to
replace the "good" with the "best." Amen.

A Love Song

*I will sing of the L*ORD*'s unfailing love forever!*
Young and old will hear of your faithfulness.
PSALM 89:1 NLT

. . . .

A changed heart is a happy heart, one filled with a new song, ready to be sung. Maybe you can relate. You've been through changes. Major transformations have taken place, not just in your heart but in your thinking, as well. God has lifted your feet from the miry clay and placed them on a rock. He's brought you through the valley to a season of great joy.

Now you want to share the news with everyone you meet. Your testimony leads the way as you have conversation after conversation with friends, family, coworkers, and neighbors. You can't help it. You're so grateful at all God has done that you want others to see His goodness too.

Today why not go even further? Don't just spread your joy in conversation. Sing praises to the Lord! Let your mouth sing—and others hear—what your heart is already celebrating!

Prayer Prompt:

What has God done in your life? During your prayer time, sing a love song to Him, thanking Him for His work in your life.

....

....

....

....

....

....

....

....

....

....

....

....

....

....

....

Lord, I choose to praise You today! You're so worthy, Father! I will not just share the stories of what You've done in my life—how You've changed and transformed me, re-created me, given me a new sense of purpose and wonder. But with my whole heart I will praise You in song, telling all of Your unfailing and forever love. Amen.

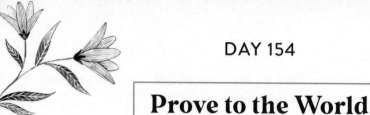

Prove to the World

"So now I am giving you a new commandment: Love each other.
Just as I have loved you, you should love each other. Your love for
one another will prove to the world that you are my disciples."

JOHN 13:34–35 NLT

. . . .

Of all the things we need to share with the world, love tops the list. Love bears witness to our relationship with Christ. It leads, guides, motivates, and transforms even the toughest situations. When the world watches our reactions to difficult situations, what do they see? If our hearts are in the right place, they see truth spoken in love and seasoned with grace and mercy.

Sure, it's easy to fall out with people, especially in today's volatile political climate. But God longs for His kids to enjoy fellowship. Don't rob yourself of that by letting animosity get in the way. Tear down walls. Learn to love so that a watching world will catch a glimpse of Jesus from your example. As God transforms your heart, offer it to others as a gift.

Prayer Prompt:

Who do you find it hard to love? During your prayer time, ask God to fill you with love for that person or persons.

....

....

....

....

....

....

....

....

....

....

....

....

....

....

....

....

Father, I want to prove to the world that I'm a lover not a hater. It's not easy, I confess. So many times I just want to prove that I'm right and the other guy is wrong. But You've shown me in Your Word, Lord, that there's a better way to be a light to others. Show me how to love even the toughest person, I pray. Amen.

Troublemakers

There happened to be a troublemaker there named Sheba
son of Bicri, a man from the tribe of Benjamin. Sheba
blew a ram's horn and began to chant: "Down with the
dynasty of David! We have no interest in the son of Jesse.
Come on, you men of Israel, back to your homes!"

2 SAMUEL 20:1 NLT

. . . .

They're everywhere. Troublemakers. And they don't care if they hurt you. In fact, that's part of their plan, their scheme. That's why you have to be on the lookout at every turn. Sometimes people want you to think they're trustworthy, but they're not.

What troublemakers have you come in contact with lately? Were they stumbling blocks in your walk of faith? Did they throw you off course? Did they threaten to undo the work God has already done in your heart?

When faced with those who are bent to take you down, use caution! Yes, God wants you to love everyone. No, He doesn't want you to be in relationship with everyone. In fact, there are some people you may need to take a giant step away from. . .possibly today. Ask God for His wisdom to guide you.

Prayer Prompt:

Who causes you trouble and makes you uneasy? Ask God for wisdom to deal with them.

....

....

....

....

....

....

....

....

....

....

....

....

....

....

....

Lord, I hate the idea of having to distance myself from some people. But I can see that many have an agenda. They won't rest until they knock me off course. So as an act of obedience to You, Father, I'll do my best to steer clear of those bent on pulling me off Your path. Amen.

Anointed, Sustained

"I have found David my servant; with my sacred oil I have anointed him. My hand will sustain him; surely my arm will strengthen him."

<small>PSALM 89:20–21 NIV</small>

. . . .

God has promised to sustain you, no matter what valleys you walk through. Even if you're in the deepest pit, His hand is right there, ready to lift you up and give you the necessary strength. Yet what does this promise mean, specifically? Will He deliver you from your situation? Maybe not. But He promises to give you the physical and emotional strength to bear up under any burden.

To be anointed by God means you're covered. His protective hand will shield you, lead you, guide you, sustain you. When He has anointed you for a task, you have nothing to be afraid of. No enemy can penetrate the anointing.

What are you waiting for? If God has called and anointed you for the task ahead, then run toward the goal, your willing heart leading the way.

Prayer Prompt:

What has God anointed you to do? Ask Him to prepare you for the task and to strengthen you when obstacles appear.

....

....

....

....

....

....

....

....

....

....

....

....

....

Father, I read about so many men and women in the Bible who were anointed for specific tasks. I wonder what it would feel like to have Your anointing. Then I'm reminded that You have anointed me as well. You've called me to reach my community, my circle, for You. Thank You for preparing me for the task at hand, Lord, for sustaining and strengthening me. Amen.

Guided into Truth

"But when he, the Spirit of truth, comes, he will guide you into all the truth. He will not speak on his own; he will speak only what he hears, and he will tell you what is yet to come."

JOHN 16:13 NIV

Isn't it amazing to realize the Spirit of God is guiding you, even now? He's like the rudder on a ship, nudging it in the direction it needs to go. The Holy Spirit is gentle and comforting, but He always aims you toward truth, for life is found in truth alone. That's why He's so keen on playing the leader while you do the following. Left to your own devices, you might veer off course.

So many people are aiming themselves at happiness instead of following the Spirit's lead toward truth. What good would it do you if you found one but missed the other?

Today, yield to the Holy Spirit. Follow His course. Relinquish yourself to the sovereign hand of God. He wants the very best for you and is the only one capable of bringing you into the fullness of His truth.

Prayer Prompt:

Are you searching for happiness or truth? Allow the Holy Spirit to guide you into God's truth.

Father, thank You for the reminder that this Christian walk isn't just about my happiness, though I know You want me to experience fullness of joy. It's about finding truth in You. Guide me, Holy Spirit; nudge me in the direction I need to go. Amen.

Take Heart

"I have told you all this so that you may have peace in me.
Here on earth you will have many trials and sorrows.
But take heart, because I have overcome the world."

JOHN 16:33 NLT

When you read the words *take heart,* what image comes to mind? Do you see your broken heart cradled in your hands, being massaged back to life? Do you envision a frown turning into a smile, anguish replaced with peace? Perhaps you see yourself drawing in a deep breath and putting one foot in front of another, determined you can make it the rest of the way if you just have faith.

When Jesus says to "*take* heart," He's implying that somewhere along the way you may have *lost* heart. But not to worry. As God transforms your life, He will gift you with His courage and peace, hope and confidence, joy and patience. For He works to replace your fearful, discouraged, worry-filled, and broken heart with His. When you yield yourself to the Master's ministrations, you'll experience His supernatural ability to overcome any circumstance that might come your way. What an amazing heart swap that would be!

Prayer Prompt:

Have you lost heart somewhere along the way? In prayer, ask God to transform your heart, restoring what was lost.

....

....

....

....

....

....

....

....

....

....

....

....

....

....

....

....

Father, how grateful I am that You have overcome the world! I would despair, otherwise. Thank You for the reminder that You're my courage giver, my peace, my overcomer. Without You, I would surely crater, Lord. With You, I can face any obstacle. Amen.

Before the Mountains Were Born

Before the mountains were born, before you gave birth to the earth and the world, from beginning to end, you are God.

PSALM 90:2 NLT

When you stop to think about Creation week, what do you envision? Perhaps you imagine hearing a majestic soundtrack, a heavenly choir ringing out as oceans roared. You see mountains rise and Technicolor canyons being carved by the tip of God's finger.

God (literally) took nothing and transformed it into something. And He's still in the transformation business, isn't He? Yet, although it's remarkable to think that "something" came from nothing during Creation week, it's even more astounding to realize that God, the Creator, was there, long before it all.

What was He doing before Creation, do you suppose? Communicating with the angels? Envisioning the world (and people) to come? Here's a fun fact: God, the Almighty, infinite Father of all, already had *you* in mind, long before this world came into being. What a remarkable notion!

Prayer Prompt:

God knew you before you were born. As you pray, remember His creative power and thank Him for giving you life.

....

....

....

....

....

....

....

....

....

....

....

....

....

....

....

Lord, You were there all along! Before the stars were flung into space. Before the rivers ran or the mountains trembled, You were right there, envisioning it all. You were thinking of me, Father. You knew my hair color, my skin tone, and even my personality. And You loved me even then. What an amazing Creator You are! Amen.

An Understanding Heart

"Give me an understanding heart so that I can govern your people well and know the difference between right and wrong. For who by himself is able to govern this great people of yours?"

1 KINGS 3:9 NLT

What does it mean to have an understanding heart? When you're fully in sync with the Lord, when His Spirit speaks to you and imparts wisdom that you can share with others, then you're "in understanding."

Not that this is an easy task. It's so tempting to fall out of step, spiritually speaking, to stop caring about the things that God cares about. But He longs for you to understand His thoughts, His wisdom, so that you can impart these nuggets of truth to others and live a fulfilled, transformed life.

Are you walking in sync with the Lord? Do your choices, words, and actions line up with His heart, His Word, His best? There's always room to draw closer, so take the time to do that even now, that you might better touch others with His amazing message.

Prayer Prompt:

What is keeping you from having an understanding heart? Ask God to give you a heart to know Him and walk in sync with Him.

....

....

....

....

....

....

....

....

....

....

....

....

....

....

....

Father, I don't want to have the kind of understanding that the world offers. Humankind's viewpoint is often so skewed, so self-focused. Help me understand the way You do, Lord. I want to be in sync with You to the point where my heart aches for the things that break Yours. May I always be in tune with You, I pray. Amen.

DAY 161

Resting in His Shadow

Whoever dwells in the shelter of the Most High will rest in the shadow of the Almighty. I will say of the LORD, "He is my refuge and my fortress, my God, in whom I trust."

PSALM 91:1–2 NIV

Part of the transformation process is simply learning how to rest in God's presence. Yet it's hard for the twenty-first-century woman to quiet her thoughts long enough to do that. Life's noises scream from every direction—kids crying, television blaring, video games chirping, horns honking, coworkers chattering. Whew! It's all she can do to think straight.

Oh, but finding the time to bask in God's presence, resting heart, mind, and spirit, is critical to survival! The Lord longs for you to draw close, to experience His goodness, His heart, His words of wisdom for whatever situation you happen to be walking through.

Where are you today? Are you resting in God's shadow or striving in the shadows of life? Run to Him right now and experience true rest.

Prayer Prompt:

What is keeping you from resting in the shadow of the Almighty?
When you pray, shut out the noise of life and listen for His voice.

....

....

....

....

....

....

....

....

....

....

....

....

....

....

....

*Father, I'm so tired of striving! I'm constantly going, 'round the
clock, trying to figure things out on my own. I give up! Help
me learn how to rest in You. Here I am, sitting at Your feet,
ready to bask in Your presence, to hear Your voice, to feel
Your heartbeat. Here I find true and lasting rest. Amen.*

The Man in the Middle

*Carrying his own cross, he went out to the place of the Skull
(which in Aramaic is called Golgotha). There they crucified him,
and with him two others—one on each side and Jesus in the middle.*
JOHN 19:17–18 NIV

Picture this: Jesus Christ—our Lord and Savior, King of all kings—hung on a cross between two thieves. On one side, a man who sought peace and redemption. On the other, a man who refused to repent.

Somehow, even in His deepest agony, Jesus managed to minister to the one who sought truth. He offered forgiveness, love, and eternal life, though the thief had done nothing to deserve it.

Today you may find yourself wedged between all sorts of people—coworkers, fellow students, family members, neighbors, friends. Some are open and ready to hear the gospel. Others, like the one thief who refused to repent, are not.

No matter what you're walking through, God can and will use you to reach others for Him. Keep your eyes wide open. Look to the right and the left. Then speak up as the Lord leads. You never know—you could very well open the door for someone to spend eternity with Jesus.

Prayer Prompt:

Who is in the circle of people around you? Make a list. When you pray, ask God for words of encouragement to speak to each of them.

Father, I want to be aware of the people You've placed all around me. Many are lost in sin. Still others are hurting and wounded. Use me to reach those who need You, Lord. I want to be available to minister as You lead. Amen.

DAY 163

His Glorious Presence

When the priests came out of the Holy Place, a thick cloud filled the Temple of the LORD. The priests could not continue their service because of the cloud, for the glorious presence of the LORD filled the Temple of the LORD.

1 KINGS 8:10–11 NLT

. . . .

What a day that must have been! The presence of God was so thick, so tangible, that the priests had to stop ministering and just breathe in His goodness. The entire temple was filled, top to bottom, side to side. Wow! Even Hollywood couldn't have done the scene justice!

What do you picture as you read those words—a magnificent cloud, weighty with the glory of God? The hum of an angelic chorus with an unfamiliar but heavenly melody pouring forth? Goosebumps on your arms and shivers running down your back?

If you've ever been in a service where God's presence was undeniable, then you've had a small foretaste of what's to come once you make the transition to heaven. Until then, keep pressing in. Draw close. Experience God's glory on a new level. Make room for the Spirit of God, and He will overwhelm You with His presence.

Prayer Prompt:

What do you desire from God today? During your prayer time, ask Him to reveal Himself to you.

....

....

....

....

....

....

....

....

....

....

....

....

....

....

....

Father, I want to know You more! I want to experience Your glorious presence, as men and women did in days of old. You're a God who never changes. If You revealed Yourself in such a marvelous way to believers back then, I know You'll do so again. Fill me today, Lord. Amen.

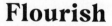

Flourish

*But the godly will flourish like palm trees
and grow strong like the cedars of Lebanon.*
PSALM 92:12 NLT

God never intended for us to live subpar lives. He desires His very best for us. Sure, we'll walk through valleys. We'll trudge through hard times. But even during those seasons, He longs for us to flourish, like leaves on a healthy vine. For when we're tied into Him, when we've given heart, mind, soul, and thoughts to Him, we receive the nourishment we need to overcome and to experience victories that make no sense in the natural.

So how do you begin the process of flourishing? Picture yourself like a small rosebush, freshly planted. Allow your roots to sink down deep in His Word. Let the water of His Spirit saturate the deepest places, removing any pain or unforgiveness. Then allow the sunlight of His presence to strengthen you from the inside out. Before long you'll be strong and hearty, a woman transformed.

Prayer Prompt:

What do you need to do to flourish in your walk with God? Pray for a deeper experience of God's presence in your life.

....

....

....

....

....

....

....

....

....

....

....

....

....

....

....

....

Father, I want to flourish. I don't want to live a subpar life, one where I'm just barely scraping by. I want the fullness that comes with knowing and loving You. Hold me close, I pray, that I might receive all You have for me. Feed, water, nourish . . .that I might flourish and grow strong in You. Amen.

So Send I You

Again Jesus said, "Peace be with you!
As the Father has sent me, I am sending you."
JOHN 20:21 NIV

So many great men and women have been nudged from the nest—to serve their countries, to run for political office, to pastor churches, to serve as missionaries, to adopt or foster children, to work in social services, to wear the badge, to pick up the fire hose. All over this globe, people are responding to various calls on their lives, saying, "Here am I, Lord. Send me!"

What does it mean to receive a call from God? Will you hear an audible voice, as Isaiah did when God's presence filled the temple, or will there be a gentle whisper from the Holy Spirit, prompting you to step out of your comfort zone? Only the Lord knows! But when He has a task for you (and He will), you've got to be ready to jump and run! A battle cry will ring out, a trumpet will sound, or a whisper will tickle your ear, signaling you to the front lines. There's no time to waste, so learn all you can now, while you're waiting.

Prayer Prompt:

What has God called you to do? In prayer, surrender to that call from Him, praying for His direction as you go.

....

....

....

....

....

....

....

....

....

....

....

....

....

....

....

....

Here am I, Lord. . .send me! I don't know where.
I don't know when. I don't know how. But I submit
myself to the process, Lord. I want to be usable,
pliable, ready to respond when You sound the cry.
Begin to prepare my heart even now. Amen.

As It Was Before

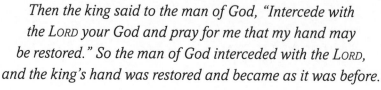

Then the king said to the man of God, "Intercede with the LORD your God and pray for me that my hand may be restored." So the man of God interceded with the LORD, and the king's hand was restored and became as it was before.

1 KINGS 13:6 NIV

Do you ever wish you could go back to the good old days? Do you find yourself reminiscing over how much simpler, kinder, or easier things were back then?

God is very specific that you're not to spend a lot of time looking over your shoulder because what lies before you is greater than what lies behind you. Not only will tomorrow be "as good as" yesterday, it can be better! Your best days are waiting for you around the bend in the road. (See Luke 9:62; 17:32; Genesis 19:26; Philippians 3:13–14; Isaiah 43:18–19.)

As you read those words, how does your heart respond? Does it feel possible, or have you given in to the mind-set that your glory days are behind you? God wants to reactivate your faith, which is why He longs for you to be forward thinking. So brace yourself! Exciting things are coming!

Prayer Prompt:

What are your plans for the future? Ask God to show you His plans for your future and give you a willing heart to change what you had planned.

....

....

....

....

....

....

....

....

....

....

....

....

....

....

....

....

Father, I keep thinking my best days are behind me.
Thank You for the reminder that Your plans for me are
vast, great, mighty. You've only scratched the surface
of what You plan to do in my life. I can't wait to
see what You have in store for me. Amen.

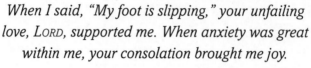

It's You, Oh Lord

When I said, "My foot is slipping," your unfailing love, Lord, supported me. When anxiety was great within me, your consolation brought me joy.

Psalm 94:18–19 niv

. . . .

If you've ever walked through a particularly difficult period, you know what it's like to feel deflated. Perhaps there were moments when you wondered if you would make it through, when you felt like giving up. Isn't it remarkable to know that God was right there, even in the midst of your pain? He never left you. He never forsook you. And He never will.

When you hit your jumping-off point, He's right there, catching you midleap. When your feet are stuck in clay, He reaches down and plucks you up again. When the stresses are weighing you down, bringing nothing but tears and despair, He consoles and brings joy.

God cares deeply about your situation and He longs to be your all-in-all. Don't give up on Him. He will never give up on you.

Prayer Prompt:

What is troubling you today or causing you to despair? Talk to God about it. He cares about your situation.

....

....

....

....

....

....

....

....

....

....

....

....

....

*I needed that reminder, Lord, that You will never give up
on me. I've given up on myself more times than I can count.
But You, oh Lord, go on supporting me. You go on consoling.
You continue to give joy. So many times, my feet have
slipped out from under me, but I can count on You not to
let me go, Father. I'm so very grateful for that. Amen.*

In One Accord

*Then the apostles returned to Jerusalem from the Mount of
Olives, a distance of half a mile. When they arrived, they went
to the upstairs room of the house where they were staying. . . .
They all met together and were constantly united in prayer.*

ACTS 1:12–14 NLT

We're living in a crazy time, when people (even within the body of Christ) can't seem to agree on much. Whether it's politics, doctrine, or even church music choices, people prefer arguing and bickering over finding common ground.

Why do you suppose God cares that we pray in one accord? Does He expect us all to be clones, replicas of one another? Of course not! But He understands that there's power in unity. When people come together, when they're all pointed in the same direction, passionate about the same thing, energy arises. Foes are vanquished.

It's time for people of the church to step into the boxing ring and do battle with the enemy of our souls. He's out to get us, and we have to fight. But we have to do it hand in hand, heart to heart. Only then will we ever stand a chance.

Prayer Prompt:

Are you a part of the problem or the solution? Ask God to show you how to be a part of the solution in working with those around you.

....

....

....

....

....

....

....

....

....

....

....

....

....

....

....

....

....

....

Sometimes I wonder if anyone out there agrees with me, Lord. I feel like the Lone Ranger, singing my own tune and marching to my own drumbeat. Put me in the company of like-minded people, I pray. Surround me with others who love You as I do. Together, we will be a force to be reckoned with. Amen.

Among the Nations

Sing to the LORD; praise his name. Each day proclaim the good news that he saves. Publish his glorious deeds among the nations. Tell everyone about the amazing things he does.
PSALM 96:2–3 NLT

. . . .

What a remarkable time we live in! Even fifty years ago, the idea of proclaiming the good news "among the nations" felt like an impossible task. Only missionaries could do that, and their commitment involved leaving home and friends behind, often to travel to other continents.

These days, we have access, via the internet, to almost any place in the world. With just a sentence or two on social media, we can impact a watching world. Suddenly, this notion that God's message can be spread across the nations isn't just a dream, it's a reality! How remarkable, to think that God knew (even before the Bible was penned) that we would one day have this capability. We can truly "publish" (with our words) His glorious deeds. What an amazing gift, to share His transformative power with people we've never even met.

Prayer Prompt:

What can you do to share the good news with other nations? Ask God to point you in the direction of those who need to hear the gospel.

....

....

....

....

....

....

....

....

....

....

....

....

....

Father, I'm so excited to live in a day and age where I can post a message on social media and watch it travel around the globe in milliseconds! You knew this day was coming, Lord, and placed me on planet Earth "for such a time as this" (Esther 4:14 NIV). My heart is attuned to Yours, Father. May my words travel across the nations, wooing others to You! Amen.

Between Two Opinions

*Then Elijah stood in front of them and said, "How much
longer will you waver, hobbling between two opinions?
If the Lord is God, follow him! But if Baal is God, then
follow him!" But the people were completely silent.*

1 Kings 18:21 NLT

. . . .

Have you ever had a hard time making up your mind? Maybe you've been torn over which way to vote. You listened to one candidate and felt persuaded, then listened to his or her opponent and got tugged in the opposite direction.

That unsettled feeling isn't good, is it? Oh, but when you finally make up your mind—when you settle the issue in your heart—what an amazing feeling that is! Suddenly you're invincible. You can conquer the world once your mind is fully made up.

God wants us to settle the issue of who He is. He's Lord and Savior, our God and King. He wants us to accept Him as such and to stop waffling between the world and the truth. The world will never be able to offer what He can—eternal life. So make up your mind to follow after God, and God alone.

Prayer Prompt:

Whose side are you on, God's or the world's? Ask the Lord to give you a mind to serve Him without wavering between two opinions.

....

....

....

....

....

....

....

....

....

....

....

....

....

....

Father, I'm going to stop waffling from one opinion to the next! My mind is made up. I'm on Your team from now on, Lord. Together, with Your hand in mine, I'll witness miracles! Praise You! Amen.

Devoted

All the believers devoted themselves to the apostles'
teaching, and to fellowship, and to sharing in meals
(including the Lord's Supper), and to prayer.

ACTS 2:42 NLT

. . . .

When you hear the word *devoted*, what comes to mind? Perhaps you think of a loved one who took the time and energy to care for a spouse with cancer. Or maybe it puts you in mind of a mother tending to her baby, tending to its every need.

To devote yourself to someone means you give of your time, your resources, and your emotions. So who are you devoted to? Who's devoted to you? Would you say that you're as devoted to the Lord (and to prayer, Bible reading, etc.) as you are to your friends, family, and children?

Those are tough questions, aren't they? Truth be told, most of us overlook daily time with the Lord because we're so busy. Today, why not recommit yourself to spending time in God's presence (and His Word), no matter how busy your life might get.

Prayer Prompt:

Who or what are you devoted to? Where do your strongest feelings lie? Spend time in God's presence, committing yourself to Him.

....

....

....

....

....

....

....

....

....

....

....

....

....

....

Lord, as we head into this new summer season,
I want to rededicate myself to You, Your will,
Your Word, and Your plan for my life. You are
so trustworthy, Father! As I devote myself to You,
I praise You for Your devotion to me. Amen.

Preserved

You who love the LORD, hate evil! He preserves the souls of His saints; He delivers them out of the hand of the wicked.

PSALM 97:10 NKJV

. . . .

Have you ever preserved a food product, such as making freezer jam, canning vegetables, or dehydrating meat? If so, then you understand the process of longevity. You've given a particular food a longer shelf (or refrigerator/freezer) life. By adding preservatives (or drying the product out), you've taken something that was destined to shortly die and transitioned it into a long-lasting state.

Did you realize that God longs to preserve—not just your life, your family, your relationships—but your very soul? He pours Himself out—like a holy preservative—and says, *"Your shelf life just got a l-o-t longer. You're going to live not just in this life but for all eternity."* Wow!

Today, take some time to ponder where your life would be without the Lord. Would you still be here? Would you have hope and a future? What a radical difference your God makes!

Prayer Prompt:

What would happen if God didn't preserve you? Thank Him today for His preserving power in your life.

....

....

....

....

....

....

....

....

....

....

....

....

....

....

Father, I'm so grateful You've extended my shelf life.
I get to live forever with You. And what a sweet
preservative You've given me, one seasoned
with forgiveness, grace, joy, and so much more.
Thank You, Lord, for preserving my soul. Amen.

Filled with the Spirit

And when they had prayed, the place where they were assembled together was shaken; and they were all filled with the Holy Spirit, and they spoke the word of God with boldness.

ACTS 4:31 NKJV

. . . .

What a day that must have been, when the Holy Spirit swept through the room and shook believers to the core. What power must have entered into each heart, what boldness! Can you even imagine what they heard, what they saw with their own eyes, and what they felt as the Holy Spirit took control of the room? The energy must have been overwhelming!

Is that what you're lacking in your life today, dear one? Do you have a rock-solid belief in God, but little power to back it up or to help you make the right decisions? Ask the Holy Spirit to sweep away the cobwebs in your heart and give you greater zeal, new energy. He desires to empower you so that you can be an effective witness for Him, one overflowing with strength. Not only will you impact those around you, you will grow in faith as God moves through you, touching others.

Prayer Prompt:

How are you allowing the Holy Spirit to work in your life? Ask God for an infilling of His Spirit that will energize you for Him.

....

....

....

....

....

....

....

....

....

....

....

....

....

....

....

....

Father, I want the power that only You can bring through Your Holy Spirit. Today I say, "Fill me, Lord! Rush in, Holy Spirit, and brush away any cobwebs. Use me as only You can. Give me the power to affect lives around me and to live fully for You, I pray." Amen.

A Just King

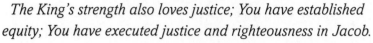

The King's strength also loves justice; You have established equity; You have executed justice and righteousness in Jacob.
PSALM 99:4 NKJV

. . . .

Justice. What comes to mind when you hear that word? Perhaps you think of social justice—where all people are treated fairly and not discriminated against. Maybe the word *justice* brings to mind a particular friend or loved one who was treated unjustly by a spouse or boss. Perhaps you can relate because the same thing has happened to you. And you know there's nothing worse than feeling like you've been discriminated against, especially when you know you did nothing to deserve it.

Aren't you glad God is a just King? He doesn't discriminate. He doesn't just randomly issue orders for one person to rule over another. He longs for equity and righteousness. Today, if you've been treated unjustly—at the hands of someone you thought you could trust or someone in your school or workplace—give your situation to God. He longs to heal the pain caused by the unjust treatment. At the same time, He wants to show *you* how to treat others fairly.

Prayer Prompt:

What does the word *justice* mean to you? Ask God to show you how to treat others and forgive those who have treated you unjustly.

What seems "just" to some might be unjust to You, Lord. I'm so glad You're a just Father, one who makes all things right in the end. Thank You, Father. Amen.

What Do You Have?

Elisha said to her, "What shall I do for you? Tell me,
what do you have in the house?" And she said, "Your
maidservant has nothing in the house but a jar of oil."
2 KINGS 4:2 NKJV

If you've ever been through a season of lack, you can appreciate this story. A poor widow, whose sons were about to be indentured by a creditor, pleads for help from Elisha. So he asks her an odd question: "What do you have in the house?" She had little. Very little—"nothing but a jar of oil."

Maybe you can relate. You open your pantry and there's little there. Or you check your bank balance and groan because it's so low. Perhaps you look at your gas gauge and realize it's nearing E.

Yet God can take your "little" and grow it into something big, just as He did for this woman. He took her one jar of oil and increased it to the point where she could not only pay her dead husband's debts but live on the money left over.

What do you have to offer God today? He will take what you have and multiply it if you just release your hold on it.

Prayer Prompt:

What do you want God to do for you today? Tell Him what you have to offer and then give it to Him.

....

....

....

....

....

....

....

....

....

....

....

....

....

....

*Lord, I feel as if my spiritual, emotional,
physical, and financial cupboards are bare
at times. I don't seem to have much to offer
You. I release what little I do have and give it
to You. Multiply it as only You can. Amen.*

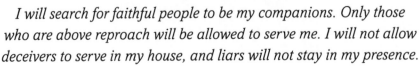

Above Reproach

I will search for faithful people to be my companions. Only those who are above reproach will be allowed to serve me. I will not allow deceivers to serve in my house, and liars will not stay in my presence.

PSALM 101:6–7 NLT

. . . .

It's always heartbreaking to see people—pastors, politicians, TV and movie stars, and so forth—fall from grace. We gasp, horrified and shocked to hear the news of what they've done in the shadows. Perhaps this is because we had elevated them to a position of fame or because we somehow felt they were above reproach.

Meanwhile, God is searching the earth for people who want to live godly lives, people who've turned their back on sin and are willing to follow wholeheartedly after Him. And He's not just looking at famous/ well-known people either. He's checking out the supermarket clerk, the mail carrier, the single mom, the CEO, the high school coach, the secretary, and so on. And He's finding willing candidates, those who say, "I will do my best to live for You and not bring shame to Your name, Lord."

Have you made a faith-filled commitment to your heavenly Father? If not, today is the perfect day to do so.

Prayer Prompt:

What can you do to be a woman above reproach? Ask God to show you how to live godly and follow Him with your whole heart.

....

....

....

....

....

....

....

....

....

....

....

....

....

....

....

....

....

....

....

....

Father, today I recommit myself to You. May I never bring shame to Your name (or my own, for that matter). I want to be who I say I am, a woman above reproach. May my name always bring joy to Your heart, Lord. Amen.

Holy Ground

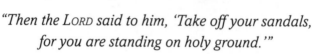

*"Then the LORD said to him, 'Take off your sandals,
for you are standing on holy ground.'"*
ACTS 7:33 NLT

. . . .

Have you ever felt the presence of God so acutely, so powerfully, that you felt you had no other choice but to drop to your knees? There are moments in life when the tangible, overpowering presence of God compels us to leave the ordinary things behind. We toss the shoes and dance in His presence, hands uplifted, words of praise on our lips. What else can we do but praise Him when we're standing on holy ground?

The Bible is filled with such stories of men and women encountering the tangible, overpowering presence of God, people such as Moses, Isaiah, Job, Amos, Hagar, Jacob, Gideon, and Manoah and his wife, to name a few. Just one moment in His presence and lives were forever changed. Isn't it remarkable to know that God is the same—yesterday, today, and forever? If He drew men and women into His holy presence back then, He will do it again today.

Prayer Prompt:

What would you do if you found yourself standing on holy ground?
Spend time praising God and rejoicing in His presence.

....

....

....

....

....

....

....

....

....

....

....

....

....

....

....

*Oh, how I long to spend time with You, Father! Your
transforming presence is all I need to turn life's situations
around. Just one minute with You and I'm reminded that
nothing else matters. Change me, heal me, touch me.*

The Prayer of the Destitute

He shall regard the prayer of the destitute,
and shall not despise their prayer.
Psalm 102:17 NKJV

- -

God cares about every human being—every situation, every pain, every heartbreak. It doesn't matter if you're the richest CEO or the poorest beggar in the street. God sees every tear and wants to heal every broken heart.

Aren't you glad the Lord cares? And isn't it comforting to know that He doesn't divide us into categories by race, color, or class? All are loved, and every prayer counts. Whether it's uttered by the man driving the BMW or the homeless veteran with no safe place to lay his head, the woman deep in sin or the mother trying to walk the straight and narrow. God doesn't discriminate. If He does something for one person, He will do it for the other.

Today, as you lift up your own needs to the Lord, why not take a few moments to pray for those in dire situations—the beggar, the prostitute, the homeless child. They need your prayers, your love, and your understanding.

Prayer Prompt:

What situation are you facing today? God doesn't show partiality. Take your need and the needs of those around you to Him.

Lord, thank You for the reminder that You do not discriminate. I want to be like You in that regard, Father. May I see every man, woman, and child as You do. Help those in need today, I pray. Amen.

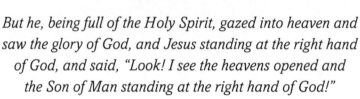

Face-to-Face

But he, being full of the Holy Spirit, gazed into heaven and saw the glory of God, and Jesus standing at the right hand of God, and said, "Look! I see the heavens opened and the Son of Man standing at the right hand of God!"

ACTS 7:55–56 NKJV

. . . .

What a majestic scene! Can you imagine seeing beyond the horizon to what Stephen saw that amazing day? What would it be like to peel back a corner of the curtain and see into heaven right now? What would you see? Angelic choirs? Streets of gold or mansions of splendor? Loved ones who've gone before you?

Heaven will be wonderful, but our focus won't be on all of the shimmer and shine. It will be on the one at the right hand of the Father—Jesus, our Savior. All that we've waited for, all that we've longed for, will be complete in that moment as we gaze at Him face-to-face.

As you think about eternity, don't let fear take root. You won't be losing your life here—or there! You'll be gaining an amazing life that will continue forever in the presence of God.

Prayer Prompt:

What are some of the things you're looking forward to in heaven? Ask Jesus to give you a greater desire to make heaven your eternal home.

....

....

....

....

....

....

....

....

....

....

....

....

....

....

....

....

....

....

....

Father, I can hardly wait to see heaven for myself. How glorious it will be. You've given me tiny peeks as I've worshipped at Your throne, but that's only a foretaste of what's to come. Thank You for giving me eternal life with You! Amen.

Forget Not His Benefits

Bless the LORD, O my soul, and forget not all His benefits:
Who forgives all your iniquities, Who heals all your diseases,
Who redeems your life from destruction, Who crowns you with
lovingkindness and tender mercies, Who satisfies your mouth
with good things, so that your youth is renewed like the eagle's.
PSALM 103:2–5 NKJV

Your friendship with the Creator of the universe comes with many benefits that are simply out of this world. Did you know, for example, that God not only forgives all of your sins, but He's a healer of diseases, a redeemer from destruction, a crowner of loving-kindness, and the ultimate satisfaction? He's the be-all and end-all, capable of fulfilling every need you could ever have in your life—emotional, physical, or spiritual.

Why does God offer so much to those He loves? Because He's a good, good Father. And it doesn't stop there. He longs for complete renewal in your life. He's waiting for you to take off like an eagle, soaring over your circumstances. It all starts with your acceptance of His benefits. So what are you waiting for? Spread those wings and fly, girl!

Prayer Prompt:

Make a list of all the benefits God has for you. Spend some time thanking Him for all He has provided.

....

....

....

....

....

....

....

....

....

....

....

....

....

....

....

Father, I don't deserve Your goodness, but You lavish it on me anyway. Thank You, from the bottom of my heart—not just for Your benefits but Your never-ending love. I'm so blessed, Lord. Amen.

Blinded by the Light

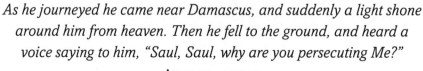

As he journeyed he came near Damascus, and suddenly a light shone around him from heaven. Then he fell to the ground, and heard a voice saying to him, "Saul, Saul, why are you persecuting Me?"
ACTS 9:3–4 NKJV

If you've ever walked out into the sunlight after being in a dark place, you know how blinding the sun can be. Imagine being in Saul's shoes! He was minding his own business, walking down the road, when suddenly a bright light shot down from heaven, knocked him off his feet, and completely blinded him—not just for a few seconds but for days!

You may have heard the old expression "He never knew what hit him." In Saul's case, he figured it out in a hurry when Jesus' voice rang out: "Saul, why are you persecuting Me?"

Perhaps God had to go to such extremes to get Saul's attention because he wouldn't have believed it otherwise. What about you? Has God ever had to go to extreme circumstances to get your attention? What did it take to finally stop you in your tracks so you would listen—truly listen—to God?

Prayer Prompt:

Why is God doing something to get your attention and what is He doing? Draw close to Him in prayer to hear His voice today.

....

....

....

....

....

....

....

....

....

....

....

....

....

....

....

....

....

Lord, I don't want to make it hard on You, so I choose to truly listen to You. May You never have to go to extremes to get my attention, Father. Amen.

Regain Sight

So Ananias went and found Saul. He laid his hands on him and said, "Brother Saul, the Lord Jesus, who appeared to you on the road, has sent me so that you might regain your sight and be filled with the Holy Spirit." Instantly something like scales fell from Saul's eyes, and he regained his sight. Then he got up and was baptized. Afterward he ate some food and regained his strength. Saul stayed with the believers in Damascus for a few days.

ACTS 9:17–19 NLT

Imagine for a moment that a longtime ailment you had was instantly healed. Or that a problem or situation you'd been praying about for a really long time was finally solved, your request addressed. Or maybe your prayer was granted soon after someone took time to simply pray with you. These situations are reminders that God is at work.

The same God who helped Saul regain his sight is the same God who wants to help you regain eyes of faith. If you don't know where to start, look up and praise God for the good things He has already done. Praise Him for how He wants to increase your faith. Then when He works in Your life, let all that you are praise the Lord (Psalm 103:22).

Prayer Prompt:

What do you need God to do for you today? In prayer, open your heart to Him and allow Him to work.

....

....

....

....

....

....

....

....

....

....

....

....

....

....

....

....

....

....

....

Jesus, I'm in need of Your touch. Help me regain strength in You and have the faith to believe You are transforming me.

Hold On Tight

Hezekiah trusted in the LORD, the God of Israel. There was no one like him among all the kings of Judah, either before him or after him. He held fast to the LORD and did not stop following him; he kept the commands the LORD had given Moses. And the LORD was with him; he was successful in whatever he undertook. He rebelled against the king of Assyria and did not serve him.

2 KINGS 18:5–7 NIV

Take inventory of the past few months with your relationship in Christ. Now compare that to when you first accepted Jesus into your life. Chances are a lot has changed. You realize you've been transformed. Your faith has grown. You have testimonies to remind you of God's faithfulness.

Like Hezekiah, or the apostles in Acts, you have been learning what it means to abide in the Lord. You have been learning to trust Him, the one who is in control of all things (Psalm 104:1–9).

Like a child who clings to her favorite stuffed animal, cling to God. He is enough and will not let go of you! He loves you not because of anything you have done, but simply because You are His child. So keep holding on!

Prayer Prompt:

Are you having a hard time with something today? Pray and ask God to strengthen your hold on Him.

....

....

....

....

....

....

....

....

....

....

....

....

....

....

....

....

....

Father, thank You for never letting go of me. Though I may loosen my grip with You at times, help me to hold on tightly to Your words so that my character may be transformed.

Power of Prayer

And Hezekiah prayed before the Lord and said: "O Lord, the God of Israel, enthroned above the cherubim, you are the God, you alone, of all the kingdoms of the earth; you have made heaven and earth."

2 KINGS 19:15 ESV

· ·

As a woman of God, you probably know by now that transformation doesn't happen overnight (although sometimes you may wish it would). It takes a lot of time, patience, and prayer.

In today's readings, found in 2 Kings and Acts 10, you learn about courageous leaders of the faith who prayed to God. Their words were humble ones. Yet God heard their prayers—each and every one. (For example, see Acts 10:30–31 ESV.)

When you pray, know this: God hears you! You might not see anything happen immediately, right before your eyes. But you can trust that the God of the universe is listening and moving behind the scenes for your good. And even though you might not even feel any different after you pray, you can be sure you've done something courageous. You humbled yourself enough to seek God.

Prayer Prompt:

What changes are you looking for in your life? As you pray, trust that God has heard you and will answer in His time.

....

....

....

....

....

....

....

....

....

....

....

....

....

....

....

Lord, as I read Psalm 104:10–23, I reflect on how
You are constantly at work in creation. Help me to
trust that You are working on me, sanctifying me,
molding me to be more of who You desire me to be.

Declare Dependence in Christ

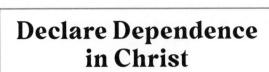

O Lord, what a variety of things you have made! In wisdom you have made them all. The earth is full of your creatures. Here is the ocean, vast and wide, teeming with life of every kind, both large and small. See the ships sailing along, and Leviathan, which you made to play in the sea.
PSALM 104:24–26 NLT

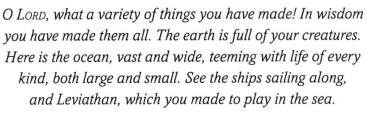

On this day, throughout the entire nation, we celebrate America's birthday. On July 4, we remember the public declaration of independence from Great Britain in 1776.

As a woman of Christ, today and every day you can choose to remember the freedom that you truly have. Every single day is a celebration of the forgiveness of sins and the hope of a transformative life found in Jesus.

So however you plan to celebrate this holiday—whether it will be watching fireworks or attending a barbecue with your family—remember all God has done in your life. As one who, like Peter's listeners, has received the Holy Spirit (Acts 10:44–47), recount your day of independence from the ways of this world. Remember when you accepted Christ into your heart and declared dependence in Him alone, the Creator who supplies and satisfies His creation (Psalm 104:27–28).

Prayer Prompt:

What are you celebrating today in your spiritual life? During prayer time, thank God for the freedom that you have.

....

....

....

....

....

....

....

....

....

....

....

....

....

....

....

....

....

....

....

....

Jesus, I declare that my dependence is in You alone!
Thank You for the freedom You so richly supply!

With All Your Heart

*I will sing to the L*ORD *as long as I live; I will sing praise
to my God while I have my being. May my meditation
be sweet to Him; I will be glad in the L*ORD.*

PSALM 104:33–34 NKJV

. . . .

King Josiah lived out what God called and commanded him to do through scripture. As a leader of the faith, he helped point God's children back to true worship. He turned away from idols and helped people refocus their thoughts toward their Creator. Because of his commitment to God, scripture says: "Now before him there was no king like him, who turned to the LORD with all his heart, with all his soul, and with all his might, according to all the Law of Moses; nor after him did any arise like him" (2 Kings 23:25 NKJV).

Wouldn't you want to be as committed as Josiah was, seen as a woman who loves the Lord with all her heart, soul, and might? One way to do this is to praise and worship God. To educate others about His goodness. And to yield to God's powerful transformative process as you read and meditate upon His Word.

Prayer Prompt:

As a woman, how can you be as committed as Josiah was? As you pray, ask God to open His Word and transform your life.

....

....

....

....

....

....

....

....

....

....

....

....

....

....

....

....

Father God, like so many of the great leaders and prophets that have gone before, may I be Your vessel. May I be Your conduit used to bring transformation to those wandering in their faith. Help me to do so with all my heart.

Chosen Child

While they were worshiping the Lord and fasting, the Holy Spirit said, "Set apart for me Barnabas and Saul for the work to which I have called them." So after they had fasted and prayed, they placed their hands on them and sent them off.

ACTS 13:2–3 NIV

. . . .

In Acts 9 we read about Saul, a Jew who was persecuting Christians—until he suddenly sees the light and converts to Christianity. Later, in Acts 13:9, Saul is called Paul. For this apostle, his story—and name change—is about the transformative power of Christ. Because of a supernatural experience, he turned from his former lifestyle and way of thinking and began sharing the gospel message with many people.

As a daughter of Christ, you too have a transformation story. One that's beautiful and amazing! One that has the power to change a life and remind others they are also God's chosen.

If you haven't done so already, take some time to write down your testimony. "Remember the wonders he has performed, his miracles" (Psalm 105:5 NLT). Then pray and ask God to show you who to share your story with. He'll be sure to give you the strength to do it (Psalm 105:4).

Prayer Prompt:

As you write your testimony, ask God to remind you of things you may have forgotten. Pray for the anointing of the Holy Spirit over your written words.

....

....

....

....

....

....

....

....

....

....

....

....

....

....

....

....

Lord, I'm so grateful for how You have changed me from the inside out! Thank You for showing me that I'm Your dearly loved chosen child. I love You!

A Total Life Change

*"From out of David's descendants God produced a Savior
for Israel, Jesus, exactly as he promised—but only after John
had thoroughly alerted the people to his arrival by preparing
them for a total life-change. As John was finishing up his work,
he said, 'Did you think I was the One? No, I'm not the One.
But the One you've been waiting for all these years is just around
the corner, about to appear. And I'm about to disappear.' "*
ACTS 13:23–25 MSG

John the Baptist paved the way for the coming Messiah. He alerted the people about Jesus' arrival and prepared them for someone awesome. Yet John wasn't preparing them for a minor makeover or even a do-over. He was preparing them for a *total* life change, a major transformation! John was then humble enough to step aside so that Jesus could do what He was called to do—lead God's children into a new and everlasting life!

You are a precious daughter of God. Think about that for a moment. *You* belong to a God who remembers His covenant to a thousand generations, who Himself never changes, and is as good as His word (Psalm 105:8–15). And His promised Son, your Messiah, has called you to follow Him. So hold on tight as Jesus leads you into a total life change as an ever-evolving creation in Christ.

Prayer Prompt:

What might you need to turn over to Jesus as He leads you into a total life change? Pray for a willing heart as the change takes place.

....

....

....

....

....

....

....

....

....

....

....

....

....

....

....

....

....

....

....

*Abba Father, I commit my life to You. I want
to see You do a total transformation in me.*

Standing in Faith

In Lystra a certain man without strength in his feet was sitting,
a cripple from his mother's womb, who had never walked.
This man heard Paul speaking. Paul, observing him intently and
seeing that he had faith to be healed, said with a loud voice,
"Stand up straight on your feet!" And he leaped and walked.

ACTS 14:8–10 NKJV

The Gospels and the book of Acts contain numerous accounts where people who had challenging health ailments were miraculously healed. Many times, those who were conduits of God's healing power, such as Paul (who's mentioned in the story above), noticed something very important about those in need: the person with a malady had faith to be healed. And because of that faith, God was able to work in that person's life.

When you have faith in God, others will notice it, including Him. Because of that faith, God will not just help you to stand—but to leap and walk!

If you want God to perform a miracle in your life, shore up your faith by spending time in His presence. Open yourself up to His Word. And pray, asking God to work in your life.

Prayer Prompt:

What miracle do you need in your life? Spend time in prayer, asking God to give you faith to believe and receive that miracle.

....

....

....

....

....

....

....

....

....

....

....

....

....

....

....

....

....

....

Lord, help me shore up my faith. Show me how to pray for the areas in my life where I desire to see You work for my good and for Your glory.

Tribulations to Transformation

After preaching the Good News in Derbe and making many disciples, Paul and Barnabas returned to Lystra, Iconium, and Antioch of Pisidia, where they strengthened the believers. They encouraged them to continue in the faith, reminding them that we must suffer many hardships to enter the Kingdom of God.

ACTS 14:21–22 NLT

As a daughter of Jesus, have you noticed something about seasons of testing? When you feel like you're under a lot of pressure, going through one trial after the next, you might feel weighed down and burdened. But with the eyes of faith, you can stand encouraged that God really is at work. For the good news reminds you that on the other side of tribulation comes transformation, and on the other side of a test comes a testimony.

When you're in the midst of the battle, cry out to God and He'll give you victory, as He always does for those who rely on, cling to, and trust in Him (1 Chronicles 5:20 AMPC).

Whatever you might be going through, cry out to Jesus. Cling to Him. Trust that He's moving mountains on your behalf. That He is all that you need.

Prayer Prompt:

How do you respond to testing? Ask God to give you strength to face whatever comes your way.

....

....

....

....

....

....

....

....

....

....

....

....

....

....

....

Lord, lead me on the pathway to be encouraged by You and other followers in the faith. Help me stand firm in what You say about me. May I cling to You and Your Word. May I rely on You and trust in You alone.

Instruction Manual

So he brought his people out of Egypt with joy, his chosen ones with rejoicing. He gave his people the lands of pagan nations, and they harvested crops that others had planted. All this happened so they would follow his decrees and obey his instructions. Praise the LORD!

PSALM 105:43–45 NLT

. . . .

When you buy something that has to be assembled at home, do you usually follow the instructions word for word? Chances are the step-by-step process might be time consuming, even frustrating. The manual might be hard to understand. In fact, you might need to consult others for wisdom, advice, help, and encouragement. And in the end, there's no telling if the completed product will leave you feeling weary or wonderful.

The same holds true for you as a woman of God. You might want a changed heart, a new situation, some kind of transformation, or better yet sanctification. But to get there requires time, patience, prayer, and an instruction manual—the Bible. It means reading God's Word, finding tools and resources to help you interpret and understand it, and having discussions about it with others (Acts 15).

The point is, you won't know how to put together a godly life until you read God's instruction manual. Consider where you can start that step-by-step transformational process today, leaving the final results in God's hands.

Prayer Prompt:

What kind of help do you consult for direction in life? Pray that God will bless your time with His Word, which is the ultimate instruction manual.

....

....

....

....

....

....

....

....

....

....

....

....

....

....

....

....

....

Father, inspire me to read Your instruction manual for my life, then obey it and live it out in such a way that true transformation takes place.

Spring in Your Step

*Praise ye the L*ORD*. O give thanks unto the L*ORD*; for he is good:*
for his mercy endureth for ever. Who can utter the mighty
*acts of the L*ORD*? who can shew forth all his praise?*

PSALM 106:1–2 KJV

What prompts you to praise God when all is going well? What prompts your praise when things aren't going well? Is it listening to other people's testimonies? Recalling the times God has been faithful to you? Hearing an encouraging message preached? What gives you the glimpse of hope and encouragement you're craving?

In the early days of the church, a message was delivered to the Antioch believers, bringing the new Christians great joy as it was read aloud. Then the prophets Judas and Silas spoke to "the believers, encouraging and strengthening their faith" (Acts 15:32 NLT).

If you need an extra dose of support and encouragement, consider tapping into old messages that have buoyed your faith in the past—or seek out new ones. As you do so, God's joy will bubble up within you, giving you that extra spring in your step and prompting praise to roll off your lips.

Prayer Prompt:

What causes you to give praise to God? Ask Him to remind you of
those things and use them to stir up the praise within you.

....

....

....

....

....

....

....

....

....

....

....

....

....

....

....

....

....

....

....

....

*Father God, whether I'm in a season of harvest or
a season of drought, help me to praise You. If joyful
words are not flowing from my mouth, help me get there
by reading or hearing the encouraging messages of others.*

Keep Pressing On

*All Israel gathered before David at Hebron and told him. . .
"In the past, even when Saul was king, you were the one
who really led the forces of Israel. And the LORD your
God told you, 'You will be the shepherd of my people
Israel. You will be the leader of my people Israel.' "*

1 CHRONICLES 11:1–2 NLT

The people of Israel wanted David to be king. That's what God had promised them (1 Chronicles 11:3). In fact, the Lord had already turned the kingdom over to David because Saul had become unfaithful to God. For he'd sought the guidance of a medium instead of God and failed to obey the Lord's instructions (1 Samuel 13:5–14; 15:1–35).

When you are walking through times of questioning and doubt, feeling like your prayers are hitting a roadblock, it can be tempting to take matters into your own hands. Instead of turning away from the faith, keep pressing on. Be like the mighty fighters who stood for God and supported David. But do so without their armor and swords. For you, woman warrior, will be able to stand your ground with God at your side, armed with the weapons of His Word of truth, the power of your prayers, and the strength of your praise.

Prayer Prompt:

Why do you sometimes feel the need to take matters into your own hands? Talk to God about this need to take charge.

Lord, when I'm tempted to go in another direction, help me find scripture to hold on to. May I keep pressing through with prayers and praise.

Mountain Mover

Around midnight Paul and Silas were praying and singing hymns to God, and the other prisoners were listening. Suddenly, there was a massive earthquake, and the prison was shaken to its foundations. All the doors immediately flew open, and the chains of every prisoner fell off!

ACTS 16:25–26 NLT

. . . .

Paul and Silas had been beaten then put into prison. They were in the inner dungeon with their feet clamped into the stocks. Ouch! Not a very cozy and comfy predicament to be in. But their conditions didn't stop them from praying and singing to the one they were so amazingly passionate about.

Within an instant their figurative mountain was literally moved right before their very eyes. An earthquake shook the prison's foundation, doors flew open, and chains fell away. The men who were once prisoners were now free! All of this transformed the heart of their jailer, who "fell down trembling before Paul and Silas. . .and asked, 'Sirs, what must I do to be saved?' " (Acts 16:29–30 NLT)!

Want a prayer life that transforms you as well as others? If so, commit to doing as Paul and Silas did. Pray to and praise God—and you too will see your mountains move!

Prayer Prompt:

What keeps you from having a transformational prayer life? Ask God to remove the obstacles so you can experience freedom.

....

....

....

....

....

....

....

....

....

....

....

....

....

....

....

....

Jesus, help me to pray to and praise You during good times and bad, leading me to the freedom that will transform my situation and the hearts of others.

Transformation Proclamation

Sing to the LORD, all the earth! Tell of his salvation from day to day. Declare his glory among the nations, his marvelous works among all the peoples! For great is the LORD, and greatly to be praised, and he is to be feared above all gods.

1 CHRONICLES 16:22–25 ESV

Have you noticed a difference in your thought life or a change in your overall attitude since you became a believer? Chances are you have witnessed some improvements. Or maybe someone has told you she sees a change in you. Maybe certain situations just don't have the same effect on you as they once did.

When going through tests or trials, you may be tempted to entertain negative thoughts or adopt a bad attitude. If that happens, if your old ways begin to rise up in your heart and mind, rest assured that God sees you and He understands! He has compassion for you. And because of that compassion, He has a word for you, a scripture verse or a prayer, a transformation proclamation that you can write down, one that reminds you that you're a new creation. That the old way of thinking and reacting is gone. That you have been transformed by the renewing of your mind.

Prayer Prompt:

What can you do to ward off negative thoughts and a bad attitude?
Spend time with God, asking Him to transform your mind and spirit.

....

....

....

....

....

....

....

....

....

....

....

....

....

....

....

*Lord, You are the Great Equipper. As I read Your
Word, You transform my mind and attitude. As I
pray, look upon me with compassion. Lead me
out of all darkness and into Your light.*

Potter and Clay

"He is the God who made the world and everything in it. . . . He himself gives life and breath to everything, and he satisfies every need. . . . He is not far from any one of us. For in him we live and move and exist."

ACTS 17:24–25, 27–28 NLT

. . . .

God created the world and everything in it—including you. He gave you life and breath. He can, does, and will satisfy your every need. For He is never far from you. Because it is in Him that you live, move, and exist.

Yet that's not the end of the story. For God continues to transform, to re-create you. God, the grand master, the potter, is molding you, the clay, to be more like the woman He desires for you to be, changing your thoughts and attitudes, even your actions and behavior. Making you a vessel through which He can shine His light for the whole world to see.

As a new creation in Christ, God has put His desires in your heart. Your prayers are now more powerful, meaningful, able to affect not just you and others but the world that surrounds you. For He has a plan in mind, and you are a part of that plan.

Prayer Prompt:

How can your prayers become more powerful and meaningful? Pray for a deeper prayer life that will affect everything you do.

....

....

....

....

....

....

....

....

....

....

....

....

....

....

....

....

Father, may You, the potter, mold me, the clay,
into more and more of what You desire.

Speak Out

*One night the Lord spoke to Paul in a vision and told him,
"Don't be afraid! Speak out! Don't be silent! For I am
with you, and no one will attack and harm you, for many
people in this city belong to me." So Paul stayed there for
the next year and a half, teaching the word of God.*

ACTS 18:9–11 NLT

As God continues to mold and shape you into the woman He desires you to be, there will be milestone moments in your faith journey. Paul's milestone moment was a vision from God that encouraged and strengthened his faith.

For you it might not be a vision. It might be someone's prayer for you, something you read in God's Word, or a Christian song you heard on the radio. Or another of a myriad of ways God reaches His people.

When God does speak to you, make note of it. Write it down. Then, as the Lord leads you, "Speak out! Tell others" how He's touched you (Psalm 107:2 NLT).

The more you expect and look for those milestone moments, the more of them you'll have. And the more you'll find yourself praising "the LORD for his great love and for the wonderful things he has done" (Psalm 107:8 NLT).

Prayer Prompt:

Can you think of some milestone moments in your life? Ask God to show you what those moments mean.

....

....

....

....

....

....

....

....

....

....

....

....

....

....

....

....

....

....

Jesus, as I continue to let You transform me from the inside out, give me the boldness to speak out about my faith in a way that's loving and glorifies You!

Lift the Load

Then they cried to the LORD in their trouble, and he saved them from their distress. He brought them out of darkness, the utter darkness, and broke away their chains. Let them give thanks to the LORD for his unfailing love and his wonderful deeds for mankind, for he breaks down gates of bronze and cuts through bars of iron.

PSALM 107:13–16 NIV

· ·

The above words give one hope. Why? Because no matter how deep your trouble or how great your distress, God can hear your cry and save you—even if you, like these people, are in "darkness, the utter darkness," words that describe the deep abyss in which they find themselves, the magnitude and weight of the heavy chains binding them.

Your encouragement lies in the idea that no matter how far down you are, no matter how burdensome your circumstances and worries might get, God is able to free you from the chains. He's ready and willing to lift the load off your shoulders.

And when He frees and lifts you, thank Him. For it is then that things begin to shift. Confining gates come down and bars break.

Prayer Prompt:

What kind of darkness are you facing today? Ask the Lord to shine His light into that darkness.

....
....
....
....
....
....
....
....
....
....
....
....
....
....
....
....

Lord, no matter how deep down I go, You can raise me up. No matter how heavy my load, You can lift it from me. For this and more I give You thanks.

Clean House

Thus the Word of the Lord [concerning the attainment through Christ of eternal salvation in the kingdom of God] grew and spread and intensified, prevailing mightily.

ACTS 19:20 AMPC

. . . .

There's a backstory to Acts 19:20. The Word of the Lord grew and spread after a major transformation took place in the minds and hearts of many people. These people were ones who'd formerly put their faith, hope, and trust in things that were not of God. The new believers got rid of these things, all to make room in their hearts and minds for the gospel message. In essence, they cleaned house to make room for the magnifying greatness of God.

Because you're a woman who's in the process of being transformed, this message might speak to you. Perhaps there are material things in your house that God would have you sweep away. Or maybe there are some intangible things that are hindering you from having the very best relationship with God. Maybe you're spending more time watching television than reading your Bible or spending more time "talking" on social media than to God. Whatever may be standing between you and the Lord, ask God for the help to make more room for Him so that His Word will grow and spread inside of you.

Prayer Prompt:

What kind of cleaning do you need to do in your life? Ask the Lord to show you what and where to clean.

....

....

....

....

....

....

....

....

....

....

....

....

....

....

....

Lord, have Your way in my heart, mind, body, soul, spirit, and home. Show me what I can do to make more room for You; then give me the strength and the ability to do so.

Lasting Impression

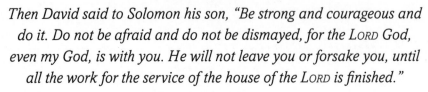

Then David said to Solomon his son, "Be strong and courageous and do it. Do not be afraid and do not be dismayed, for the LORD God, even my God, is with you. He will not leave you or forsake you, until all the work for the service of the house of the LORD is finished."

1 CHRONICLES 28:20 ESV

David gave a charge to his son Solomon to build a house for God. David's words were strong, passionate, encouraging, and inspirational. He wanted Solomon to know that God would be with him, helping him every step of the way. That God would not leave Him until the work was done.

Chances are there have been women who have gone before you who have mentored or commissioned you in some way. These ladies left an imprint on your heart and mind to carry out the faith in a bold way.

Reflect on these people, and take some time to thank God for them. These individuals laid a groundwork, a lasting impression, that has impacted your soul! Without God placing them in your life, He wouldn't have been able to mold you into the person you are today.

Prayer Prompt:

Who made a lasting impression in your life? Ask God to make you a lasting impression for Him on someone else.

_____

_____

_____

_____

_____

_____

_____

_____

_____

_____

_____

_____

_____

_____

Savior, thank You for placing people in my life who've made a lasting impression on me. Like David, who inspired and emboldened his son Solomon, show me how I can do the same for others so they can witness Your transforming power in their own lives.

Perfect Alignment

"Because your greatest desire is to help your people, and you did not ask for wealth, riches, fame, or even the death of your enemies or a long life, but rather you asked for wisdom and knowledge to properly govern my people—I will certainly give you the wisdom and knowledge you requested. But I will also give you wealth, riches, and fame such as no other king has had before you or will ever have in the future!"

2 CHRONICLES 1:11–12 NLT

Solomon was only twenty years old when he became king of Israel, charged with not only ruling the Israelites but building a temple for God. One night, after Solomon was worshipping in the tabernacle, God came to him, asking what he wanted. In response, Solomon made an admirable prayer request, asking God for wisdom and knowledge to lead His people.

Solomon's request revealed that the desires of his heart were in perfect alignment with God's. Because of this, God blessed Solomon immensely, not only answering his prayer but giving Solomon everything else he *could* have—but hadn't—asked for: wealth, riches, and fame.

This God who worked in the life of Solomon is the same God working in you right now! Today, spend time worshipping God. Ask Him to align your desires with those He has in mind for you. Then make your prayer request as admirable as Solomon's.

Prayer Prompt:

What "greatest desire" do you need to ask God for? Pray that your desires are in line with His will.

Abba Father, give me the wisdom and knowledge to fulfill the dreams and desires You have for me.

Hard Heart Work

*"So the LORD has fulfilled His word which He spoke, and I have
filled the position of my father David, and sit on the throne of Israel,
as the LORD promised; and I have built the temple for the name of
the LORD God of Israel. And there I have put the ark, in which is the
covenant of the LORD which He made with the children of Israel."*

2 CHRONICLES 6:10–11 NKJV

. . . .

Letting God work in you isn't easy. It requires a spirit that remains obedient, confident, humble, and reliant on God.

For Solomon, he remained in tune, in step, with God. Every single detail of God's blueprints for His new "home" was attended to. Every piece of furniture, column, bit of gold and silver was put into place within His temple. A temple that David had "very much wanted to build" (2 Chronicles 6:7 MSG) but hadn't. For God had told him "Your son . . .will build it" (2 Chronicles 6:9 MSG). So David submitted to God so Solomon could fulfill the work. That was hard heart work on David's part.

Today, ask God to shore up your faith so that you, like David, can yield to what God has for you. Then you can sing as David did, using the words he wrote.

Prayer Prompt:

In what way are you submitting to God even though it may be hard? Ask God for a humble, obedient heart that submits to Him.

....

....

....

....

....

....

....

....

....

....

....

....

....

....

....

....

"My heart is confident in you, O God; no wonder I can sing your praises with all my heart!" (Psalm 108:1 NLT).

A God-Incidence

When Solomon finished praying, a bolt of lightning out of heaven struck the Whole-Burnt-Offering and sacrifices and the Glory of GOD filled The Temple. The Glory was so dense that the priests couldn't get in—GOD so filled The Temple that there was no room for the priests! When all Israel saw the fire fall from heaven and the Glory of GOD fill The Temple, they fell on their knees, bowed their heads, and worshiped, thanking GOD: Yes! God is good! His love never quits!

2 CHRONICLES 7:1–3 MSG

It was a celebration that started off with a bang—literally! Solomon and the people of Israel were dedicating the temple when a bolt of lightning came down from heaven. A coincidence? No. A God-incidence!

Chances are you too have experienced God-incidences. It's when your faith aligns with reality and crosses over into your everyday life. It's those moments you look back on in awe and wonder. You tell others about the experience, and all you can do is praise God!

As you think about God at work in your life and in the lives of others you know, consider those God-incidence moments. Ask God to give you more of them, because when He does, it will increase your faith and others'.

Prayer Prompt:

What are some God-incidences in your life? Give God praise for those times and ask Him to use them for His glory.

....

....

....

....

....

....

....

....

....

....

....

....

....

....

....

....

....

*Father God, I want to experience more of You
in my everyday moments. Help me to hold on
to Your goodness and faithfulness. May I see
You at work in ordinary and extraordinary ways.*

Shift Gears

I will greatly praise the LORD with my mouth;
yea, I will praise him among the multitude.
PSALM 109:30 KJV

. . . .

Praising God might come naturally to you. Then again, it might not. Yet often it's through praising God that your thoughts become transformed. That's because your focus shifts. Instead of focusing on circumstances or the everyday events, you turn your attention toward your Creator.

Take some time today to praise God and, in turn, transform your thoughts. Here are some ideas:

- Go for a walk and, as you do, notice the beauty of creation. Thank God for all you see, hear, and smell.

- Call, text, or email a girlfriend you haven't talked with for a while. As you catch up, offer to pray for her. If she's a believer, ask her if you can share some of your prayer requests. Then pray for each other.

- Sit quietly in your house, at a nearby coffee shop, or even in your car. Turn off any source of media. Be still, and silently start praising God for the good things that come to the forefront of your mind.

- Listen to worship music. Sing or dance to it.

Prayer Prompt:

Do you find it hard to lay aside your plans and spend time with God? As you pray, ask Him to help you prioritize your days.

....

....

....

....

....

....

....

....

....

....

....

....

....

....

....

....

Lord, show me some unique ways that I can shift gears and focus on You. As I do, help me praise You in all things. As I praise You, change and transform my mind.

Called Out

"Then he told me, 'The God of our ancestors has chosen you to know his will and to see the Righteous One and hear him speak. For you are to be his witness, telling everyone what you have seen and heard. What are you waiting for? Get up and be baptized. Have your sins washed away by calling on the name of the Lord.'"

ACTS 22:14–16 NLT

. . . .

The Summer Olympics is a momentous every-four-year occasion that unites the whole world.

Over two weeks, everyone across the globe get to witness some of the most inspiring, captivating, and jaw-dropping moments in sports history. Whether it's a team or individual event, those going for the gold, athletes aspiring to attain their personal best, or those who are simply grateful to represent their country all have a story to share. Yet each participant probably has a similar universal theme: transformation. For each person will have worked tirelessly, beaten the odds, and overcome obstacles to even make it to the Olympic Games.

The Olympics are also a great opportunity for Christians of all nations to be a mouthpiece for God right at the very epicenter of global attention.

No matter where you find yourself putting your own best foot forward, consider it a place where you too are called to tell others what you have overcome in your transformational journey as a woman of faith.

Prayer Prompt:

What can you do to put your best foot forward for God? Ask Him to show you how to share your story for His glory.

....

....

....

....

....

....

....

....

....

....

....

....

....

....

....

....

....

....

....

....

*Jesus, help me to be Your passionate mouthpiece
in sharing Your good news with those around me.*

DAY 206

Walk in the Way

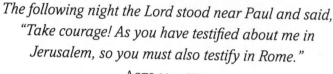

The following night the Lord stood near Paul and said,
"Take courage! As you have testified about me in
Jerusalem, so you must also testify in Rome."
ACTS 23:11 NIV

. . . .

The apostle Paul is just one of many Bible characters with a transformative testimony. He came to faith after persecuting people who believed in Jesus. What's so encouraging about Paul's story is it proves there's hope for every one of us! If God can forgive and love someone like Paul, who rejected the faith and then received it, God can do the same for all!

After accepting Christ into his life, it wasn't an easy process for Paul to walk in the ways of the Lord. It required a humble spirit and sacrifice on his part. It meant repenting and turning from his old way of life and obeying God—no matter what His request.

God is writing an awesome, transformative story with your life too. Remember that if the Holy Spirit can work in the life of Paul and use him the way He did, the Holy Spirit can work in your life and use you in a powerful way.

The impact Paul's conversion had on the church made a lasting impression then, and it still does today. Keep walking in the ways of God and you too will leave a lasting impression today and beyond!

Prayer Prompt:

What can you do to leave a lasting impression on others? As you pray, ask the Holy Spirit to anoint your life and transform your story.

....

....

....

....

....

....

....

....

....

....

....

....

....

....

....

....

....

Holy Spirit, fill me now. Use my life to be a transforming testimony of what it means to walk Your way.

Imprint It

*His work is honorable and glorious, and His righteousness
endures forever. He has made His wonderful works to be
remembered; the Lord is gracious, merciful, and full of loving
compassion. He has given food and provision to those who
reverently and worshipfully fear Him; He will remember
His covenant forever and imprint it [on His mind].*

PSALM 111:3–5 AMPC

. . . .

The Bible contains many promises. As a woman of God, consider all the promises He made to you and followed through on over the past few years. Doing so will help you realize the strength found in knowing that no matter how good or challenging life might get, God always keeps His promises to you.

In the verses above, the word *imprint* stands out. To imprint is to impress, produce, or fix firmly on the mind in memory. Here God is telling you, reminding you, that He will never forget His promises—to always be with you, go before you, love you, bless you, and so much more.

So if there are moments you forget God's promises, waver in your faith, or feel like you just don't know what to do next, take heart knowing that God has never forgotten you! And that His promises are there for the taking. Imprint them on your mind and heart, and you'll find your life, your very self, transformed.

Prayer Prompt:

What promises has God given you personally? Pray that His promises
will become more real in your life.

....

....

....

....

....

....

....

....

....

....

....

....

....

....

....

....

*Lord, help me remember Your words. Transform me by
impressing Your promises in my mind and on my heart.*

Underdog Moments

They are confident and fearless and can face their foes triumphantly.
They share freely and give generously to those in need. Their good
deeds will be remembered forever. They will have influence and honor.

PSALM 112:8–9 NLT

. . . .

In the 2000 Summer Olympics held in Sydney, Australia, US athlete Laura Wilkinson was considered the underdog heading into the finals of the women's ten-meter platform diving competition. Although she wasn't favored to win, Laura's positive, persistent spirit kept her going. More so, her faith played a pivotal role in her performance.

According to NBC commentators, in the months leading up to her competition, Laura experienced a setback. An injury to her right foot forced her to focus a lot of her training on dry land exercises and routines, as well as visualizing her dives.

On her last dive during the Olympic finals, Laura performed beautifully and won the gold medal! Following her victory, she had numerous opportunities to share her faith in Jesus Christ.

Know that, as a woman of God, there may be times when you too may feel like the underdog. Yet no matter how much the pain or how many the setbacks, like Laura, you can take heart in knowing the outcome will be beautiful. Just keep going!

Prayer Prompt:

What setbacks are you facing in your walk with God? Pray for stronger faith and perseverence in the face of obstacles.

....

....

....

....

....

....

....

....

....

....

....

....

....

....

....

....

Jesus, as You transform me, replace any doubts I may have with a steadfast assurance of who I am in You. Give me underdog moments so that I can rely more on You and not on my own strength.

God Reigns

*And Jehoshaphat stood in the assembly of Judah and Jerusalem,
in the house of the LORD, before the new court, and said,
"O LORD, God of our fathers, are you not God in heaven?
You rule over all the kingdoms of the nations. In your hand
are power and might, so that none is able to withstand you."*

2 CHRONICLES 20:5–6 ESV

As you read 2 Chronicles 20–21 and Psalm 113, can you find a common theme? It's that God reigns over all.

Psalm 113:4–6 (ESV) says: "The LORD is high above all nations, and his glory above the heavens! Who is like the LORD our God, who is seated on high, who looks far down on the heavens and the earth?"

As you think about the areas of your life in which you desire to see change, remember God reigns. If it's a relationship you have been praying about for years—God reigns. If it's a financial situation or a career decision—God reigns. He is supreme over all.

In today's passage in Acts, Paul is brought before King Agrippa. What might seem like a very intimidating situation for Paul becomes an opportunity for him to share about his conversion to Christianity. Once again, God reigns!

Whatever you face today or in the days ahead, remember: God reigns!

Prayer Prompt:

Are you facing situations that seem hopeless? When you pray, ask God to reign over those hopeless situations.

....

....

....

....

....

....

....

....

....

....

....

....

....

....

....

....

Father, You are on the throne of this world and the throne of my life. You rule over all the nations. Thank You for being in control over everything.

Real Living

"'I'm sending you off to open the eyes of the outsiders so they can see the difference between dark and light, and choose light, see the difference between Satan and God, and choose God. I'm sending you off to present my offer of sins forgiven, and a place in the family, inviting them into the company of those who begin real living by believing in me.'"
ACTS 26:17–18 MSG

. . . .

Paul went before King Agrippa and shared with him his testimony—a story about transformation from an old way of thinking and believing to a whole new way of life. As Paul noted, it was *real living*.

This new way of life was a huge change for Paul. Acts 26:19–20 (MSG) says:

"What could I do, King Agrippa? I couldn't just walk away from a vision like that! I became an obedient believer on the spot. I started preaching this life-change—this radical turn to God and everything it meant in everyday life—right there in Damascus, went on to Jerusalem and the surrounding countryside, and from there to the whole world."

Dear daughter of Christ, what has this "real living" looked like for you? Today, as you continue on your journey of faith, consider where God may be calling you to take inventory once again.

Prayer Prompt:

Have you been "real living" or just going through the motions? In prayer, ask Jesus to help you begin living the real life He has for you.

....

....

....

....

....

....

....

....

....

....

....

....

....

....

....

....

....

Jesus, I want to continue on this path to real living with You! Show me how I can be more like the apostle Paul, who turned from his old way of life and obeyed You!

Helper and Shield

O Israel, trust and take refuge in the Lord! [Lean on, rely on, and be confident in Him!] He is their Help and their Shield. O house of Aaron [the priesthood], trust in and lean on the Lord! He is their Help and their Shield.

PSALM 115:9–10 AMPC

Have you ever thought of God as being your Helper and Shield?

A helper is a person who provides assistance or support. A shield is a piece of armor, varying in size, that is used to protect in defense of weapons like swords or arrows.

To think that God can be gentle and affirming, as well as warrior-like, is amazing!

Consider all the instances you've witnessed God being your Helper. Although not physically seen right there beside you, He provided people to come alongside you, to support and encourage you. Likewise, consider the times God has been your Shield. Although you may not have seen Him there, you may recall situations that turned out better than they could have.

Today and every day, continue to invite God to be your Helper and Shield, confident that He's always with you as He continues to mold and shape you.

Prayer Prompt:

How many ways has God been your Helper and Shield? As you pray, invite Him to be your Helper and Shield today.

....

....

....

....

....

....

....

....

....

....

....

....

....

....

....

....

Lord, You mean so much to me! There are so many ways about You that I have yet to fully understand. I invite You into all that I am so that I can experience more of Your presence. Make Yourself known to me as a Helper and a Shield.

Flourish

The LORD remembers us and will bless us: he will bless his people Israel, he will bless the house of Aaron, he will bless those who fear the LORD—small and great alike. May the LORD cause you to flourish, both you and your children. May you be blessed by the LORD, the Maker of heaven and earth.

PSALM 115:12–15 NIV

. . . .

In Acts 28 the apostle Paul survives a shipwreck *and* the attack of a snake. After the viper bit his hand, "Paul shook the snake off into the fire and suffered no ill effects" (Acts 28:5 NIV). The people on the island of Malta were amazed. So amazed, they thought Paul was a god.

Although Paul wasn't a god, he was a very faithful and obedient servant of the one true God. It was He who protected Paul on the open waters. It was He who helped Paul with the viper. No matter what trials and tribulations Paul was going through, God was watching over and blessing him, causing Paul to flourish. In the end, people noticed there was something very different about this child of God.

Prayer Prompt:

How is your life affecting those around you? When you pray, ask God to help you be a blessing and example to others for Him.

....

....

....

....

....

....

....

....

....

....

....

....

....

....

Lord, when I run into challenging situations, help me to lean in to You, knowing You're watching over me, using Your transforming power to help me to flourish. I want to shine for You in such a way that people will take notice and give You the glory.

New Courage

And the [Christian] brethren there, having had news of us, came
as far as the Forum of Appius and the Three Taverns to meet us.
When Paul saw them, he thanked God and received new courage.
ACTS 28:15 AMPC

The apostle Paul had been arrested, bound in chains, threatened by religious leaders, then put under guard on a ship to Italy where, as a Roman citizen, he would take his appeal to Caesar. Along the way, he was shipwrecked on the island of Malta. There he was bit by a snake yet lived to heal many of the islanders. After three months, Paul was picked up by another ship and sailed to Italy. It was in Rome where he met up with some fellow Christians. Seeing them, Paul felt his courage renew within him.

When you need a break, when you're disheartened and dispirited, when nothing seems to be going your way, take heart. God will send just what you need at just the right time to give you new courage. To lighten your heart, spirit, and mind. To renew you.

Today, thank God for seeing you through some dire situations. And when He sends others to come alongside you, lift up your heart and voice in praise. His help and their encouragement will make a new woman out of you.

Prayer Prompt:

What kind of break do you need today; what will make a new woman out of you? Trust God to bring it to pass.

....

....

....

....

....

....

....

....

....

....

....

....

....

....

....

....

Thank You, Lord, for seeing me through so many things and for sending brothers and sisters in Christ to renew my courage.

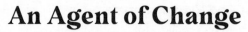

An Agent of Change

*GOD is gracious—it is he who makes things right, our most
compassionate God. GOD takes the side of the helpless;
when I was at the end of my rope, he saved me. I said to myself,
"Relax and rest. GOD has showered you with blessings."*

PSALM 116:5–7 MSG

· ·

Looking for reasons to love the Lord? Check out Psalm 116, and you'll
find a myriad of them!

You've a God who hears when you cry out (v. 1). He bends down
close, listening intently as you pour your heart out to Him in prayer
(v. 2). When troubles—spiritual or physical—seem to surround you,
threatening your mental and emotional health, you can call out to a God
who's gracious to you. The one who, in His compassion, will make things
right (vv. 5–6). He comes alongside you, helping you when you feel
helpless. He dries your tears and steadies your feet. He prompts you to
relax and rest as you marvel at His showers of blessings (vv. 7–8).

All that God does to turn your life around gives you a new purpose
and perspective, making you want to "give back to GOD. . .the blessings
he's poured out on" you (v. 12). That, in turn, prompts you to reach out
to others, to help transform their circumstances and perspectives as He
works through you to make their lives a little more "right."

Prayer Prompt:

What can you do to be an agent of change in someone else's life?
Ask God for the wisdom to become an agent of change.

Lord, thank You for all the blessings that
make me an agent of change for You!

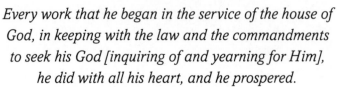

Heart Smart

*Every work that he began in the service of the house of
God, in keeping with the law and the commandments
to seek his God [inquiring of and yearning for Him],
he did with all his heart, and he prospered.*

2 CHRONICLES 31:21 AMPC

Unlike his father, King Hezekiah of Judah did things that were right in God's eyes. He repaired and restored worship at God's temple then took down the altars of idols. And because Hezekiah did those things and sought God with his *whole* heart, God blessed him.

Later, when Sennacherib of Assyria and his army surrounded Jerusalem, Hezekiah's relationship with God gave him the courage to fortify the city walls *and* shore up the faith of his people. He told them to be strong and courageous, "for there is Another with us greater than [all those] with him. With him is an arm of flesh, but with us is the Lord our God to help us and to fight our battles" (2 Chronicles 32:7–8 AMPC). In the end the Lord sent an angel to destroy the enemy army (2 Chronicles 32:20–21).

The only thing that ever led Hezekiah away from God and His blessings was his prideful heart. But when Hezekiah changed, humbling his heart once again before God, he and his people were saved (2 Chronicles 32:25–26). That's heart smart.

Prayer Prompt:

What can you do to become heart smart? Ask God to give you a humble heart before Him.

....

....

....

....

....

....

....

....

....

....

....

....

....

....

....

....

....

Lord, I want to be smart, following You with all my heart. Rid me of any pride that may come between us.

Finding Your Way Back

Manasseh sought the LORD his God and sincerely humbled himself before the God of his ancestors. And when he prayed, the LORD listened to him and was moved by his request.

2 CHRONICLES 33:12–13 NLT

. . . .

When Hezekiah died, his son Manasseh became king of Judah. But he followed idols, built up the high places where he burned his children as sacrifices, and, even worse, made altars to worship foreign gods—in God's house! *And* his people followed his reckless behavior.

God tried to turn His people around to bring them back to Him, but they wouldn't listen. So God allowed Assyria to take Manasseh prisoner. "They put a ring through his nose, bound him in bronze chains, and led him away to Babylon" (2 Chronicles 33:11 NLT).

That's when Manasseh prayed to God who, in His compassion, listened to the king and brought him back to Jerusalem. That's when "Manasseh finally realized that the LORD alone is God!" (2 Chronicles 33:13 NLT).

No matter what you've done, if you sincerely repent (turn around), if you change and come back to God, you can move the one who moves the world.

Consider where God may be speaking into *your* life, where He may be wanting you to change. Then pray, knowing God is listening and, if you're sincere, will be moved by your plea—and will bring you back home to Him, where you belong.

Prayer Prompt:

What area in your life is God speaking to you about? During prayer time, repent if you need to and open your heart to God.

....

....

....

....

....

....

....

....

....

....

....

....

....

....

....

....

....

God, open my ears to Your voice.
Help me find my way back home to You.

Opening the Gates

Open for me the gates where the righteous enter, and I will go in and thank the Lord. These gates lead to the presence of the Lord, and the godly enter there. . . . This is the day the Lord has made. We will rejoice and be glad in it. . . . The Lord is God, shining upon us.

PSALM 118:19–20, 24, 27 NLT

No transformation can take place unless you're in sync with God, walking in step with Him, following His every prompt, nudge, whisper. That requires you lowering your resistance to God and His will. Trust Him enough with yourself, your loved ones, your present and future, everything you have and are, and walk through the gates that lead to God's presence.

Today, consider areas in your life in which you may not be giving God full sway. Where are you feeling resistance to His message, hints, and commands? What things or people have you not turned over to Him, surrendered to His gentle care and touch? Which worries are leading you to places of doubt and fear?

Ask God to open your eyes to concerns that are best left in His care. Then surrender them to Him as you walk through the gates that lead to His presence. And rejoice, for God has made this day for you.

Prayer Prompt:

What barriers are keeping you from surrendering all to God? Pray for His direction as you tear down barriers and walk through the gates toward Him.

....

....

....

....

....

....

....

....

....

....

....

....

....

....

....

....

Lord, reveal, then tear down any barrier that exists between me and Thee. For I long to enter Your gates with praise upon my lips.

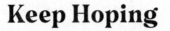

Keep Hoping

Abraham believed in the God. . .who creates new things out of nothing. Even when there was no reason for hope, Abraham kept hoping. . .fully convinced that God is able to do whatever he promises.
ROMANS 4:17–18, 21 NLT

. . . .

The Bible is full of God's promises to you, ways He intends to bless you. Yet you need not conform to a certain law or do any one thing to receive those promises, because they're founded on your faith.

The faith-filled Abraham believed God could do anything—including create "new things out of nothing"! God cannot only do that but has a habit of speaking "of the nonexistent things that [He has foretold and promised] *as if they [already] existed*" (Romans 4:17 AMPC, emphasis added)!

Case in point: Abraham's original name, *Abram*, means "high, exalted father" (Genesis 17:5 AMPC). But God changed his name to Abraham, meaning "father of a multitude" (Genesis 17:5 AMPC). God did this when Abraham was already ninety-nine years old and Sarah was eighty-nine, well past childbearing years! In other words, God spoke of Abraham being the father of many before he even had his son, Isaac, with Sarah!

God is already changing things in your life, creating something new for you out of nothing. So be like Abraham. Hope even when you see no reason for hope, fully convinced God is doing and has the power to do whatever He's promised.

Prayer Prompt:

What would you like God to speak into existence as if it already
existed? When you pray, believe, exercise the faith He has given you.

....

....

....

....

....

....

....

....

....

....

....

....

....

....

....

....

....

Lord, my hope lies in You!

DAY 219

Word and Spirit

*The LORD fulfilled the prophecy. . . . He stirred the heart
of Cyrus to put this proclamation in writing and to send it
throughout his kingdom: "This is what King Cyrus of Persia
says: The LORD, the God of heaven. . .has appointed me to
build him a Temple at Jerusalem, which is in Judah."*

EZRA 1:1–2 NLT

Over one hundred years before Cyrus became king of Persia, Isaiah
foretold that a person named Cyrus would command the temple in
Jerusalem be rebuilt (Isaiah 44:28) and that God would empower Cyrus
to complete such a feat (Isaiah 45:1).

The interesting thing is that Cyrus was not an Israelite. He was a foreign king, one who ruled over Babylon and founded the greater Persian
Empire. Yet God was able to speak to Cyrus through His Word and stir
his kingly heart.

At this very moment, God is stirring the spirit of someone you may
consider an enemy, an oppressor. God is speaking to that person through
His Word. And with His tools of Word and Spirit, God is transforming the
world for the good of His people, of which you are one.

Today, know that God is the supreme agent of change. He can transform that which seems untransformable. And all for His glory and to
your good.

Prayer Prompt:

As the supreme agent of change, what do you want God to do? Thank Him in advance for the change He's going to bring.

....

....

....

....

....

....

....

....

....

....

....

....

....

....

....

....

....

The power of You, Your Word, and Your Spirit never ceases to amaze me, Lord. Knowing You can move in the hearts of those who seem to be against Your people gives me hope.

The Power of the Hidden Word

Do not let any part of your body become an instrument of evil to serve sin. Instead, give yourselves completely to God, for you were dead, but now you have new life. So use your whole body as an instrument to do what is right for the glory of God.

ROMANS 6:13 NLT

. . . .

As a believer, you've been "joined with Christ Jesus" (Romans 6:3 NLT) in life and death. And just as Jesus was raised by God's power so that He could walk in the newness of life, you too have been raised to live a new life (Romans 6:4). In the verse above, the apostle Paul urges you to give yourself completely to God. To not let any part of you become an instrument of wrongdoing. But instead to use your entire body as a tool to do what's right.

That sounds like an enormous challenge. But God's Word holds the key to keeping you on the "right track." For as you hide God's Word in your heart (Psalm 119:11), you will find the hope, light, wisdom, and strength you need to choose God's way over any other and you will experience the resulting peace that follows.

Today, choose a verse or perhaps just a phrase that speaks to your soul deep within. Then learn those words by heart, where they'll remain to keep you on the straight and narrow.

Prayer Prompt:

What do you need to do to give yourself completely to God? Read His Word, then pray that those words will take root in your heart.

....

....

....

....

....

....

....

....

....

....

....

....

....

....

....

....

....

....

I'm resolved, Lord, to hide Your
Word and its power in my heart.

Don't Walk—Run!

I will [not merely walk, but] run the way of Your commandments, when You give me a heart that is willing.
PSALM 119:32 AMPC

. . . .

After God's people had been exiled to Babylon, God "turned the heart of the king of Assyria" so His people could return to and rebuild Jerusalem. At the same time, God put His "good hand" upon the scribe Ezra so he could help lead God's people back to His ways. Yet God's hand was upon Ezra *because* he had "prepared and set his heart to seek the Law of the Lord [to inquire for it and of it, to require and yearn for it], and to do" it (Ezra 7:10 AMPC)!

So somewhere along the line, Ezra must have applied to God, asking for "a heart that is willing" to seek and follow Him. And he got it.

When you ask God for a willing heart, when you ask Him to help you understand His way, ensuring Him you're ready to meditate upon His Word, God will put His good hand upon you too. *And* He'll transform your heart so you'll not only crave God's Word but do it!

Today don't just walk to God—run and ask for a willing heart!

Prayer Prompt:

How can you prepare and set your heart to seek the Law of the Lord?
As you pray, ask God for a heart to know Him.

....

....

....

....

....

....

....

....

....

....

....

....

....

....

....

....

....

....

*Lord, give me a willing heart that seeks You and craves
Your Word so I can run—not walk—where You lead!*

DAY 222

God-Speak

We don't know what God wants us to pray for. But the Holy Spirit prays for us with groanings that cannot be expressed in words. And the Father who knows all hearts knows what the Spirit is saying, for the Spirit pleads for us believers in harmony with God's own will.
ROMANS 8:26–27 NLT

. . . .

At times, you may not know how to put your request to God into words. Perhaps you've lost a dear loved one and are too stunned to adequately express yourself. It may be that some other event has left you without words.

In those situations, remember that even when you don't know what to say to God, the Holy Spirit is with you. As you wordlessly pray, He comes alongside and hears your groans and moans. He gets down to the heart of your matter and uncovers exactly how you feel, what you truly desire. He searches out and then transforms your "unspeakable yearnings and groanings too deep for utterance" (Romans 8:26 AMPC) into God-speak and brings them to the throne, pleading on your behalf "in harmony with God's will" (Romans 8:27 AMPC).

So don't let your not knowing what to say keep you from going to prayer. Just sit before God, seeking His light with all your heart, soul, and mind. And let the Spirit take care of the rest.

Prayer Prompt:

What are you having trouble praying about? Begin by telling God
how you feel and then allow the Holy Spirit to do His part on your
behalf.

_Be with me, Holy Spirit. Search my heart
and lift my wordless prayer to God's ear._

DAY 223

One Thing Certain

And we know that God causes everything to work together for the good of those who love God and are called according to his purpose for them. For God knew his people in advance. . . . And having chosen them, he called them to come to him.

ROMANS 8:28–30 NLT

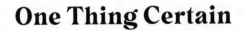

No matter what happens in your life, no matter what changes come—expected or unexpected—there is one thing of which you can always be certain. Everything that happens is according to God's plan for you. And He means you nothing but good.

God has known you from the beginning, known you'd love Him and be a follower of Jesus. That you would seek out the Light. So no matter how things look on the surface, God *is truly* making everything work for your good. Why? Because He loves you. And nothing on heaven or earth can separate you from that love (Romans 8:38 NLT).

Revel in that love that comes from the most powerful force in the universe. Know that all that happens will work for your good. Believe that nothing can separate you from Jesus' love and light. And live out your purpose with the assurance that you have a role to play: to become like Christ (Romans 8:29), the Son of love.

Prayer Prompt:

If you feel like giving up, don't do it. Seek God for His plan, and remember that all things will work out because you belong to Him.

....

....

....

....

....

....

....

....

....

....

....

....

....

....

....

....

....

Lord, thank You for calling me, loving me,
transforming me to be more and more like Jesus.
Help me spread His light and love today.

DAY 224

Power Tool

Then the king said to me, "What do you request?"
So I prayed to the God of heaven.
NEHEMIAH 2:4 NKJV

. . . .

When Nehemiah, cupbearer to the king of Persia, received news of the destruction of Jerusalem, he wept for days. With a heavy heart, he fasted then prayed to God (Nehemiah 1:4–11), speaking of His kindness for His people who love Him and keep His commandments. He asked God to hear his prayer for the Israelites, acknowledging they'd behaved badly. Then Nehemiah reminded God that He'd promised to bring them back if they changed their ways.

The following day, the king noticed Nehemiah's sadness. Knowing there was something on his cupbearer's mind, he said, "How can I help?" Before speaking, Nehemiah "prayed to the God of heaven" (Nehemiah 2:4 NKJV). Then he asked the king to send him to Jerusalem to rebuild it.

Prayers come in all different shapes and sizes. That's because different situations require different prayers. Nehemiah's first and longer prayer was his way of unburdening himself. It also allowed him to remind God (and himself) of His promises—and to ask for help. But the next day, before the king, Nehemiah wisely used an arrow prayer, a quick opening up to God for help to speak wisely.

No matter what the length or content of your prayer, be assured of its power to transform you, your words, and the situation at hand.

Prayer Prompt:

What kind of prayer do you need to pray today? Send that prayer to God and believe in Him to answer.

....

....

....

....

....

....

....

....

....

....

....

....

....

....

....

....

....

....

Thank You, God, for gifting me
with the tool and power of prayer.

DAY 225

Imprinting God

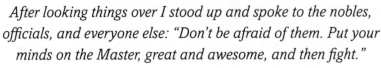

After looking things over I stood up and spoke to the nobles,
officials, and everyone else: "Don't be afraid of them. Put your
minds on the Master, great and awesome, and then fight."
NEHEMIAH 4:14 MSG

· ·

Once Nehemiah began overseeing the reconstruction of Jerusalem's walls, he was met with anger and opposition from neighboring rulers. They didn't want to see Jerusalem become a stronghold once more, so they decided to muster an army against the Jews.

In defense, Nehemiah and the people "countered with prayer to our God and set a round-the-clock guard against them" (Nehemiah 4:9 MSG). Yet the workers on the wall were still frightened. That's when Nehemiah told the people, "Do not be afraid of the enemy; [earnestly] remember the Lord and imprint Him [on your minds]. . .and [take from Him courage to] fight" (Nehemiah 4:14 AMPC).

When you come up against resistance to doing God's will and work, go to God and ask Him for divine aid. Then take what steps you can to protect your work. Most importantly, don't give in to fear. Instead, put all your focus on God. Imprint Him and His Word upon your mind. And your fear will be transformed into courage, enabling you to make God's plans for you come to completion.

Prayer Prompt:

What is hindering you in your Christian walk? Ask God for help and follow His instructions. Don't allow the enemy to discourage you.

Lord, You know what I'm up against. Give me the help and courage to see things through.

DAY 226

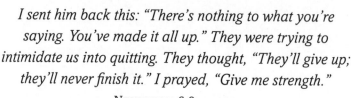

Staying Firm

*I sent him back this: "There's nothing to what you're
saying. You've made it all up." They were trying to
intimidate us into quitting. They thought, "They'll give up;
they'll never finish it." I prayed, "Give me strength."*
NEHEMIAH 6:8–9 MSG

. . . .

While overseeing the rebuilding of Jerusalem, Nehemiah met with con-
tinual opposition. At one point, a local leader named Sanballat threatened to send out a news release proclaiming that once the walls were
reconstructed, the Jews planned to make Nehemiah the king of Judah!

Yet Nehemiah stayed firm in his resolve to not be intimidated. He
saw the report for what it was: an attempt to keep the Jews from doing
what God had called them to do. So instead of giving in, changing his
mind because of outside pressure, Nehemiah prayed for God to give him
strength. In the end, the wall was finished in fifty-two days. And when all
the Israelites' enemies heard about it, they "totally lost their nerve. They
knew that God was behind this work" (Nehemiah 6:16 MSG).

Don't let the falsehoods of others intimidate you. Don't let lies and
bullies keep you from doing what God has called you to do. Instead, go
to God for strength to persevere in your endeavor. And in the end, all
who witness the completion of your work will realize it was God's doing
after all.

Prayer Prompt:

Who is trying to intimidate you? Seek God and keep your eyes on Him. Pray for courage to continue the work God has called you to do.

....

....

....

....

....

....

....

....

....

....

....

....

....

....

....

....

....

Give me strength, Lord, to stay on Your
track and not be influenced by others.

Joy-Filled Reading

*They read from the Book of the Law of God and
clearly explained the meaning of what was being read,
helping the people understand each passage.*
NEHEMIAH 8:8 NLT

Knowing that God's Word draws you closer to Him, you've made it a point to read your Bible through once, twice, maybe eight times. Then one day in church your pastor explains a familiar verse, digging deep into its meaning. Suddenly, a lightbulb goes off in your mind! *So that's what it truly means!*

That's what happened to the Jews when their spiritual leaders explained God's book to them. A lightbulb went off in their heads, not just transforming their thoughts but making them realize they'd fallen very short of God's desire for them, so much so that they began to weep. Yet once again, their leaders stepped in, telling them not to mourn but to celebrate. For the joy of their reunion with God was their strength (Nehemiah 8:10).

God delights to forgive you, to save you. He loves to shower His affection upon you when you willingly come to Him with a mind and heart open to His Word.

Today, trust that God would put people in your life to help you understand His Word. Know that when you open yourself up to Him and His Word, when you become reunited with Him, His joy in you—just as you are—will indeed become your strength.

Prayer Prompt:

How much time do you spend reading God's Word? Ask the Holy Spirit to make God's Word come alive for you.

....

....

....

....

....

....

....

....

....

....

....

....

....

....

....

....

....

Thank You, Lord, for the joy and strength I find in You and Your Word!

The New You

Don't copy the behavior and customs of this world,
but let God transform you into a new person by changing
the way you think. Then you will learn to know God's
will for you, which is good and pleasing and perfect.

ROMANS 12:2 NLT

. . . .

It's so easy to get caught up in the ways of the world. To bow under the pressure of the people surrounding you. To envy someone else and say to God, "I'll have what she's having." But rather than being a world *wanter*, God would have you be a world *changer*. How? By being like His Son, Jesus.

So how do you get there from here? It begins with offering all you have and are to God (Romans 12:1). It's about being open to God and following His way for you, knowing that's the best possible way. It's about fixing *all* your attention on God. For then "you'll be changed from the inside out" (Romans 12:2 MSG). And the new you will "readily recognize what he wants from you, and quickly respond to it" (Romans 12:2). You'll then be on the rise. Because "Unlike the culture around you, always dragging you down to its level of immaturity, God brings the best out of you" (Romans 12:2 MSG).

How wonderful to be the best version of yourself you can be. How transformational!

Prayer Prompt:

How can you keep from conforming to the world? When you pray, surrender all that you are to God.

....

....

....

....

....

....

....

....

....

....

....

....

....

....

....

....

Lord, here I am! Make me a new person by changing me—and my thoughts. My eyes are on You!

Rising Above
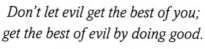

Don't let evil get the best of you;
get the best of evil by doing good.
ROMANS 12:21 MSG

. . . .

Some people say it's only human nature to want to give back tit for tat, to seek revenge upon someone who wrongs you. But, as missionary Rose Sayer (played by Katharine Hepburn) tells Charlie Allnut (played by Humphrey Bogart) in *The African Queen*, "Nature, Mr. Allnut, is what we are put in this world to rise above."

The apostle Paul (who wrote Romans) and Jesus Himself agree. Paul wants you to rise above your natural inclinations. To go against all norms. To provide food and drink to your enemy if she's hungry or thirsty (Romans 2:21). For when you love others—even those who offend you—you're doing just what God has commanded you do (Romans 13:8). Along the same vein, Jesus says if someone slaps you, offer her your other cheek; if someone takes your shirt, give her your coat (Luke 6:29).

So, want to fight evil? Return all the wrongs done you with good. And watch a transformation take place—perhaps not in your offender, but in yourself and all who witness your words and actions.

Prayer Prompt:

What tends to bring you down? Pray for strength to rise above that thing.

....

....

....

....

....

....

....

....

....

....

....

....

....

....

....

....

....

*I find it hard, sometimes, to be kind to someone who
has wronged me. But I know that's exactly what You
would have me do. Make me more like You, Lord.
Help me get the best of evil by doing good.*

A Word of Guidance

The entrance and unfolding of Your words give light. . .
understanding (discernment and comprehension) to the simple. . . .
Establish my steps and direct them by [means of] Your word.
PSALM 119:130, 133 AMPC

Every day you make a multitude of decisions, some say as many as thirty-five thousand per day. Assuming you get at least eight hours of sleep a night, that amounts to over two thousand decisions every hour you're awake! That may seem like a really high number, but if you think about it, it may just be true. You made a decision to get out of bed, open this book, and read these words. Soon you'll make a decision as to whether to continue to read this or not.

So let's assume you make lots of little decisions each day and perhaps several big ones. But what are your decisions based on? If it's the Word of God, you're heading in the right direction. For if you read, delve into, and live out God's Word, His wisdom will give you all the light and guidance you need as you take each step, keeping you close to God and away from the pitfalls of life.

Today, allow God's Word to shine upon your path as you stand at the crossroads of decisions—big and little. Doing so will keep you in the way, truth, and light of Jesus.

Prayer Prompt:

Who or what directs your mind as you make decisions? Pray for God's wisdom in every decision. He gives it freely.

....

....

....

....

....

....

....

....

....

....

....

....

....

....

....

....

....

*Lord, help me look to You with each decision
I make. I want to be walking Your way.*

Wade Right In

Each one of us needs to look after the good of the people around us, asking ourselves, "How can I help?" That's exactly what Jesus did. He didn't make it easy for himself by avoiding people's troubles, but waded right in and helped out.
ROMANS 15:2–3 MSG

· ·

When Jesus walked upon this earth, He spent time with sinners, prostitutes, and tax collectors who cheated hardworking people out of their money. He allowed people who were unclean—lepers and the woman with the issue of blood—to approach Him, sometimes even touch Him. He reached out to those who were dying, already dead, or possessed by demons. He healed the afflicted. He loved the hated and befriended the unfriendly.

In doing all these things, Jesus went against societal norms. Some thought He also went against all human reasoning. Yet nothing could deter Him from helping the helpless. And so He transformed this world and continues to do so through those who follow in His footsteps.

You too can transform the world, or at least your little part of it, by reaching out to others. By asking yourself, *How can I help that person?* And then actually helping. For you have been called to "follow in His footsteps" (1 Peter 2:21 AMPC).

Prayer Prompt:

Who can you help in the world around you? Ask Jesus to show you those who need your help.

....

....

....

....

....

....

....

....

....

....

....

....

....

....

....

....

....

Jesus, I want to transform this world, just like You transformed mine. Show me how I can help someone today. Be with me as I follow in Your footsteps.

For Such a Time and Place as This

*Who knows but that you have come to the kingdom
for such a time as this and for this very occasion?*

ESTHER 4:14 AMPC

Esther was a Jewish orphan who'd been raised by her cousin Mordecai. When King Xerxes of Persia sent away his queen, he chose the beautiful Esther as her replacement. Yet Esther kept her Jewish heritage a secret (Esther 2:20).

Later, when Mordecai learned of a plot to annihilate his fellow Jews, he sent word to Esther, urging her to save her people by going to the king and pleading for them. But Esther told Mordecai that to go before the king without being summoned was punishable by death. Yet, knowing of God's saving power, Mordecai continued to press her, saying, "Who knows but that you're here, in this place, for this very reason." So after requesting the prayer and fasting of her people, Esther did indeed see the king, changed the path of destruction, and saved her people.

You too have been put here on this earth, at such a time and in such a place, to change things for the better. Perhaps to even save others. Today, consider what God is calling you to do to change your path and, in turn, the paths of others.

Prayer Prompt:

What can you do to change things for those around you? Ask God to show you what to do in the place where you are now.

....

....

....

....

....

....

....

....

....

....

....

....

....

....

....

....

....

....

....

....

Sometimes, Lord, I'm not sure of my purpose for being here in this time and place. Please show me what You'd have me do to change this world for the better.

DAY 233

Restless Nights

The king had trouble sleeping, so he ordered an attendant to bring the book of the history of his reign so it could be read to him. In those records he discovered an account of how Mordecai had exposed the plot. . .to assassinate King Xerxes.

ESTHER 6:1–2 NLT

. . . .

Queen Esther's cousin Mordecai, a Jew, refused to bow down to anyone other than God. This enraged the honor-craving Haman, a servant of King Xerxes. So Haman urged the king to send out a decree to annihilate the Jews. Later he went a step further and had gallows built on which he planned to have Mordecai hanged.

That night, King Xerxes had trouble sleeping. He was so restless he had someone read the memoirs of his reign. That's when he learned Mordecai had once saved his life and hadn't been recognized.

From that point on, God ended up turning things around, changing circumstances in a profound way. For that night, the king decided to honor Mordecai and later commanded that Haman be executed on the very gallows he'd had built for Mordecai's demise!

God has a way of reaching us, of getting our attention by any means available. When you find yourself persistently restless, spend some time before God. Go deep. Ask Him what He wants you to know, to do. Then watch how God begins to turn things around.

Prayer Prompt:

How has God turned things around for you? Ask Him to use you to help turn someone else's circumstances around.

_____

_____

_____

_____

_____

_____

_____

_____

_____

_____

_____

_____

_____

_____

_____

_____

Lord, You have my full attention. What do You want me to know, to do, to help You turn circumstances around?

God the Guardian

GOD's your Guardian, right at your side to protect you—shielding you from sunstroke, sheltering you from moonstroke. GOD guards you from every evil, he guards your very life. He guards you when you leave and when you return, he guards you now, he guards you always.

PSALM 121:5–8 MSG

When you find yourself stuck in a cycle of worry and anxiety, when you really need to change things up, to get your faith back in God's camp, ask yourself just one question: Where are you looking for help? For strength?

Perhaps it's time to look up—not at the mountains but to God (Psalm 121:1). Because He's the one who made those mountains. He's the one who holds all the power and strength you need—emotionally, physically, mentally, and spiritually.

God is the one who guards you, stands at your side protecting you, shielding you, and sheltering you, keeping evil at bay. He sees and guards you as you're going out and coming in—and will do so always.

Go to God day and night for all the comfort, help, strength, and protection you need. Know He's never far. If you're worried, it's you that's moved, not Him. So snuggle up close, knowing God's on the job, ever awake and ever vigilant.

Prayer Prompt:

Who do you go to for help and comfort? Turn to God in prayer; He's your keeper.

....

....

....

....

....

....

....

....

....

....

....

....

....

....

....

....

....

....

Thank You, Lord, for keeping such a close watch over my coming and going. Help me stay attuned to Your presence by my side, this day and always.

Think Again

"The LORD gave me what I had, and the LORD has taken it away.
Praise the name of the LORD!" . . . "Should we accept only good
things from the hand of God and never anything bad?"

JOB 1:21; 2:10 NLT

. . . .

What do you do when everything seems to be going against you? Consider Job.

Job had everything—fields, herds, servants, children, money, and more. And he led an exemplary life. Then one day Job lost everything but his wife and health. Yet still he gave credit where credit was due. He said the Lord gave him all he'd had and now the Lord had taken it away. And he praised God.

Sometime later, Job found himself stricken with terrible boils. To find relief, he scraped his skin with a shard of pottery. That's when his wife advised him to "curse God and die" (Job 2:9 NLT). But Job kept his faith and devotion to God by saying, "Should we take just the good and not the bad from God?"

When you're feeling down, thinking things couldn't get any worse, think again. Instead of lamenting your woes, feeling sorry for yourself, or cursing God, remember that He loves you like no other. That He has a plan for your life. That you can trust Him to make something good come out of the worst of circumstances.

Prayer Prompt:

What kinds of things are happening in your life? Give God praise whether it's good or bad.

....

....

....

....

....

....

....

....

....

....

....

....

....

....

....

....

....

Lord, I'm not sure why certain things have happened,
but I trust You'll see me through. Praise be to You!

Rock-Solid

Those who trust in GOD are like Zion Mountain:
Nothing can move it, a rock-solid mountain you
can always depend on. Mountains encircle Jerusalem,
and GOD encircles his people—always has and always will.

PSALM 125:1–2 MSG

. . . .

Everything changes—almost. You change. Those around you change. The earth changes. The weather changes. But there's one thing that'll never change—God (Hebrews 13:8; Malachi 3:6; James 1:17; Numbers 23:19; Isaiah 40:8; Psalm 102:25–27). Nor will His Word—the extension of God and who He is—ever change (Psalm 33:11; 119:89; 90:2).

That means you can trust God. You can depend upon His power and His promises. You can rely on not just the idea but the very fact that the God who is everlasting keeps His promises. That He has been, is now, and always will be surrounding you.

And the great thing about all this is that when you trust in this God and His Word that never change, *you* will be rock solid. You *yourself* will not be able to be moved. *You* will stand fast and abide forever!

So trust in God. Lean on Him when you need to. Hope in all He is, does, and has. Rely on His Word, knowing it will never change. And nothing will topple you in this world or the next.

Prayer Prompt:

Who or what are you leaning on today? Ask God to renew your trust in and dependence on Him.

....

....

....

....

....

....

....

....

....

....

....

....

....

....

....

Thank You, Lord, for being the one thing I can always count on to help, strengthen, and rescue me. Surround me now, forever and ever, and I will stand immovable in You.

A God-Centered Life

Except the Lord builds the house, they labor in vain who build it;
except the Lord keeps the city, the watchman wakes but in vain.
It is vain for you to rise up early, to take rest late, to eat the bread
of [anxious] toil—for He gives [blessings] to His beloved in sleep.
PSALM 127:1–2 AMPC

God wants to be involved in every aspect of your life. Your home, work, play, family, church, neighborhood, and country. When He is, you get closer to what He intends, not just for you but for the people around you.

At the same time, God wants you not to work yourself to the bone. Nor to be anxious about the results of your endeavors. Instead, you are to leave all outcomes of your efforts to Him.

The Lord knows that a life lived without Him at the center is a life not worth living. So be sure to put God in the center of your processes as you build your life with Him by your side. As you do so, you will find yourself blessed with peace and so much more, including a good night's rest.

Prayer Prompt:

What is your life centered around? Ask the Lord to help you get your priorities in line with Him being the center of your life.

....

....

....

....

....

....

....

....

....

....

....

....

....

....

....

....

....

....

Lord, too often I get so wrapped up in my work, family, and church that I forget to include You in the process. Remind me each day to look to You for all things, to do my best in all endeavors, and to leave all the results to You.

God Only Knows

[Only] with [God] are [perfect] wisdom and might; He [alone] has [true] counsel and understanding. Behold, He tears down, and it cannot be built again. . . . He withholds the waters, and the land dries up; again, He sends forth [rains], and they overwhelm the land or transform it. With Him are might and wisdom; the deceived and the deceiver are His [and in His power].

JOB 12:13–16 AMPC

. . . .

Some days you may have a million questions as to why God has allowed certain things to happen. Why does He withhold the rains, then later pour them out in a flood that transforms the land? Why does He allow good people to die too soon and the seemingly not-so-good people to live into their nineties?

Instead of getting caught up in trying to figure out the whys of God, trust that He knows best. Eckhart Tolle says, "Sometimes surrender means giving up trying to understand and becoming comfortable with not knowing."

God alone has perfect wisdom and might. He's in total control, knows what He's doing, and has a plan for His people—including you. So no matter what happens, relax. Everything in this world is under God's power. You need not understand everything—but God does. And that's all you need to know.

Prayer Prompt:

What questions are troubling you today? In prayer, give those questions to God and trust and accept that He will take care of them.

....

....

....

....

....

....

....

....

....

....

....

....

....

Sometimes, Lord, I have trouble accepting certain things. Help me to surrender to Your wisdom and might, to acknowledge the idea that I don't have to understand everything, but simply trust You for everything.

Perfect Timing

I wait for the Lord, I expectantly wait, and in His word do I hope.
I am looking and waiting for the Lord more than watchmen for
the morning, I say, more than watchmen for the morning.
PSALM 130:5–6 AMPC

. . . .

Years ago, in the days when there were no emails or texts, Facebook or Twitter, it took days for messages and life updates from friends and family members to arrive in handwritten letter form through the post office. But today, it takes only seconds to get and receive information, post and upload pictures, make comments on other people's lives. And even then, we may find ourselves impatient for the replies or remarks from others once we've put something out into cyberspace.

So it's no surprise when we find ourselves waiting on God and getting impatient as hours turn into days, days into weeks, weeks into months, and months into years. For His timetable is certainly not ours.

Yet God wants us to learn how to wait. To expect He will answer when the time is absolutely right. For as we watch and wait, our faith and expectations grow, making us ever stronger and dependent on Him.

So instead of tapping your toes with arms folded, be still and open to the knowledge that God loves you. And He will act when the time is just right.

Prayer Prompt:

What are you feeling impatient about, and is that impatience directed toward God? Ask Him to show you how to leave it in His hands.

....

....

....

....

....

....

....

....

....

....

....

....

....

....

....

....

....

....

On You, Lord, I wait, leaving all things to Your perfect timing and continuing to hope in Your good Word.

A Quiet Heart and a Calm Soul

GOD, I'm not trying to rule the roost, I don't want to be king of the mountain. I haven't meddled where I have no business or fantasized grandiose plans. I've kept my feet on the ground, I've cultivated a quiet heart. Like a baby content in its mother's arms, my soul is a baby content.

PSALM 131:1–2 MSG

Oh, if only you had your way, if only people would listen to you, if only you could be queen, you could straighten out this world.

Have you ever felt like that? If so, that's the exact opposite of what God wants you to be feeling. He loves the humble, those who long to surrender to Him and serve others. When you leave all your plans and worries in His hands, He lifts you up (1 Peter 5:6–7; James 4:10), guides you, and teaches you what's right (Psalm 25:9). When you give Him complete control, God transforms your defeat to victory (Psalm 149:4).

Jesus said the kingdom of heaven was made up of people who were like little children (Matthew 19:14). So ask God to help you cultivate a quiet heart. To make you a trusting daughter, one whose soul is calm, just like a baby who finds her contentment in her mother's arms.

Prayer Prompt:

Who or what do you feel the need to control or fix? In prayer, surrender those people and things to the Lord and give Him complete control.

....

....

....

....

....

....

....

....

....

....

....

....

....

....

....

....

Lord, transform my heart and soul. Help me trust You with all things, stay humble, have a quiet heart and a calm soul, content in Your loving arms.

With Peace You Prosper

"Submit to God, and you will have peace;
then things will go well for you. Listen to his
instructions, and store them in your heart."

JOB 22:21–22 NLT

. . . .

Different Bible versions use different words for *submit* in the verses above, words such as *acquaint* or *agree* or *give in*. But they all mean the same thing. When you know God, trust Him, and yield to Him, allowing Him to have full sway over you, then and only then will you have the peace you crave. And when you have that peace, "[you shall prosper and great] good shall come to you" (Job 22:21 AMPC).

Part of that yielding, that surrendering, involves listening to God's Word, instructions, and wisdom, and storing all those things up in your heart so that when you need them, you'll know how to respond in thought, word, and deed in every situation.

Begin today. Consider the areas of your life where you've not given God full rein. Think about what situations are fractious or where you feel angst. Then ask God to help you submit to Him, His instructions, His wisdom, whatever He has in mind. Before you know it, you'll not only have more peace, but much good will come from your efforts. For God can do amazing things when you yield yourself to Him.

Prayer Prompt:

What are you withholding from God's control? In prayer, submit that area to God and allow Him to bring you peace.

....

....

....

....

....

....

....

....

....

....

....

....

....

....

....

....

....

Show me where I need to yield to You,
Lord, for I so crave Your gift of peace.

Life Defined

Don't be wishing you were someplace else or with someone else. Where you are right now is God's place for you. Live and obey and love and believe right there. God, not your marital status, defines your life. . . . The really important thing is obeying God's call, following his commands.

1 CORINTHIANS 7:17, 19 MSG

God has called you to live this life in Christ. To obey Him and love Him with all you are. To serve Him and live out your calling right here, right now, exactly where you are.

First Corinthians 7 makes it clear you don't have to change your status to fulfill your calling. For your status—married, widowed, slave, free, doctor, lawyer, housewife, CEO, and so on—has nothing to do with your fitness to serve God. All God wants you to do is be yourself and follow His commands. For it is He who "defines your life."

In her book *Do It Afraid!* Joyce Meyer writes, "God wants us to be ourselves so that we can fulfill the call He has placed on our lives." God chose you for a reason, wanting you to use your innate talents, intelligence, and aptitudes to serve Him. If any changes are to be made, you'll be sure He'll provide the opportunities in which to do so. For now, be who you are, serving the Great I Am.

Prayer Prompt:

What is defining your life right now? Ask God to give you
contentment where you are today and allow Him to define you.

....

....

....

....

....

....

....

....

....

....

....

....

....

....

....

....

....

....

....

....

I'm ready to serve You, Lord, here and now,
just as I am. What would You like me to do?

Never Out of Date

GOD, your name is eternal, GOD, you'll never be out-of-date.
GOD stands up for his people, GOD holds the hands of his people.
PSALM 135:13–14 MSG

Although you and all the things, places, and people around you will change in one way or another, there is one thing that never changes: God. For not only is His name eternal, but He and His Word are never out of date.

Of course, people may tell you otherwise. They may say God is dead. Or that all those Bible stories took place so long ago, they have no relevance to you or your world in this day and age. Yet the amazing thing is they do! Although we may not wear the same clothes or speak exactly like the people in the Bible, their life lessons hold all the wisdom we need to walk and grow in God today.

> *Even if it was written in Scripture long ago, you can be sure it's written for us. God wants the combination of his steady, constant calling and warm, personal counsel in Scripture to come to characterize us, keeping us alert for whatever he will do next.*
> ROMANS 15:4 MSG

You can depend on God and His Word to give you all the wisdom, guidance, and instruction you need to speak into your life every day, to help you find where God is nudging you, helping you, showing you His way.

Prayer Prompt:

How do you feel about God's Word in today's world? Ask God to open your understanding of His Word, and then apply it to your life.

....

....

....

....

....

....

....

....

....

....

....

....

....

....

....

....

....

....

....

Thank You for Your Word, Lord. Show me
what You'd have me know today.

DAY 244

Counting Every Step

"Does he not see my ways and count my every step?"
JOB 31:4 NIV

For most of us, the thought of God seeing everything we do and watching every move we make often does not bring comfort. We know how often we stumble. We know our thoughts are not pure and our hearts are often swayed to follow paths that do not lead to God. And though we know God sees all and knows all, we don't like to think about it.

But here Job is calling on God as a witness to his character. He is asking God to testify on his behalf. Line after line, Job lists examples of sins and wrongdoing—seemingly confident that he has had no part in any of it. He claims his innocence. He calls on God to write out the case against him, because he feels so sure that there is not one.

And even as he stands before his friends and before God, laying his life out for everyone to judge, perhaps the one thing Job missed in his list was pride. Because if he knows God sees his ways and counts every step, then he also knows God does not need his testimony. The Almighty does not need Job's account. But Job was too busy defending himself to realize that he already had a Defender.

Prayer Prompt:

What things in your life make you uncomfortable knowing God sees and hears them? Ask the Lord to help you surrender those things to Him.

....
....
....
....
....
....
....
....
....
....
....
....
....
....
....
....

Lord, may I remember Your mercy
with every step of every day. Amen.

Run to Win

Don't you realize that in a race everyone runs,
but only one person gets the prize? So run to win!

1 CORINTHIANS 9:24 NLT

. . . .

Every day he runs. Rain or shine. Freezing cold or oppressively hot. No matter what happens, he runs. Some days he can only stand a few minutes, but he still runs. Some days he goes for hours.

Marathon runners may seem like aliens to some of us—superhumans who have powers of endurance and levels of pain tolerance we cannot fathom. But every runner knows one thing. You have to keep putting one foot in front of the other.

Surely it helps if you have put in the time and the work beforehand to train your body to do that. The muscles must learn what it feels like to stretch and contract and stretch again in response to the pavement. The bones and joints have to get used to the bending and bouncing that come with every step. The mind has to become familiar with the passing of time that's required and learn to stay attentive for every inch of the twenty-six miles (plus some).

This kind of transformation doesn't just happen. It requires work. Practice. Training. Humility. Dedication to a goal and an understanding of why that goal matters. Whether running a race or living as a follower of Christ, seek to run with purpose.

Prayer Prompt:

What do you need to do to win the race for Christ? Ask the Lord to lead you through the training you need.

....

....

....

....

....

....

....

....

....

....

....

....

....

....

....

....

....

*Lord, help me change to become what I
need to be to win hearts for You. Amen.*

DAY 246

Whatever You Do

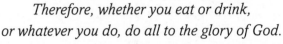

Therefore, whether you eat or drink,
or whatever you do, do all to the glory of God.
1 CORINTHIANS 10:31 NKJV

It seems there has never been a time before now when so many words were written about and so many pictures taken of what we eat and drink. Everywhere, on every page of social media, at any time, you may see photos of glorious meals and confessions of indulgences and commitments to the latest diet discipleship plan of the day.

Does any of it really matter? Paul says, "All things are lawful for me, but not all things are helpful; all things are lawful for me, but not all things edify. Let no one seek his own, but each one the other's well-being" (1 Corinthians 10:23–24 NKJV).

What might happen if, instead of caring so much about what we eat or drink, we applied some of that thinking and planning and talking to the needs of others and how to help meet those needs? What would happen if, instead of worrying so much about what we put into our mouths, we concerned ourselves with the words coming out? What if, instead of merely worshipping God during Sunday services, our worship of God really and truly began when we stepped outside the doors to serve? Doing it all to the glory of God.

Prayer Prompt:

What does it mean to "do all to the glory of God"? When you pray, ask God to show you areas where you need to glorify Him.

*Lord, change my filter and my
focus so I can glorify You. Amen.*

Life Lived Large

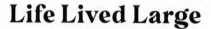

The moment I called out, you stepped in;
you made my life large with strength.
PSALM 138:3 MSG

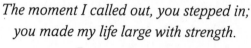

The one who spoke light into being speaks to us through His Word—the words that He made sure, even through the centuries, that we could hold in our hands. The one who planned the universe has a plan for each of us. The one who shaped mountains would move mountains just to get to us. The one who so loved the world that He gave up everything, gives up time still now to listen to our worries and our wants.

Since this God—this almighty, all-seeing, all-good God—is on our side, how can we ever feel weak? All we have to do is call out, and He answers—He will be our strength. He will help us when we can't see a way out of our troubles. He will walk with us when we are in the middle of difficult situations. He will keep the ground where we are standing firm when everything and everyone else is crumbling away.

So how should we live? We should live large—not filled with our own pride, but as humble servants emboldened by the holy, glorious, mighty power of God. We should lean on Him into every challenge we face—knowing He is faithful and He will never leave us.

Prayer Prompt:

How has God helped you to "live large"? Thank Him for those times when He has enabled you to live large for Him.

....

....

....

....

....

....

....

....

....

....

....

....

....

....

....

....

....

....

Lord God, thank You for being my strength. Amen.

Finding Meaning

*Yet when I surveyed all that my hands had done and
what I had toiled to achieve, everything was meaningless,
a chasing after the wind; nothing was gained under the sun.*
ECCLESIASTES 2:11 NIV

Every person comes to this moment at some point. For some, it comes early—perhaps in adolescence. For others, it comes later in life, after retirement. It might even come at several points. It's the moment of meaning—the moment we stop and wonder what in the world we are doing on this earth, asking, *Does any of it matter?* It's a moment of awareness and accounting. It's a moment of honest reflection. And for some, it's a moment of utter despair.

The words of the writer of Ecclesiastes often sound to the modern reader like someone singing the blues. They are the words of Eeyore—nothing ever matters. Nothing ever happens. Nothing ever changes.

But if we look more closely at this little book in the Bible, we see a different message. We see that God "has made everything beautiful in its time. He has also set eternity in the human heart; yet no one can fathom what God has done from beginning to end" (Ecclesiastes 3:11). We ask these questions about meaning because God put the questions inside us. Because He wanted us, through the questioning, to find Him. To know that our meaning is found in Him.

Prayer Prompt:

What things give your life meaning? Ask God to remind you of His blessings and His purpose for you.

....

....

....

....

....

....

....

....

....

....

....

....

....

....

....

....

....

Lord, thank You for the longing for
purpose that leads me to You. Amen.

Wonderful Works

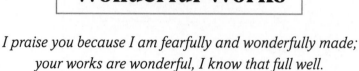

I praise you because I am fearfully and wonderfully made;
your works are wonderful, I know that full well.

PSALM 139:14 NIV

. . . .

What causes you to gasp in awe? What image or landscape or event have you ever witnessed that took your breath away with its beauty? What things in nature amaze you or delight you? Think for a moment about those things. Or walk outside and look up at the sky or down at the tiny ant making his way to his task. Consider the vastness of the expanse above you and the intricately designed details of the world living at your feet.

Now consider that, as wonderful or beautiful or amazing or delightful as those things are, you are in the same category. Because you are one of the wonderful works of God.

What do you think of that? Is it hard for you to believe? But it's true. We know full well God's works are wonderful. And we know He knit us together in our mother's wombs (Psalm 139:13).

Go ahead. Go outside. Look and gasp in wonder at the beauty around you. Then go back in and look in a mirror and say, "I am a wonderful work of God." What difference will that make for you—or *to* you—today?

Prayer Prompt:

Name one thing that causes you to gasp in awe at God's greatness.
Give Him praise for all He has created.

....
....
....
....
....
....
....
....
....
....
....
....
....
....
....
....
....
....
....
....

Lord, remind me that I am made by You,
and because of that, I am valuable. Amen.

Search Me

Search me, God, and know my heart; test me
and know my anxious thoughts. See if there is any
offensive way in me, and lead me in the way everlasting.
PSALM 139:23–24 NIV

. . . .

When our cars aren't working properly, we take them to the experts—the mechanics. When we feel something isn't quite right in our bodies, we see our doctors. When we want to know if our finances are in order, we ask an accountant.

And sometimes, when we ask for help from the experts, we come to them in fear and embarrassment. We come that way because we know that what we've been doing on our end to take care of things ourselves has been less than perfect. But we still come because we need the help. We need the expert wisdom. We need guidance.

When our spiritual fitness is in question, shouldn't we then go to the expert? We must go to God, ask Him to test out our systems and tell us what's gone wrong. Instead of just worrying about our troubles, we should bring them to Him and ask Him to sift through them, to tell us what's at the heart of our problems.

Today, ask God to look into your heart, and then be ready to listen to what He tells you. It will no doubt be a painful process, but it is the only way to life everlasting.

Prayer Prompt:

What might bother you about God testing your heart? When you pray, ask Him to give you courage to allow His inspection.

....

....

....

....

....

....

....

....

....

....

....

....

....

....

....

....

....

Lord, I'm anxious about many things.
Show me what truly matters. Amen.

By Grace

But whatever I am now, it is all because God poured out his special favor on me—and not without results. For I have worked harder than any of the other apostles; yet it was not I but God who was working through me by his grace.

1 CORINTHIANS 15:10 NLT

He can make the sick well. He can make the blind see. He can bring the dead to life again. He can turn doubters into believers and murderers into miracle workers.

Yet somehow still we sometimes fall into the habit of thinking that God cannot do anything with us. That the God who crafted Saul the persecutor into Paul the propagator cannot change us and use us to expand His kingdom.

Even Paul felt he was "not even worthy to be called an apostle" (1 Corinthians 15:9 NLT). But the difference between Paul and many others who feel unworthy is that Paul didn't let his feelings get in the way of God's faithfulness. Grace does that for us. Grace gives us a position we have no right to take and access to power we have no authority to use in exchange for nothing we can do or deserve.

Grace is the beautiful, life-changing, heart-shaping gift of your loving God. Whatever you are or will be is because of His grace.

Prayer Prompt:

How are you allowing God's grace to work in your life? Thank Him for His grace during your prayer time.

....

....

....

....

....

....

....

....

....

....

....

....

....

....

....

....

....

Lord, thank You for Your gift of grace.
Help me to use it to work for You. Amen.

Changed by Love

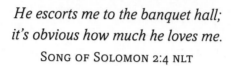

He escorts me to the banquet hall;
it's obvious how much he loves me.
SONG OF SOLOMON 2:4 NLT

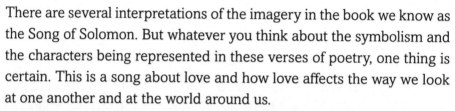

There are several interpretations of the imagery in the book we know as the Song of Solomon. But whatever you think about the symbolism and the characters being represented in these verses of poetry, one thing is certain. This is a song about love and how love affects the way we look at one another and at the world around us.

When we fall in love, a beautiful transformation takes place. A person, who perhaps a day before was just like anyone else walking on the streets, suddenly becomes beautiful to us—precious. Someone we want near us. Someone we want to know every little thing about. Someone we want to know us.

And that same beautiful transformation happens to everyone through the love of Christ—including you. Instead of nothing special, you become one of the favored ones of the King of kings. Instead of being lost in sin, you are found at His feet. Instead of being an embattled soul, you become an instrument of His peace. And instead of being a stranger on the street, you become a guest of honor at His banquet table.

It should be obvious to us how much God loves us—it is written all over His hands and feet.

Prayer Prompt:

How has the love of Jesus transformed you? Spend some time in
prayer telling Him how much you love Him in return.

Lord, thank You for loving me so completely. Amen.

DAY 253

Kind Rebukes

Let a righteous man strike me—that is a kindness;
let him rebuke me—that is oil on my head.

PSALM 141:5 NIV

. . . .

To have a person in your life who's willing to tell you the truth about yourself and to examine your actions in the cold light of God's day is a precious blessing.

But, let's face it, it doesn't always feel that way. Rebukes, especially from people we respect and admire, are hard to take. They can be embarrassing and sound harsh to the ears of the guilty, even when delivered with the gentlest spirit. But there comes a time (or two or two thousand) when everyone needs a righteous slap in the face.

The best thing we can do to help guard ourselves from making bad decisions in the first place is to surround ourselves with honest, kind souls who're willing to make us hurt a little to prevent us from hurting a lot. For we're our own worst enemies, and we need someone around to save us from ourselves.

There's no shame in being rebuked by a godly person. Shame comes when we hide from rebuke, refuse to receive forgiveness, and ignore instruction. But to be humbled by a rebuke is to be offered the chance to see ourselves as we truly are and to recognize the righteousness of God. That kindness shows our place before God. And that place is the place of grace.

Prayer Prompt:

How do you react when someone corrects you? Ask the Lord to give you the grace to receive a godly rebuke knowing it's for your good.

....

....

....

....

....

....

....

....

....

....

....

....

....

....

....

....

*Lord, thank You for the kindness
of righteous rebukes. Amen.*

In Community

Watch, stand fast in the faith, be brave,
be strong. Let all that you do be done with love.

1 CORINTHIANS 16:13–14 NKJV

. . . .

These final pieces of advice from Paul come in the middle of news about various other members of the Christian community. Paul talks about welcoming one another, submitting to one another, and supporting one another. So when he encourages and challenges the Corinthians, it is in the context of this community of believers.

They should watch—be on the alert—not just for their own security but looking out for every member of the community. They should stand firm in the foundations of their beliefs because each member is leaning on the others for support. They should be brave because, when troubles come, everyone looks around to see how others are behaving. If they run away, others are more likely to run away and doubt and fear. But if they bravely face the trials, others will stand with them. They should be strong because the weaker members of the community will need their support. And in all these things, they should remember that the reason to do any of it is love.

How fitting it is to be reminded that we are all members of a greater community, that we must strengthen and lift up one another. And above all, love each other.

Prayer Prompt:

How do you stand firm in the face of trouble? Ask the Lord to give you courage to stand even when others flee.

....
....
....
....
....
....
....
....
....
....
....
....
....
....
....
....

Lord, help me to be strong and brave
in my love for others. Amen.

Woe to Those

Woe to those who call evil good, and good evil;
who put darkness for light, and light for darkness;
who put bitter for sweet, and sweet for bitter!
ISAIAH 5:20 NKJV

. . . .

Have you ever had friends who were so wrapped up in a relationship that they couldn't see that the fantasy did not match reality? That is, the object of their affection was not worthy of all the love and attention and time and energy they were doling out? Or worse yet, that the so-called significant other was actually inflicting on them significant harm?

It can be heartbreaking to have to watch such a relationship from the outside and not be able to convince a friend of the truth. There are times when we just can't see the danger in front of us because we've become too use to tolerating the evil all around us. Our filters are off. Our sensors are no longer sensitive. So when something slightly better than the surrounding options comes along, we call it good.

But good only comes from God. This is why it's so important to steep in His Word, to dwell in His truth, and to train ourselves to look through His eyes. Then, with His help, we will be able to see clearly and distinguish light from dark, sweet from bitter, and good from evil.

Prayer Prompt:

How can you know the difference between good and evil, light and darkness? Ask God to fill you with His Spirit so you can discern the difference.

....

....

....

....

....

....

....

....

....

....

....

....

....

....

....

....

....

Dear Father, I'm sorry for the times when I
have judged poorly. Please correct me. Amen.

Morning Guidance

Let me hear of your unfailing love each morning, for I am
trusting you. Show me where to walk, for I give myself to you.
PSALM 143:8 NLT

. . . .

The sunlight stretches through the curtains, into your room, lying warm and golden on the top of your bed. It is a beacon, calling you to sit up and greet the day.

The first light of the day, whether it comes from the lamp beside your bed or from the sunrise, can serve as a reminder that today is a new beginning. The first page of a new chapter. The first line of a new story. Whatever has gone before need not be forgotten—in fact, it's good to remember the days that have passed and to recall the times God has been with you, each step of the way showing His love for you. And on this new day, in full confidence of His unfailing love, you can commit once again to put your life in His hands. You can trust Him. He will not lead you down a wrong path. He will not leave you to walk any path alone.

When you start the day off in God's Word, you start the day knowing truth, gaining wisdom, and confirming His love for you. Can you think of a better way to begin any adventure?

Prayer Prompt:

How do you begin each day? Greet the Lord with a conversation about what's on your heart.

....

....

....

....

....

....

....

....

....

....

....

....

....

....

....

....

....

....

....

....

Lord of love, call me every morning
to wake up in Your Word. Amen.

Citizens

For to us a child is born, to us a son is given,
and the government will be on his shoulders.
ISAIAH 9:6 NIV

. . . .

Certainly, even the nonbelievers among us wouldn't mind having a political leader like the Messiah—the one who is called wonderful Counselor, mighty God, everlasting Father, Prince of peace. This is the sort of person who could bear the weight of governing a nation—even a whole world. This is the sort of person who would never be corrupted by power or weakened by arrogance. This is the sort of person who could judge fairly and choose wisely. This is the sort of person who could establish justice and righteousness forever.

But the country our Lord rules over is not one formed by politically drawn borders. Instead, it is a nation of hearts, a land of lives, a union of souls. Whatever happens in the governments of human creation, we can be sure that the kingdom of God will stand. This kingdom God planned for generations ago is still here today, and we can be citizens of it. We can carry on the reign of Christ through the way that we treat one another, forgive one another, and love one another. We can teach others about the law that brings freedom. We can demonstrate what it looks like to live as servants of the King of kings.

Prayer Prompt:

How can you show others the way to live as a servant of the King of kings? Spend time in prayer, getting to know the King better.

....

....

....

....

....

....

....

....

....

....

....

....

....

....

....

....

Lord, let love govern us all. Amen.

DAY 258

Transformed in Glory

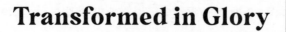

And we all, who with unveiled faces contemplate the Lord's glory, are being transformed into his image with ever-increasing glory, which comes from the Lord, who is the Spirit.

2 CORINTHIANS 3:18 NIV

In the days of the Israelites of old, Moses would go to meet the Lord and talk with Him. And whenever he returned to the people, for a time after meeting with God, Moses would cover His face. Just being in the presence of God was so glorious, it would cause Moses' own face to shine and radiate and reflect that same glory to such a degree, the Israelites became afraid. The veil acted as a filter through which the Israelites could stand to look on Moses again and come near to hear what he had to tell them.

Now we can come into God's presence on our own and hear His Word at any moment. Not only that, but when we turn to the Lord, we can receive His Spirit to dwell in our hearts. Through His Spirit, we are being changed, day by day, into beings that not only can look on His glory without fear, but into creatures shaped in His image, bearing His glory ourselves, living in that glory, and increasing that glory through spreading the good news of Jesus Christ.

Prayer Prompt:

How can people tell if you have spent time with Jesus? When you pray, take your time. Let Him transform you.

Lord, thank You for shaping me into something that can bring You glory. Amen.

Watching Over

*The LORD watches over the foreigner and sustains the fatherless
and the widow, but he frustrates the ways of the wicked.*
PSALM 146:9 NIV

. . . .

Lost. Abandoned. Neglected. Forgotten. There are times in each of our lives when we may have these feelings. And we don't have to be a refugee or an orphan or have lost a spouse to feel lonely. But because we do feel these ways, we should be able to imagine all the more what it must be like to be in a position in which you have suddenly lost everything that makes home feel like home and all the things that are familiar and bring comfort. And we should then be able to have compassion for those who are in such a position.

Yet our gentle, loving, ever-present Father God transforms us. He watches over us and cares for us and provides for us. In His love, we are changed—those who are lost are found. Those who are fatherless are welcomed into Daddy's arms. Those with broken hearts are made whole again. God's love is powerful and surprising, showing up in some of the most mysterious places. And every time we are met with unconditional love, with unmerited favor, with generous gifts of grace, we can know that we are experiencing the love of our perfect Father.

Prayer Prompt:

What are some ways you can show compassion to others? Ask the Lord to fill you with His love for those less fortunate.

....

....

....

....

....

....

....

....

....

....

....

....

....

....

....

....

....

Lord, thank You for Your gentle love
that makes me Your child. Amen.

New Life

*Now we look inside, and what we see is that anyone
united with the Messiah gets a fresh start, is created
new. The old life is gone; a new life emerges!*

2 CORINTHIANS 5:17 MSG

Rosh Hashana is when those who follow the Jewish tradition welcome a new year. They welcome it with penitence and reflection—with expressing all their sorrow for wrongs that have been done and handing over their shame to God. It is a time when Jewish people are called to wake up and notice the world and who they are in the world, when they are called to be their best selves. It is a time when they recommit to trying to be the creatures God designed them to be.

But when we accept the salvation of Jesus Christ our Lord, we are given the gift of a new life with a new hope. We no longer have to be ashamed. We no longer have to perform acts to try to get rid of our sins—which no person can do. We can rest in the Spirit of God, united with Christ in the death of our old selves and joined with Him on a new path. Our heart is made clean once and for all. Our minds look to Jesus to understand better how to follow Him—not because we must do better, but because His love compels us to become more like Him, to come close to Him.

Prayer Prompt:

How can you rest in the Spirit of God, unashamed for the past? As you pray, accept the complete gift of new life that Christ brings.

....

....

....

....

....

....

....

....

....

....

....

....

....

....

....

....

....

....

Lord, thank You for a new life! Help me live it well. Amen.

Something's Stirring

He sends his word and melts them;
he stirs up his breezes, and the waters flow.
PSALM 147:18 NIV

. . . .

There is something about the holy Word of God. It is alive with meaning, sparking within us motivation and inspiration. It breathes into us a breath of energy and conviction, striking right to the heart of the truth of what's weighing us down, keeping us from knowing God more. It is invigorating—like a swift, cool breeze running through autumn trees, making the leaves dance and fly away. God's Word blows out the cobwebs of stubborn patterns of thinking and invites us to run with those who mount up on wings like eagles—never getting weary, never stumbling, always moving forward.

God's Word can do all these things because God is present in His Word. His wisdom is there. His love is there. His righteousness is there. His clarity is there. His comedy is there.

God becomes alive to you through His Word, and you become alive through studying what He says to you. Through taking in the bits of His mind that He lets you glimpse. Through realizing over and over again, verse after verse, how much He loves you.

Allow God's Word to bestir you today.

Prayer Prompt:

How can you receive more from God's Word as you read? When you pray, ask for understanding and an open mind to receive His Word.

....

....

....

....

....

....

....

....

....

....

....

....

....

....

....

....

God, thank You for the gift of Your Word
that leads me every day to You. Amen.

Swallowed Up

*On this mountain he will destroy the shroud that
enfolds all peoples, the sheet that covers all
nations; he will swallow up death forever.*

ISAIAH 25:7–8 NIV

Starting a new life means the beginning of many things. A new job could mean a new office, a new desk, a new boss, or new employees. A new diet will mean new food, new recipes, and new habits. A move to a new city will mean new opportunities for new relationships, new places to visit, new patterns to develop.

But with each new beginning comes a parting from the old ways. For some, this parting can be sad. Perhaps we aren't quite ready to let go of the old way of life. Maybe there are people and memories we want to hold on to tightly and take with us into the new beginnings.

Yet God promises a new beginning that has no sadness. Through Jesus, we can say good-bye to the punishment of death and to everything that comes with it. We can put away the symbols and suffering of dying. God, ruler of all, will put an end to the need for tears. He will ban death from the earth. And He will take away all our shame. No more condemnation. No more debts to pay. We can live freely now, confident of the life God has created for us.

Prayer Prompt:

If you're facing a new beginning, what are some ways to handle it? As you pray today, ask the Lord to guide you in your new life.

_____

_____

_____

_____

_____

_____

_____

_____

_____

_____

_____

_____

_____

_____

_____

_____

_____

_____

_____

Lord, help me to live each day in the freedom You have granted me, through the freedom of Your promises. Amen.

An Autumn Hymn

Let everything that breathes sing praises to the LORD!
PSALM 150:6 NLT

. . . .

Let the colors of the trees reflect the variety of His blessings. Let the crisp, fresh air remind you of the life He breathes into your lungs. Let the birds that greet the sun give thanks for the new day. Let the fox that slips through the shadows of the night bow in submission to the Lord of all creation. Let the wings of the geese that migrate beat out the rhythm of His provision. Let the deer freeze in poses of graceful beauty, revealing the thoughtful details of His design. Let the flowers that close their petals to the cold and the fronds that curl in the dew show you the intricate miracles He works around you every day.

Let the school buses full of laughing, howling children speak of the glories of innocence and renewal and joy. Let the parents waiting at the bus stops remind you of His ever-watchful, tender care. Let the drivers of all the cars in all the lines of traffic tell of the numbers of souls He came to save. Let the congregations that sit, stand, or dance rejoice in the ever-increasing majesty of your Maker.

Let people sing and talk and shout and laugh and pray and cry and hug and hold and bow down. Let every breath be a song of praise. Let every life breathe it out every day.

Prayer Prompt:

What do you see when you look around you? During prayer, thank the Lord for all that you observe and give Him praise for His creation.

....

....

....

....

....

....

....

....

....

....

....

....

....

....

....

....

....

Lord, You're so beautiful; I praise You and You only. Amen.

Sow Now

Remember this—a farmer who plants only a few seeds will get a small crop. But the one who plants generously will get a generous crop.
2 CORINTHIANS 9:6 NLT

. . . .

Imagine the farmer. He works hard—clearing his fields, digging up and throwing out the rocks, turning the soil over and making it ready for the seeds. The little packages of promise that he will put into the ground, water, and pray over, hoping for a fruitful crop. If he thinks the seeds will do good—will grow and produce valuable resources—why would he ever just plant a few? Wouldn't he plant as many as he could? Wouldn't he use every inch of land and every seed he could buy?

There is one fact we can be sure of. God will do good with whatever we give Him. So if we know that to be true, wouldn't we want to give everything we have to God? Wouldn't we want to give Him every coin we could spare? Wouldn't we want to hand over to Him every gift, every thought, every moment?

What you give to God, He will multiply. He will maximize your investments beyond any earthly calculations. And He will supply you with more than you need and so much more than you deserve. Just try Him.

Prayer Prompt:

What are you sowing in your life? As you pray, ask God to give you a generous spirit to sow into His work.

....

....

....

....

....

....

....

....

....

....

....

....

....

....

....

....

....

....

....

....

....

Lord, I want to give everything to You. Help me to let go of my worries and give generously today. Amen.

Paths to Avoid

Such are the paths of all who go after ill-gotten gain;
it takes away the life of those who get it.
PROVERBS 1:19 NIV

. . . .

When we read such verses in the book of Proverbs, we often tend to separate ourselves from the image being presented. We are not such people, we might say. We are not wicked. We are not interested in plundering the innocent or ambushing some harmless person. We are not going to try to trap people and take their possessions.

Yet do we ever find ourselves caught up in earning money so much that we forget our families, our friends, and our faith? Do we become proud of providing for ourselves to such an extent that we forget to depend on God? Do we take advantage of others or judge those who don't have as much material wealth as we do—or as much education, or as much social capital?

It is not just crooks and robbers who can be turned into prisoners. We can walk down a path to imprisonment if we fail to rely on God and instead keep going after things that don't matter. We can imprison ourselves in a cell of pride and selfishness, pushing everyone else away. We can lose our lives to the pursuit of the not-so-precious. But we don't have to do that. We can choose to step in the paths of righteousness instead.

Prayer Prompt:

What is turning you or those around you into prisoners? Pray for wisdom to follow paths of righteousness, not ill-gotten gain.

....

....

....

....

....

....

....

....

....

....

....

....

....

....

....

....

Lord, stop me from stepping in paths
that lead to corruption. Amen.

Blooming Glory

The desert and the parched land will be glad;
the wilderness will rejoice and blossom.

ISAIAH 35:1 NIV

. . . .

Come to the desert on one day and you'll find dry, cracked earth with not a drop of moisture in sight. The sun will beat down, driving you to find any tiny bit of shade. Signs of life will be scarce as every animal tries to conserve energy and hide from the overwhelming weight of heat.

But then the rains come.

And the next day, in the space of hours, spores burst forth, blooms open, and a great hallelujah of light and life explodes into sight with all the beauty of the rainbow. Like a painter's palette fresh from a masterpiece, vibrant hues cover the drab background. The earth rejoices!

The same change can occur in your life. Once thirsty for meaning, you can find soul refreshment in Him. Once parched and weary, weighed down with the monotony of life, you can find purpose in His plan. Once aching for relief, you can rest in the glorious pleasure of His forgiveness and grace.

Your God is the one who can strengthen the feeble and steady the unstable. He's the one who can turn fear into courage and doubt into bravery. He's the one who can open blind eyes, unstop deaf ears, and cause mute tongues to shout for joy (Isaiah 35:3–6). And for all this and more, you follow Him.

Prayer Prompt:

What kind of rejuvenation do you need today? Spend time in prayer, drinking in the spiritual refreshing that Jesus gives to all who thirst after Him.

....

....

....

....

....

....

....

....

....

....

....

....

....

....

....

....

....

....

Lord, thank You for glorious change. Amen.

Weak Made Strong

Therefore I will boast all the more gladly about my weaknesses, so that Christ's power may rest on me.

2 CORINTHIANS 12:9 NIV

· ·

How is power made perfect? More importantly, how is God's power made perfect? Isn't it perfect already?

Of course it is. But the perfecting being talked about here is not something that happens to God—it's what happens to us. When our weaknesses are displayed to the world, and yet God's power, God's strength, and God's majesty shine through, everyone witnesses the completeness of the work of God. A god who could use the strongest beings to show strength is one thing. But *our* God uses the weakest things and transforms them into the most valuable, the most mighty, the most wise. This is the perfecting power of God Almighty.

So it is that Paul is delighted by his own failures and losses—in the insults that are hurled at him and in the difficulties he faces and in the persecution he suffers. For he knows that through all these things, he is being made into a more perfect witness of the glory of God. And that witness doesn't just testify to others, but it serves as a daily reminder to us of the God who loves us so much and loves us exactly as we are.

Prayer Prompt:

What weaknesses do you deal with in your life? When you pray, offer your weaknesses to Him so His power can rest on you.

....
....
....
....
....
....
....
....
....
....
....
....
....
....
....

Lord, when I am in the middle of hard times,
help me to lean fully on You. Amen.

Treasure of Wisdom

*For the L*ORD *grants wisdom! From his mouth*
come knowledge and understanding.
PROVERBS 2:6 NLT

. . . .

"School is pointless," says the teenager with a sigh. "Why do I even have to go? I'm not learning anything!"

Children often find it hard to believe their parents' suggestions that school is important, worthwhile, or necessary. Instead they often believe it to be, at best, an utter waste of time and, at worst, some kind of perverse punishment designed to torture them. They believe they could figure out the world on their own—perhaps just by looking up everything on the internet.

But education, one realizes once one becomes a bit older and has had some experience, *is* valuable. Gaining understanding is what allows a person to grow and accept new challenges. And gaining knowledge of God is the best kind of education.

As you study God's Word and concentrate on what He's trying to teach you, you'll not only become smarter, you'll become something different. You'll be changed into a woman who is more like the person God created you to be. And with His wisdom, you gain His protection—a shield that guards your hold on your faith and your character. You'll be kept safe from bad choices and evil people. Instead of being a waste of time, this kind of learning keeps you from losing your whole life.

Prayer Prompt:

In what way are you willing for God to change you? Pray for understanding of His Word as you study it.

....

....

....

....

....

....

....

....

....

....

....

....

....

....

....

....

....

Lord God, help me to follow the way to wisdom.
Grant me insight and understanding. Amen.

Marvelous

*But even before I was born, God chose me
and called me by his marvelous grace.*
GALATIANS 1:15 NLT

• •

What is so astonishing about the grace of God? What is it that makes us read about it and think about it in absolute wonder? It's just that it is there at all. To be given this position of favor and blessing—this gift of forgiveness and restoration—without even asking for it or having done some act of penitence or completed some method of atonement ourselves, is more than we can even comprehend.

Certainly, giving to others is an action we can see as good and helpful. But even that act of kindness is something we do because it feels good or because we feel we have a duty to do it. But God does not need us to make Him feel good. And He has no obligation to us—He doesn't owe us anything.

No, in fact God had made His plans and included us in them long before we ever even took a breath. Before our tiny fingers were able to hold a Bible, God had constructed the story of His people. And before we were able to squeak out the notes about His amazing grace, God had already composed the sweet music of forgiveness.

Prayer Prompt:

Since God chose you before you were born, how do you feel about His plans for your life? Pray for understanding of His grace.

....

....

....

....

....

....

....

....

....

....

....

....

....

....

....

....

....

....

....

Lord, I marvel at Your never-ending
kindness and love. Amen.

Rough Waters

"When you're in over your head, I'll be there with you.
When you're in rough waters, you will not go down."
ISAIAH 43:2 MSG

. . . .

In chapter 43 of the prophet Isaiah's account, we read beautiful words of God's promises. He declares we can never suffer so much that we will lose sight of Him, because He loves us—He would do anything for us: "I'd sell off the whole world to get you back, trade the creation just for you" (v. 4 MSG).

And His love is made even more apparent by the fact of our own ignorance toward Him and reluctance to depend on Him. As God's message to us through the prophet continues, we see God note, with sharp humor, that though we have been stingy as a people in our worship of God—holding back as we hold tightly to what God has given us—we have not been stingy at all with our sins (v. 24). We have indulged in our sinful nature quite liberally.

So we begin to realize that those rough waters God was talking about—those hard things we might go through—are not seas of trouble that swallow us up by accident. No, these are the floods that come when we worship idols of our own making and strive to fill our lives with emptiness. And our God still saves us—pulling us out of the waters we choose to wade into, out of arrogance and ignorance.

Prayer Prompt:

What rough waters are you sailing into today? As you pray, lean on God, depending on Him to save you when you get in over your head.

God, thank You for saving me from myself. Amen.

How Foolish

How foolish can you be? After starting your new lives in the Spirit,
why are you now trying to become perfect by your own human effort?
GALATIANS 3:3 NLT

. . . .

Would you ever try to create a flower? Not just plant the seed and water it and watch it grow, but shape it out of nothing? Pull a blossom out of the air? Speak petals into existence with a breath?

Of course not.

Why is it then that we so often think we can shape the stories of our lives out of nothing and completely on our own? Why is it that we live as though we are working it all out—that everything we gain and every step forward we take is only achieved through our own effort and will? Why do we get so caught up in following rules we write for ourselves instead of listening to what God tells us?

Perhaps we want to make it easy. We want a three-step process to eternal life, a program to follow. And maybe we like the idea of having some standard we can judge others by along the way too.

But God isn't fooled by our foolishness. He's not impressed with our efforts. Our great and glorious and gracious God just looks down on us and reminds us again and again that He's the only one who can shape us into beings ready to walk through eternity with Him.

Prayer Prompt:

What are you trying to accomplish on your own today? Ask God to work it out for you. His way is so much better than ours.

....

....

....

....

....

....

....

....

....

....

....

....

....

....

....

....

....

Lord, thank You for looking past my folly. Amen.

Inheriting Honor

He mocks proud mockers but shows favor to the humble and
oppressed. The wise inherit honor, but fools get only shame.
PROVERBS 3:34–35 NIV

How many times do you see commercials showing poor people sliding behind the wheel of a luxury vehicle? Or how often do you see oppressed people walking down red carpets and receiving awards in glamorous ceremonies?

While the world has its own set of standards about what makes a person rich, admirable, successful, or worthy of honor, God's standards are pretty simple. The people He honors are those who do two things— love Him and love others.

In God's kingdom, those who are humble are highly favored. Those who are pushed down by the world are lifted up in His hands. If we want to be among those inheriting honor from God, we have to be wise in His sight. We have to listen to Him and follow Him. We have to be people who are generous and open with our neighbors—people who trust God and are trustworthy. People who choose peace over violence, care over conflict, and love above all.

There will be some no doubt who mock us for the way we choose to live our lives. There will be many who don't understand. But perhaps when they see the blessings of God we receive—the peace and quiet, happy confidence that comes through living for Him—they will stop their mocking and be drawn to Him too.

Prayer Prompt:

Which is more important to you—the world's standards or God's standards? As you pray, ask God for help to follow His standard of living.

....

....

....

....

....

....

....

....

....

....

....

....

....

....

....

....

Lord, keep me humble. Amen.

No Longer a Slave

So you are no longer a slave, but God's child; and since
you are his child, God has made you also an heir.
GALATIANS 4:7 NIV

. . . .

Waiting. Hoping. Longing. Imagine for a moment being an orphan—a child left without parents for whatever reason—and anticipating the day when you might be adopted. For some, this may be an exercise in memory instead of imagination. But put yourself in the shoes of a child who wants very much to be part of a loving family. What feelings would you have? What dreams would you envision about what your home could someday be?

Think about children who sometimes wait day after day and year after year to hear what they want so much to hear—that they have been chosen. That they are wanted. That they are valuable and loved.

This is the message God wants you to hear. Before you know God, you are a slave to the impulse of your nature and a slave to the rules you create for yourself. But when you know God and accept His salvation, you don't just become a member of a group of believers. You become His child—His. He adopts you, making you His daughter—an heir to the inheritance of eternal life with Him. You are no longer an orphan. No longer a slave. You no longer have to live in fear or wonder about your worth. You are a child of the King.

Prayer Prompt:

What words would you use to describe being an heir of God? Spend some time thanking Him for adopting you into His family.

....

....

....

....

....

....

....

....

....

....

....

....

....

....

....

....

....

....

....

....

Lord, I'm so glad I'm Yours! Amen.

The Bearer of Good News

How beautiful upon the mountains are the feet of him who brings good news, Who proclaims peace, Who brings glad tidings of good things, Who proclaims salvation, Who says to Zion, "Your God reigns!"

ISAIAH 52:7 NKJV

· ·

Have you ever considered the notion that you are a good news bearer? It's true! God has transformed you, made you into His image, not just so that you can spend eternity with Him, but so that you can shine as a light to others.

Who's most in need of that light today? A neighbor? A coworker? A child in your neighborhood? An elderly man you pass on the street corner on your way to take the kids to Little League? Your toughest critic, the thorn in your flesh?

Today, acknowledge your usability to the Lord. Say, "Okay, Father, I'm here! Send me out to share the good news." Then watch as He places you in front of people who need your compassion, friendship, guidance, or wisdom.

Get ready! God's got great plans for you today.

Prayer Prompt:

Who needs to hear the good news from you today? Pray for direction to share the light you have with the one who needs to hear it.

....

....

....

....

....

....

....

....

....

....

....

....

....

....

....

....

....

....

....

Father, it takes a lot of courage for me to say, "Use me to share the good news," because I'm not sure where You'll send me or who I'll meet. But I say those words today and mean them from the bottom of my heart. I want to be a good news bearer for You, Lord. Use me today, I pray. Amen.

No Longer Enslaved

So Christ has truly set us free. Now make sure that you stay free, and don't get tied up again in slavery to the law.

GALATIANS 5:1 NLT

Picture a slave finally breaking free from his shackles. He's never known the freedom of running or leaping or living life to its fullest because he's always been bound. But now the world is his oyster! No longer enslaved, he's free to soar, to attain new heights, witness miracles.

Why would someone who's experienced true freedom contemplate going back to his chains? Why would he reach for those shackles and restrap them to his ankles and wrists? He wouldn't!

This might seem like an extreme visual, but that's exactly what a believer—one who has been set free from sin and death—does when she wanders back into her old lifestyle or habits. She's been there before, done that before, and learned the hard lessons. So why go back?

Why, indeed?

Prayer Prompt:

What shackles did Jesus remove for you in the past? Spend time praising Him for the freedom He has given you.

....

....

....

....

....

....

....

....

....

....

....

....

....

....

....

....

....

Lord, I thank You for freeing me from the shackles of sin and shame, for delivering me from bad habits. I don't ever want to go back! I'm Yours now, Father—a child, a daughter who walks in complete freedom. No going back for me! Amen.

Leave It All at the Cross

As for me, may I never boast about anything except the cross of our Lord Jesus Christ. Because of that cross, my interest in this world has been crucified, and the world's interest in me has also died.
GALATIANS 6:14 NLT

. . . .

So often we allow the troubles and cares of life to weigh us down. We get depressed or give way to fear. During political seasons, we get worked up and allow ourselves to feel despair over the condition of our county, state, or nation.

God wants us to care about the goings-on around us, but they shouldn't be a driving force in our lives. Instead we're to drop our cares in a place where He exchanges our anguish with hope. That place is the cross.

When Jesus died on the cross, He accomplished all that needed to be accomplished. His death, burial, and resurrection didn't just ensure our place in heaven, it gave us a way to live in victory and peace, unencumbered by the troubles each day might bring.

What's holding you back today? Have you left it at the cross? Release it to the Lord and watch Him free you up to live a full, abundant life.

Prayer Prompt:

What do you need to leave at the cross today? In prayer, share your burden with the Father and then leave it at the cross.

....

....

....

....

....

....

....

....

....

....

....

....

....

....

....

....

....

Father, today I come to the cross, not just to lay my burdens at Your feet, but to thank You for being my burden bearer. How can I ever repay You? From the bottom of my heart, I bring You praise. Amen.

Bringing His People Home

*"And what do I see flying like clouds to Israel, like doves to their nests? They are ships from the ends of the earth, from lands that trust in me, led by the great ships of Tarshish. They are bringing the people of Israel home from far away, carrying their silver and gold. They will honor the L*ORD *your God, the Holy One of Israel, for he has filled you with splendor."*

ISAIAH 60:8–9 NLT

. . . .

What an amazing picture, painted thousands of years ago! The Israelites have always longed for their home, Israel. Many times, they have been stranded or enslaved far, far away, but the heart of God for His children is a glorious homegoing.

Maybe you can relate. Maybe you've felt like a child lost in the wilderness, wanting to go home. Today, God is calling you back to Himself. No matter where you are, no matter how far you've wandered, no matter how many times you've convinced yourself that going home isn't an option, He's right there, crying out for you to run into His arms.

Don't wait another minute. Like a dove, fly to your nest and find true rest in Him once and for all.

Prayer Prompt:

What obstacles keep you from going home to the arms of the Lord? If you're wandering in the wilderness, go home during your prayer time.

....

....

....

....

....

....

....

....

....

....

....

....

....

....

Lord, I want to go home! No more wandering for me. I've been in the wilderness too long. I've experienced too much. Today, I choose to run back into Your arms, as the Israelites sprinted toward Jerusalem. There's no place sweeter than being at home with You, Father. Amen.

A Lesson from the Ants

Take a lesson from the ants, you lazybones.
Learn from their ways and become wise!
PROVERBS 6:6 NLT

. . . .

Ants are frantic little creatures, aren't they? Always scurrying here and there on a mission at all times. Whether they're moving in perfect lines or parting ways, they are always on the move. Isn't it interesting that the Bible instructs us to take a lesson from these busy critters? They're not lethargic. They don't sit around eating ice cream and watching movies. They're scurrying. They're motivated. They're busy. They don't just talk about doing something. . .they actually get up and do it.

What about you? Do you tend to run on the lethargic side? Do you have hyped-up plans that are never fulfilled? Always talking a big game about the things you're going to do. . .someday? Maybe today's the day! If so, it's time to ask the Lord to bring back your zeal and to raise your energy level. He can do it, you know!

Prayer Prompt:

What do you keep talking about doing but never accomplish? Ask the Lord to give you the courage and energy to get busy for Him.

Lord, I don't want to be a woman who talks a big game but never really accomplishes anything. Turn my pipe dreams into realities, Lord. Get me up off the sofa and set my feet on a path to do great things for You, I pray. Amen.

Above All We Could Ask or Think

Now to Him who is able to do exceedingly abundantly above all that we ask or think, according to the power that works in us, to Him be glory in the church by Christ Jesus to all generations, forever and ever. Amen.

EPHESIANS 3:20–21 NKJV

God can do more. More than a rushing river. More than the strongest wind. More than a tsunami barreling toward the shore. With just a word, the universe was created, mountains rose, oceans roared, animals populated the earth.

The power of our God is so far beyond anything our finite minds can comprehend. Why, then, do we doubt Him when we pray? The same God who created everything we enjoy in this life cares about our requests, our needs. He won't leave us hanging. He's got the power to save marriages, to transform lives, to turn wayward children back toward home. And His plan for His children, including you, darling daughter, is for good, not evil.

What are you facing today? Stop fretting over what you can't do and start trusting what God can do. It will be far above anything you could ask or think.

Prayer Prompt:

What problem is overwhelming you and seems impossible to solve?
Give it to God in prayer. Nothing overwhelms Him.

....

....

....

....

....

....

....

....

....

....

....

....

....

....

....

....

*Father, I don't give You enough credit! You're the Creator
of all, all-knowing, all-powerful, and full of wisdom and
might. I know I can trust You with every facet of my
life, Lord, and today I choose to do just that. Amen.*

DAY 280

Before You Were Formed

"Before I formed you in the womb I knew you; before you were born I sanctified you; I ordained you a prophet to the nations."

JEREMIAH 1:5 NKJV

- -

How long has God known you? Most would answer, "Since I was born!" In truth, He's known you longer than that. The Bible says that He knew you before you were formed in the womb. Let that sink in. Before your parents came together. Before your grandparents were born. Before your great-great-grandparents came to this country. He knew you—every single freckle, mole, hair, blemish—the total you. And He loved you even then.

It's remarkable to think about God's vast ability to "know" His kids even before He ushers them into the world as babies. But we can see from His words to Jeremiah how much planning goes into the birth of each child: "Before you were born I sanctified you; I ordained you a prophet to the nations." God doesn't just "know" us. . .He sanctifies and ordains us. Wow, what a God we serve!

Prayer Prompt:

How do you feel about today's verse? If you feel no one understands you, spend some time with God. He formed you in the womb.

....

....

....

....

....

....

....

....

....

....

....

....

....

....

You know me, Lord. . .better than anyone. You know when I'm in a bad mood, when I'm off my game, and when I'm feeling invincible. More than anything, You know my heart, Father. You've known it all along, even before I was born. What a miraculous thought! I praise You for knowing and loving me, Lord. Amen.

Keep His Commands and Live

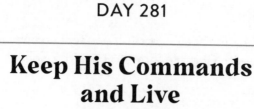

*My son, keep my words, and treasure my commands
within you. Keep my commands and live, and my
law as the apple of your eye. Bind them on your fingers;
write them on the tablet of your heart. Say to wisdom,
"You are my sister," and call understanding your nearest kin.*
PROVERBS 7:1–4 NKJV

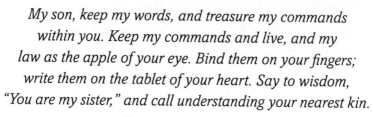

Many people believe that God's commands are restrictive, that He wants to somehow stop people from having a good time in life. Nothing could be further from the truth! His commands bring life, joy, peace, and ultimately help His children remain healthy and strong.

Don't you just love the image painted in verse 3 above? "Bind them on your fingers; write them on the tablet of your heart." What an awesome way to say, "Learn the scriptures. Keep them close by because you're going to need them."

You may not be good at memorizing scripture verses. But in God's will, you'll find a way. Today, choose several of your favorites. Write them down and post them in places around your house where you're sure to see them every day—on your bathroom mirror, refrigerator door, nightstand, and so on. The more you see the Word, the more you'll remember it. . .and that's a good thing.

Prayer Prompt:

How do you feel about God's commands—restrictive, hard to follow? Ask Him to give you love for His Word and understanding as you read.

....

....

....

....

....

....

....

....

....

....

....

....

....

....

....

....

Father, I want to immerse myself in Your Word, to bind Your commands on my fingers and keep them close to my heart. May Your words flow out of me in good times and in bad. Amen.

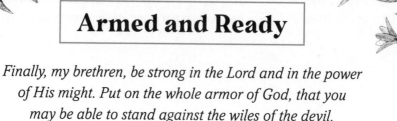

Armed and Ready

Finally, my brethren, be strong in the Lord and in the power
of His might. Put on the whole armor of God, that you
may be able to stand against the wiles of the devil.
EPHESIANS 6:10–11 NKJV

. . . .

The enemy is skilled at surprise attacks. Many times, he lashes out when we least expect it and when we're ill prepared. That's why it's important to be armed and ready at all times, not just in obvious battles. When he kicks our knees out from under us, we don't have to crater. If we're fully suited up to fight, the enemy won't get far.

God doesn't want us to be armed out of fear or intimidation. His goal isn't to weigh us down with burdensome armor. Ultimately, God longs to free us up. His armor isn't heavy; it's life sustaining, life giving. It does the job without driving us to our knees.

What enemies are you facing today? What opposing forces threaten to undo the work God is doing in your life? Suit up, my friend! You can take down this foe in the name of Jesus!

Prayer Prompt:

Whose armor are you wearing today? As you pray, suit up in the armor that God provides and you'll be ready for battle.

....

....

....

....

....

....

....

....

....

....

....

....

....

....

....

....

....

....

....

....

....

....

Lord, I want to be armed and ready. Today, I choose to step into the armor You've provided so that I'm ready for the battle ahead. No cowering. No cratering. I'm strong when I'm suited up, Lord. . .ready to fight in Your name, strength, and power. Amen.

Wisdom Is Calling

*Listen as Wisdom calls out! Hear as understanding raises
her voice! On the hilltop along the road, she takes her
stand at the crossroads. By the gates at the entrance to
the town, on the road leading in, she cries aloud.*

PROVERBS 8:1–3 NLT

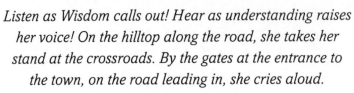

Remember, as a child, how you heard your mother's voice call out to you? Perhaps you were playing in the neighbor's backyard or riding bikes. Then, clear as day—that familiar voice: "Kids! Come home! It's time for supper!" So you ditched the games and took off for home, ready for an amazing home-cooked meal. What caused you to respond so quickly (and positively)? The familiarity of Mom's voice. You knew what that "Come home!" meant. An amazing meal was waiting.

The same is true today, only it's not Mom calling. Today's verse reminds us that wisdom cries out to us. She stands along the edge of the road and cries in a loud voice, just like Mom did. She beckons you to come home, to take the right road, to turn your back on childish decisions and put on your spiritual thinking cap.

Listen. Can you hear her?

Prayer Prompt:

Whose voice are you listening to? Ask the Lord to tune your ears to His voice so that it becomes familiar to you.

....

....

....

....

....

....

....

....

....

....

....

....

....

....

....

....

Lord, I want to live my life tuned in to Your thoughts, Your ways, Your wisdom. May I never be found guilty of following my own advice or carving my own path. I want to follow after You, Father, down a wise path. So here I am, listening, waiting to hear wisdom's familiar voice. Amen.

This Is What the Lord Says

"This is what the Lord says: 'When people fall down, don't they get up again? When they discover they're on the wrong road, don't they turn back?'"

JEREMIAH 8:4 NLT

. . . .

Think of the many times you've tripped and fallen in your life. One minute you were standing straight as an arrow; the next you were sprawled out on the sidewalk, wondering how you got there. No one likes to take a tumble, hard or soft. This is especially true as we age. Getting back up again is tougher with older, arthritic joints, and recovery takes longer.

The same thing is true in your spiritual walk. There will be seasons when you tumble, when you make mistakes. But God doesn't want you to stay down long. Sure, it's not easy to pick yourself up, admit you've made a mistake, then get back to walking the straight and narrow. But it is possible. And don't spend too much time worrying about the recovery period. God will see you through all of that, no matter how long it takes.

Prayer Prompt:

What's causing you to stumble and fall in life? Don't stay down. Ask the Lord to help you stand up and walk again.

....

....

....

....

....

....

....

....

....

....

....

....

....

....

....

....

....

....

Father, I find myself in so many messes! I've stumbled and fallen more times than I can count. Today I'm ready to admit my flaws, my imperfections. Pick me up (again), I pray. I can't promise this will be the last time, but I know You'll stick with me, no matter how many times I hit the ground. I'm so grateful for Your staying power, Lord. Amen.

DAY 285

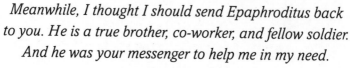

A Fellow Soldier

Meanwhile, I thought I should send Epaphroditus back to you. He is a true brother, co-worker, and fellow soldier. And he was your messenger to help me in my need.
PHILIPPIANS 2:25 NLT

Where would we be without our fellow soldiers? When we're weakened by the battle, ready to give up, they stand strong beside us (or even in front of us), unwilling to let us give in to defeat. They've got our backs. . . and we've got theirs. It's impossible to imagine doing life without them, isn't it?

Today, pause for a moment to think about the people God has surrounded you with. Are they relatives? Friends? Coworkers? Neighbors? Have any of these people stepped up to help as you powered your way through a tough situation?

Maybe you're feeling alone, wondering if anyone has your back. The best way to find a friend like this is to first *be* a friend like this. So, eyes wide open! Be on the lookout for a coworker or friend in need. Be the soldier she needs. Stand in the gap. Pray. Defend. Then watch as God brings warriors to your side when you need them most.

Prayer Prompt:

Who do you need to stand in the gap for today? Ask the Lord to show you who needs support and encouragement in their life.

....

....

....

....

....

....

....

....

....

....

....

....

....

....

....

....

Lord, I want to stand in the gap for others, to be a good soldier who cares about those I love. Today, open my eyes to see one in need, so that I can lift her arms and give her hope. Use me, I pray. Amen.

Good Judgment

*"Come in with me," she urges the simple. To those who
lack good judgment, she says, "Come, eat my food,
and drink the wine I have mixed. Leave your simple ways
behind, and begin to live; learn to use good judgment."*

PROVERBS 9:4–6 NLT

. . . .

Good judgment. Oh, how we need it—in every situation, large and small. New job opportunity. New relationship. Trouble with a friend. We rely on our judgment to help us get through these and other tough seasons.

As you look back over your life, would you say that your judgment has been mostly good or not so good? Have you been bamboozled or taken in by others? Have you opened yourself up to swindlers or cheats?

God can turn things around and give you good judgment even if you have a rough history. Today, take the time to ask the Lord to beef up this area of your life, to strengthen your discernment, and to help you make great decisions from this point forward.

No looking back! From here on out, it's good judgment all the way!

Prayer Prompt:

What caused you to make poor judgments in the past? Ask the Father to give you a discerning spirit so you won't make the same mistakes again.

....

....

....

....

....

....

....

....

....

....

....

....

....

....

Father, I'll admit—my judgment has been lacking. I've entered into relationships I shouldn't have, invested in deals I should've avoided, and gotten caught up in friendship woes that were really none of my business. All of that is behind me now, Lord. Give me discernment. Help me to make good choices from this day forward, I pray. Amen.

Return to Him

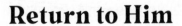

This is how the LORD responds: "If you return to me, I will
restore you so you can continue to serve me. If you speak good
words rather than worthless ones, you will be my spokesman.
You must influence them; do not let them influence you!"
JEREMIAH 15:19 NLT

So many of us depend on a GPS to get us where we're going. Back in the olden days, though, we had to rely on paper maps or intuition that sometimes wasn't the best. Perhaps you've been there. . .driving down a road for some time before realizing you're headed in the wrong direction. The only solution? Hit the brakes and turn around. Point your car in the correct direction.

The same is true in your spiritual life. No matter how far off course you've wandered, no matter how many years it's been since you spoke to God, He longs for you to hit the brakes and find the nearest U-turn. He can transform your current situation and make things right again.

So what are you waiting for? Hit those brakes, girl! Don't let another minute go by.

Prayer Prompt:

What road did you take that you realize is the wrong one? Pray to the Father, admit your mistake, ask Him for directions from now on.

....

....

....

....

....

....

....

....

....

....

....

....

....

Father, I'll admit there have been times I've wandered far from You. I've deliberately moved in the opposite direction, wanting to live my own life, do my own thing. But I can see now that moving away from You is never the answer. Today I choose to run back to Your arms. Thanks for guiding me home, Lord. Amen.

Reconciled

*Yet now he has reconciled you to himself through the death
of Christ in his physical body. As a result, he has brought
you into his own presence, and you are holy and blameless
as you stand before him without a single fault.*

COLOSSIANS 1:22 NLT

. . . .

You didn't mean for it to happen. Neither did she. But you and your good friend have had a falling-out. Your disagreement got ugly, and walls went up. Now you're wondering what it's going to take to make things right again.

God is in the reconciliation business. He longs to tear down walls—not just the ones raised between friends, but those invisible walls you've put up to keep Him out too. He wants to restore your relationships, not just put bandages on them. Does that sound impossible? Remember, nothing is impossible with God.

What relationships are you most concerned with today? Instead of stressing out over them, give them to the Lord and ask for His perfect, holy will. Then watch as He moves supernaturally in ways you never dreamed.

Prayer Prompt:

What relationships do you need to mend today? As you pray, ask God to heal and mend your relationship with Him and with others also.

....

....

....

....

....

....

....

....

....

....

....

....

....

....

....

....

Father, I've given up on some of my relationships. I know there are people I'm not supposed to be friends with anymore, but there are others who have grown distant. Today I give those relationships to You and pray for Your will to be done. Heal and mend the ones that are meant to be, I pray. Amen.

DAY 289

The Potter's Wheel

This is the word that came to Jeremiah from the LORD: "Go down to the potter's house, and there I will give you my message." So I went down to the potter's house, and I saw him working at the wheel. But the pot he was shaping from the clay was marred in his hands; so the potter formed it into another pot, shaping it as seemed best to him.

JEREMIAH 18:1–4 NIV

How many times has God shaped and reshaped you? Have you remained pliable in His hands, or do you stiffen up, unwilling to change? The Lord longs to shape and form you into His image, and the task is much easier when you submit to the process.

No matter what you've been through—whether you're soft or hard, broken or whole—God wants to keep reshaping you. Instead of fighting the process, put yourself on the wheel today and submit. He will mold you into something beautiful if you let Him.

Prayer Prompt:

In what ways do you need God to reshape you? In prayer, climb onto the potter's wheel and submit to God's shaping.

....

....

....

....

....

....

....

....

....

....

....

....

....

....

....

Father, I'll admit. . .I don't always like to be on the potter's wheel. I don't want to submit to the process. I've been too hurt, too broken. Thank You for the reminder that I can be soft in Your hands once again. Today, hard as it might be, I resubmit myself to the process of becoming pliable so that You can shape me into the woman I long to be. Amen.

Set Your Mind on Things Above

Since, then, you have been raised with Christ, set your hearts on things above, where Christ is, seated at the right hand of God. Set your minds on things above, not on earthly things.

COLOSSIANS 3:1–2 NIV

Have you ever had a mind shift? Maybe you felt one way about something and then, *bam. . .*you changed your mind. God is in the mind-changing business. No matter where your thoughts have been—good, bad, or otherwise—the Creator of the universe longs for you to shift them to Him. Why is He so keen on captivating your thoughts? Because having the mind of Christ is the only way you will survive in this life.

How, then, do you set your mind on things above? Focus on what is good, what is right, what is true, what is lovely. Ask the Lord to give you His opinion on everything (even the little things). Don't focus on self. Instead, keep your eyes on Him. That's where you will find your answers, after all.

Prayer Prompt:

What is your mind focusing on today? Talk to the Lord about what's troubling you, and allow Him to give you a mind shift.

_____

_____

_____

_____

_____

_____

_____

_____

_____

_____

_____

_____

_____

_____

_____

_____

Today I choose to set my mind on things above, Lord. I won't let the daily troubles get me down. I'll shift my eyes up, up, up to You, my Maker and Creator. You alone know how to change my thoughts from worry to praise. Thank You for this mind shift, Father. Amen.

The Lips of the Righteous

The lips of the righteous know what finds favor,
but the mouth of the wicked only what is perverse.
PROVERBS 10:32 NIV

Have you ever had a friend who only spoke positive, uplifting words? Chances are pretty good you gravitated to this friend for her positivity and her encouragement. God longs for all His daughters to be like this, to use their words as instruments of love, not hate. (The world has plenty of hate speech as it is.)

So where do you fit into that equation? Are you more prone to positive or negative speech? Do you find yourself caught up in gossip or conversations that tend toward the negative? If so, God wants to transform not just your speech, but your heart, for out of the abundance of the heart, the mouth speaks (Luke 6:45).

The question is, how do you obtain the righteous lips referred to in Proverbs 10:32? By having the mind of Christ (Philippians 2:5). The natural result of this is so powerful: When you adopt the mind of Christ, you take on the *speech* of Christ. When you think His thoughts, you naturally *speak* His words. Wow, that's amazing!

Who are you speaking for today? Just something to think about.

Prayer Prompt:

What are you speaking and thinking today? Ask the Lord to make your thoughts and the words of your mouth acceptable to Him.

....

....

....

....

....

....

....

....

....

....

....

....

....

....

....

....

Lord, may Your thoughts be my thoughts, Your words, my words. I want to have the mind of Christ and the vocabulary of Christ to match. Help me, I pray. Amen.

Ears to Hear

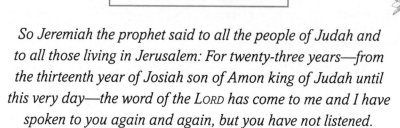

So Jeremiah the prophet said to all the people of Judah and to all those living in Jerusalem: For twenty-three years—from the thirteenth year of Josiah son of Amon king of Judah until this very day—the word of the LORD has come to me and I have spoken to you again and again, but you have not listened.

JEREMIAH 25:2–3 NIV

Sometimes we only hear what we want to hear. We walk away from conversations (or even sermons) only gleaning the phrases that jibe with our current mind-set. The rest gets tossed out.

God is interested in breaking through any walls we've put up, so He can do a real work in our lives. In other words, He wants us to really listen ...to the whole message, not just part. There's no picking and choosing with the Lord. It's all or nothing.

What has God been speaking to you lately? Which parts of His message have been hard to hear (and even harder to apply)? What will you need to do to activate your faith so you can not only listen, but obey? Today is the day.

Prayer Prompt:

What are you hearing when God speaks to you? Pray that your ears will be open to His every word.

....

....

....

....

....

....

....

....

....

....

....

....

....

....

I'll admit it, Lord—I often pick and choose which parts of Your Word I want to apply. Some of those verses are tough! Forgiving my enemies, for example. That's a hard one. But today I commit myself to listening to the whole message and applying it to the best of my ability. Give me ears to hear, I pray. Amen.

No Need for Accolades

*We were not looking for praise from people, not from you
or anyone else, even though as apostles of Christ
we could have asserted our authority. Instead,
we were like young children among you.*

1 THESSALONIANS 2:6–7 NIV

Oh, how we love those pats on the back. Those "attagirls." They encourage us when we're down and give us the tenacity to keep going, to reach our goals. Sometimes, though, we get a little too addicted to praise. We crave it, long for it, can't seem to keep going without it. We perform for the purpose of getting accolades.

Today, the Lord wants to remind you that the only praise that matters is His. He adores you and is your biggest cheerleader. So don't seek the praise of those around you. They can't give you what the Lord can. Applause is short lived, but the love of the Lord lasts forever. And best of all, He's not asking you to perform for Him. He simply wants your heart.

Prayer Prompt:

Whose applause are you listening for? Ask God to give you a heart that loves His approval more than the applause of others.

....

....

....

....

....

....

....

....

....

....

....

....

....

....

....

....

....

Father, I've been such a performer, such a people pleaser. I'll admit, the accolades felt good. But I see now that the only audience I need is an audience of one. I'm so grateful You're not asking me to perform, Lord. Whew! I can relax in Your presence and simply be. Thank You for that, Father. Amen.

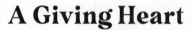

A Giving Heart

One person gives freely, yet gains even more;
another withholds unduly, but comes to poverty.

PROVERBS 11:24 NIV

Don't you just love generous people? They're always surprising others in such fun ways—groceries on the front porch, a gift card to a local restaurant, maybe even a plane ticket to see a loved one.

God loves a cheerful giver, and He wants that giver to be you! He longs for you to have a generous heart, not just willing to give away things with monetary value, but to freely give away love and adoration, as well.

Would you say that you're a generous person? Today, think of some ways that you can bless others who are going through a hard time. Get creative. Ask the Lord to help you come up with fun and random ideas; then follow through with a smile on your face and a song in your heart. God loves a cheerful giver, after all.

Prayer Prompt:

Who can you be generous to today? As you pray, ask the Father who needs to be touched by your generosity.

....

....

....

....

....

....

....

....

....

....

....

....

....

....

....

....

Father, I want to be known as a giver. Touch my heart with the things that touch Yours, I pray. Give me eyes to see those in need and ears to hear what others are going through so that I can play a role in meeting needs. What fun, to give! I'm so grateful for every opportunity, Lord. Amen.

Coming Home

*"The days are coming," declares the LORD, "when I will bring my
people Israel and Judah back from captivity and restore them
to the land I gave their ancestors to possess," says the LORD.*
JEREMIAH 30:3 NIV

. . . .

If you've ever moved away from a place you loved then returned for a
visit, you know the joy of coming home again. Sometimes the experience
exceeds your expectations. Other times it falls short because the images in
your mind are exaggerated. It's like when you go back to your childhood
home after forty years of being away. Sometimes that home isn't as big
as you remember it to be.

Yet the thing is, no matter where you currently live, no matter how
many places you have called home in the past, God longs for you to come
home to *Him*. . .to stay. When you're at home with Him, you can kick
back, put your feet up, speak your mind, and fill your heart and soul with
choice morsels from His Word.

Prayer Prompt:

Where do you feel most at home? Seek the Lord in prayer;
draw closer to Him so that you feel at home in His presence.

....

....

....

....

....

....

....

....

....

....

....

....

....

....

....

I love the phrase "There's no place like home," Lord.
I feel that way when I'm curled up on my sofa and
when I'm in communion with You. Home really
is where the heart is, Father, and my heart is
always and forever with You. Amen.

How Smart Are You?

To learn, you must love discipline;
it is stupid to hate correction.
PROVERBS 12:1 NLT

Remember, as a child, how you hated being disciplined by your mother or father? No child looks forward to being put in the corner or being punished some other way, after all. If only we could learn all our lessons during childhood! Unfortunately, we still need seasons of discipline as adults. And it's better to humbly accept the Lord's correction than to run from it or be reined in with lots of kicking and screaming.

Is it possible to love discipline? Stop and think about that question for a moment. If we learn to love discipline, we'll live obedient lives. And obedient lives have excellent outcomes—health, great relationships, safety, provision, and so much more.

If discipline leads to obedience, which leads to a rich life, then you could—and should—learn to love discipline. Better yet, make up your mind to live an obedient life so there's nothing to discipline.

Prayer Prompt:

How do you feel about being disciplined? As you pray, accept the Lord's discipline with a humble heart and learn from it.

....

....

....

....

....

....

....

....

....

....

....

....

....

....

....

....

....

I haven't always loved discipline, Lord. In fact, I can remember many times in my life when my parents or teachers disciplined me in a way that really stung. Your discipline leads to repentance, Lord, and offers me a whole, healthy life. I'll take it, Lord, and learn from it, as well. Amen.

Worthy of the Calling

We constantly pray for you, that our God may make you worthy of his calling, and that by his power he may bring to fruition your every desire for goodness and your every deed prompted by faith.

2 Thessalonians 1:11 NIV

So many of us struggle with unworthiness. We wonder if God can—or will—ever use us. Some people base their lack of worth on actions or behaviors in the past. Still others feel disqualified due to how they look—body shape/size, hair, physical flaws. Some feel like they can't—and never will—get their act together: "How can God use me when I'm such a loser?"

Isn't it refreshing to realize that God makes us worthy through the blood of His Son? The salvation process brings with it an additional gift—worthiness. In ourselves, we are not righteous. But through the blood of Jesus we are made righteous. We are made worthy. We have value because He has value. It's that simple. . .and that complicated.

God wants to use you. He has already made you worthy. So no excuses! Step up and watch as He leads you down new and exciting paths.

Prayer Prompt:

What makes you feel unworthy to be used of God? As you pray, submit to God's will and accept that Jesus' blood makes you worthy.

I've felt unusable at times due to my unworthiness, Lord. I've used it as an excuse. Thank You for the reminder that You've made me worthy. Today I step out in faith and say, "Use me, Lord." I am righteous in You and ready for whatever tasks You send my way. Amen.

Lesson Learned

*Then the word of the L*ORD *came to Jeremiah, saying: "This is what the L*ORD *Almighty, the God of Israel, says: Go and tell the people of Judah and those living in Jerusalem, 'Will you not learn a lesson and obey my words?' declares the L*ORD*."*

JEREMIAH 35:12–13 NIV

Have you ever wondered why children have to go to school for so many years? Who decided on twelve years plus kindergarten? Who came up with the plan for four years in college and so on?

The truth is, lessons never stop, whether you're in a physical classroom or the classroom of life. You're a perpetual student, always stumbling across new material. You might be in your seventies or eighties, but that doesn't mean the learning stops. In fact, God hopes you'll remain an ever-ready student because He's got a lot of lessons to teach you.

As you look back over the lessons you've already learned, which have been the hardest? Which have been the easiest? Are there any you're still struggling with? Today, the Lord wants you to know He's proud of you for your willingness to grow and change. That's what transformation is all about—taking the lessons you've learned and applying them to your life. What a great student you are!

Prayer Prompt:

What lessons in life are you struggling with? Ask the Lord to teach you, and then apply yourself to His lessons.

....

....

....

....

....

....

....

....

....

....

....

....

....

....

Father, I want to be a good student, always ready to learn whatever lessons You're sending my way. May I transform daily into Your image as I study Your Word and listen to Your voice. Amen.

Guard Your Words

Those who guard their lips preserve their lives,
but those who speak rashly will come to ruin.

PROVERBS 13:3 NIV

Oh, how easy it is to let our words flow. Oftentimes we unleash them like a river rushing downstream with no thought for how they might affect others. There are times when the Lord wants to put a clamp on our words, just as one might dam a river. Why? Because the force of those words can bring life or death. That's how powerful they are.

Since God began His transformation in your life, have you noticed a change in your speech? Are you as apt to let your thoughts flow? Are you as quick to snap to judgment? Have you given more thought to how, when, where, and why you speak?

God desires for you to guard your words. Stop. Think. Then speak. It's a habit that can be acquired, one that could potentially save relationships.

Prayer Prompt:

Do you speak first or think first? Ask the Lord to give you wisdom to know when to speak and when to be quiet.

....

....

....

....

....

....

....

....

....

....

....

....

....

....

....

....

....

....

Lord, I'm a little too wordy at times. I let my thoughts flow out, not giving much thought to how they might hurt others. Make me more cautious, I pray. Guard my lips. I want to be more careful so that my words bring life, not death. Amen.

Our Mediator

*For there is one God and one mediator between God and mankind,
the man Christ Jesus, who gave himself as a ransom for all
people. This has now been witnessed to at the proper time.*

1 TIMOTHY 2:5–6 NIV

Have you ever hired an attorney? If so, then you know what it's like to have an advocate, someone who not only believes your story but will defend you with passion.

Jesus is your mediator, your attorney, if you will. He took your case, pled your defense, and even took your punishment for sin. He stood in the gap for you, only asking for your heart, your adoration in return.

What an amazing portrait of love. Unlike any attorney you'll ever meet, Jesus Christ gave Himself as a ransom for all people. Talk about pro bono work! He poured Himself out for all people! What an amazing Savior you have. What a mediator!

Prayer Prompt:

How do you need Jesus to mediate for you today? Ask Jesus to be your advocate in that area, then praise Him for the result.

_____

_____

_____

_____

_____

_____

_____

_____

_____

_____

_____

_____

_____

_____

_____

Lord, thank You for serving as my mediator, my go-between. You did it all for me, and I'm so grateful. Thank You for pleading my case and for being my advocate. When I couldn't defend myself, You swept in and took on my cause. How can I ever repay You, Father? I'm far more than Your client. . .I'm Your child, and a grateful one at that. Amen.

Walking with the Wise

Walk with the wise and become wise,
for a companion of fools suffers harm.
PROVERBS 13:20 NIV

Think back on the many friends you've had. Go all the way back to childhood. Did you choose wisely? Did these boys and girls keep you walking the straight and narrow or take you by the hand and lead you down a different path?

Friends can make or break us, so it's important to choose wisely, not just during childhood but even as we age. They often shape our behaviors, our convictions, our beliefs. We tend to adjust our thinking to those we hang out with, so it's important to draw close to those who will elevate our thinking and help us draw closer to Jesus.

Does this mean you can't be friends with people who are different? Of course not! But when you're trying to decide who to emulate, choose the ones who represent the Lord. You can't go wrong when you glean from those who are strong in their faith.

Prayer Prompt:

What relationships dominate your life? Ask the Lord to help you choose friends that honor Him.

....

....

....

....

....

....

....

....

....

....

....

....

....

....

....

....

....

....

....

....

I'm grateful for the reminder that I've got to be careful choosing friends even as an adult. There are many who would lead me down the wrong path even now. I want to be wise, Lord. Give me discernment so that I can pull away from those who mean to harm me, I pray. Amen.

Elder Care

Do not rebuke an older man harshly, but exhort him as if he were your father. Treat younger men as brothers, older women as mothers, and younger women as sisters, with absolute purity.
1 TIMOTHY 5:1–2 NIV

If you're blessed to still have your mother, your father, or your grandparents, praise the Lord! These precious souls are a gift and not one to be taken lightly. God cares very much how you treat your elders.

What "elders" do you look up to? Parents? Grandparents? Older neighbors? Friends from church? How have they blessed you? What is your greatest joy in spending time with these people? Are there any challenges?

The Bible is very clear that you're to speak with kindness and affection to your elders, as if every one happened to be a mother, a father, or a grandparent. Today, why not reach out to someone in your community who needs to be treated with that kind of gentleness and affection? Likely, they are in need of companionship. And you have much to glean from these amazing people!

Prayer Prompt:

What can you learn from those who are older than you? Ask the Lord to give you a heart of love and respect for your elders.

....

....

....

....

....

....

....

....

....

....

....

....

....

....

....

....

....

Father, point me toward those who could use a friend.
May I be an advocate and friend for people in their
golden years. May I always be known as someone
who cared about people of all ages, Lord. Amen.

Discernment

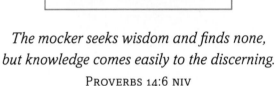

The mocker seeks wisdom and finds none,
but knowledge comes easily to the discerning.
PROVERBS 14:6 NIV

. . . .

Have you ever heard the old expression "If it'd been a snake, it would've bit me!" Some people just can't see evil for what it is, even when it's staring them in the face. That's why discernment is so important, especially in this day and age we live in. Because when we suffer from a lack of discernment, we fall into many traps.

The enemy knows just how and where to strike. He's skilled at surprise attacks. But we have a tool, a weapon, if you will—discernment. We don't have to fall prey to the enemy's attacks. We can know the truth, and it really can (as the Bible says) set us free.

Today, spend some time asking God to give you supernatural discernment. He longs for you to walk in victory, and it only comes as you discern truth.

Prayer Prompt:

What is the enemy attacking you about? Ask the Lord to give you discernment to know the spirit of truth and the spirit of error.

....

....

....

....

....

....

....

....

....

....

....

....

....

....

....

....

....

....

....

My eyes are wide open, Lord. I want to see—the good, the bad, and the ugly—so that I can avoid what needs to be avoided. May I have Your discernment, I pray, so that I don't get caught up in the enemy's trap. Guard my heart and mind, Lord. Amen.

A Way That Seems Right

There is a way that appears to be right,
but in the end it leads to death.

PROVERBS 14:12 NIV

. . . .

We are surrounded on every side by people who feel like they have the best answers, know the right way to live, see the better path. So how do we know which path to follow? These people are convinced that they're right, after all, and are aching to bring you over to their side.

The Bible warns us that there's a way that seems right to a woman, but that doesn't make it right to God. There's only one path that leads us to Him, and that's through His Son, Jesus. No matter how convincing your neighbors, civic leaders, or politicians might be, their "way" will lead to death if it doesn't involve going through the cross of Jesus Christ.

The Lord is calling on you—on all His children—to share the good news of the gospel message, not just by living a holy life in front of a watching world, but by speaking up when the occasion calls for it. You can be a compass for someone headed in the wrong direction. What greater joy could there be in this life than leading someone to the Lord?

Prayer Prompt:

What voices are you hearing around you? Ask the Lord to give you ears to hear His voice and courage to point others in the right direction.

....

....

....

....

....

....

....

....

....

....

....

....

....

....

....

Father, today I pray a simple prayer: Use me.
Give me courage to speak up and point people
to Jesus, the only true way. Amen.

Grandma's China

*In a wealthy home some utensils are made of gold and silver,
and some are made of wood and clay. The expensive utensils
are used for special occasions, and the cheap ones are for
everyday use. If you keep yourself pure, you will be a special
utensil for honorable use. Your life will be clean, and you will
be ready for the Master to use you for every good work.*

2 TIMOTHY 2:20–21 NLT

There's something thrilling about a special occasion meal, complete with fancy dinnerware, linen napkins, and the confusing extra forks. Maybe you even associate holidays or other celebration meals with heirloom china.

In Paul's second letter to Timothy, he urges his young protégé to live a pure life so God can use him like highly prized, special occasion dinnerware—set apart for important work.

How do we live a pure life? Paul explains in 2 Timothy 20:22, 24 (NIV): "Flee the evil desires of youth and pursue righteousness, faith, love and peace. . . . And the Lord's servant must not be quarrelsome but must be kind to everyone, able to teach, not resentful."

You are meant to gleam like polished silver that the master of the house is pleased to present to guests. So don't settle for being a common, everyday setting. Ask God to purify your heart and shine!

Prayer Prompt:

What kind of utensil are you? Ask God to make you shine like a precious utensil for His glory.

....

....

....

....

....

....

....

....

....

....

....

....

....

....

....

Like a priceless heirloom, I want my life to be a special, prized possession to You, Father. Amen.

Holy Health

A peaceful heart leads to a healthy body;
jealousy is like cancer in the bones.
PROVERBS 14:30 NLT

. . . .

What are your current health goals? Maybe you're trying to be more active or eat healthier to shed a few pounds. Perhaps eight-hours-per-night sleep is your aim. Destress or detox? HIIT or Fitbit? Delivery or DiGiorno?

It's easy to get discouraged by the ever-changing requirements of a "healthy lifestyle." For, as Christians, we know someday God will give us new bodies (1 Corinthians 15:35–58; 2 Corinthians 5:1–5), so appointments with the treadmill may feel like an exercise in futility (pun intended). But God cares about your physical state—values your body so much that His Holy Spirit has *chosen* to take up residence there. Paul goes on to say in 1 Corinthians 6:19–20 (NLT), "You do not belong to yourself, for God bought you with a high price. So you must honor God with your body."

Honoring God with your body starts with obeying His Word. Many of the spiritual disciplines Jesus teaches are soul matters. But a healthy spirit and soul, confidently standing in God's grace, can cultivate a contented heart, stronger relationships with friends and family, restful sleep, less stress, and a more positive outlook—all of which can have an impact on your physical health both now and in the long term.

Prayer Prompt:

What are you doing to honor God with your body? Ask Him to show you the area you need to work on to be healthy.

....

....

....

....

....

....

....

....

....

....

....

....

....

....

....

....

....

Father, give me the motivation I need to treat my earthly body as a precious gift from You. Amen.

What God Thinks of Idols

"The whole human race is foolish and has no knowledge!
The craftsmen are disgraced by the idols they make,
for their carefully shaped works are a fraud. These idols have
no breath or power. Idols are worthless; they are ridiculous
lies! On the day of reckoning they will all be destroyed."
JEREMIAH 51:17–18 NLT

Twenty-first-century idols look different than the idols of Old Testament times. Where pagan craftsmen once made figures for worship out of precious metals, wood, and stone, our idols are made out of much more sophisticated materials. Consider:

- The precision-cut glass, cobalt, graphite, lithium, silicon, and aluminum of a smartphone
- The wood, drywall, stone, marble, metal, and glass of a magazine-ready house
- The oxygen, carbon, hydrogen, nitrogen, calcium, and phosphorus that make up the human body (idols included but not limited to: our children, husbands, a celebrity, or even our own bodies)

Is there anything or anyone more important in your life than God? Do those worthless idols hold more influence than God in your life because you spend more time on them than on your relationship with Him? Remember, living a real life and obtaining real wisdom come from worshipping God the transformer, not the transformed.

Prayer Prompt:

What do you consider an idol in today's world? When you pray, ask God to remove anything that might be an idol to you.

....

....

....

....

....

....

....

....

....

....

....

....

....

....

....

God, You are better than anything I could ever put in Your place! Forgive my wayward heart. I want You and You only. Amen.

Simple Living

A wise person is hungry for knowledge,
while the fool feeds on trash.
PROVERBS 15:14 NLT

. . . .

In today's world, there's no lack of diversion to fill our eyes, ears, heads, and hearts. Books and magazines are only the beginning. From traditional TV and movies to streaming music and videos, video games, podcasts, audiobooks, blogs, social media, and every other rabbit hole, we can access lifetimes of information through the touch screen grasped tightly in our fists.

If we're honest, much of what we take in has no lasting value. And what seems harmless, simply trivial and fluffy, can do real damage to our spiritual health and heart. Most of it is *garbage*. Proverbs calls one who feasts on this trash a *fool*.

The wise person, instead, is hungry for knowledge—for ideas and entertainment that promote good in the world and will encourage one to pursue good as well. Where can you go to fill your hunger? The first and best answer is to God's Word, but there are so many other resources that are rooted in good and available to you as well. When you find one, recommend it to others—spread knowledge and take out the trash!

Prayer Prompt:

Are you hungry for knowledge or feeding on trash? Ask the Father to show you what is good for your spiritual health.

....

....

....

....

....

....

....

....

....

....

....

....

....

....

....

....

....

....

....

....

Father, I'm grateful for knowledge at my fingertips. Give me a hunger for the good and a distaste for trash. Amen.

Open Mouth

Everyone enjoys a fitting reply; it is wonderful
to say the right thing at the right time!
PROVERBS 15:23 NLT

. . . .

Open mouth, insert foot.

We've all known the taste of toe jam. We're too quick to speak and woefully shortsighted when we're being insensitive. James 3:2 tell us that if we could control our tongues, we would be perfect and could also control ourselves in every other way. But we aren't perfect, and our words indicate just that.

So how can you become a woman known for saying the right thing at the right time?

1. Hold your tongue. "Too much talk leads to sin. Be sensible and keep your mouth shut" (Proverbs 10:19 NLT).

2. Ask God for words. "Take control of what I say, O LORD, and guard my lips" (Psalm 141:3 NLT).

3. In all words, love. "Most important of all, continue to show deep love for each other, for love covers a multitude of sins" (1 Peter 4:8 NLT).

God's grace covers your sins, including the words that come out of your mouth. Getting a handle on your tongue—making your responses fitting and kind and good and helpful—is a spiritual discipline that won't happen overnight. But with work and with God's help, you can be transformed into a woman known for saying the right thing at the right time!

Prayer Prompt:

What can you do to be sure you speak at the right time? Ask God to help you control your tongue.

....

....

....

....

....

....

....

....

....

....

....

....

....

....

....

....

....

*God, help me tame this wild, unpredictable thing
inside my mouth. I can't do it alone. Amen.*

God Confidence

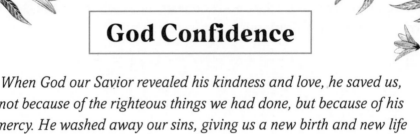

When God our Savior revealed his kindness and love, he saved us, not because of the righteous things we had done, but because of his mercy. He washed away our sins, giving us a new birth and new life through the Holy Spirit. . . . Because of his grace he made us right in his sight and gave us confidence that we will inherit eternal life.

TITUS 3:4–5, 7 NLT

· ·

When do you feel most confident? Whether it's some aspect of your career or ministry or hobby, your confidence shines brightest when you're doing something you're exceptionally good at. Confidence is empowering. Confidence is a great feeling.

But none of us is perfect, and we all have bad days that cause us to question if we know what we're doing. Setbacks can leave us frustrated and wondering why we even try.

That's why God's grace is so important in every aspect in our lives. Our old lives had moments of greatness, but ultimately were empty and worthless. Our new lives when we're born again are perfect and whole because Jesus Christ is perfect and whole. So we never have to wonder if we're good enough or if our self-confidence can carry us through. Our God confidence empowers us in this moment and through all of eternity.

Prayer Prompt:

What makes you feel confident when you're doing it? Ask the Lord to
help you do it for His glory so everyone can benefit.

....

....

....

....

....

....

....

....

....

....

....

....

....

....

....

....

....

....

Father, fill me with the God confidence that I need today.
Let Your mercy and grace fill my heart and my soul.
Breathe in me a new life every moment of every day. Amen.

Put Your Money Where Your Faith Is

And I am praying that you will put into action the generosity that comes from your faith as you understand and experience all the good things we have in Christ.

PHILEMON 6 NLT

. . . .

Generous living starts with experiencing all the good and joyful things we have in Christ. And an outcrop of our generous *living* of this good and joyful life is our generous *giving*.

Giving. Hm. Money is a tricky conversation for the church. Maybe we just feel like finances are too personal a topic to broach, but Jesus tells us in Matthew 6:21 that where we put our money shows where our hearts are.

Do you know where your money goes? That may seem like a silly question, but if you can't tell where your income is going, then you aren't managing well what God has given you.

If you do know where your money goes, do the debits in your bank account line up with who you claim to be? Are you joyfully, generously giving to the church? To worthwhile organizations that do good in the world?

Let your faith overflow into your giving, and get ready to experience a more fulfilling *living* in Christ.

Prayer Prompt:

What are your feelings toward giving money? When you pray, ask God to show you how to use what He has given you.

....

....

....

....

....

....

....

....

....

....

....

....

....

....

....

....

....

....

....

Father God, show me where You want me
to put Your money to use for Your kingdom.
I want to contribute in a real way! Amen.

He Remains

You, Master, started it all, laid earth's foundations, then crafted the stars in the sky. Earth and sky will wear out, but not you; they become threadbare like an old coat; you'll fold them up like a worn-out cloak, and lay them away on the shelf. But you'll stay the same, year after year; you'll never fade, you'll never wear out.
HEBREWS 1:10–12 MSG

"You'll understand when you're older." Remember how that answer from a grown-up really burned you up? But as you grew older and matured, you *did* start to understand there are some things you simply can't explain to someone who hasn't experienced them for him- or herself.

The more we mature, the more we realize just how little we know—especially when we consider that God has no beginning and no end (Hebrews 7:3)—that He was the first and will be the last (Revelation 22:13). That He was the past, is the present, and will be the future. If we spend too many minutes trying to find logic in such things, our little human brains might just melt. That's where faith steps in.

Within this puzzle of God's eternal nature comes comfort: God is always the same. He *never* changes. And that's true of His love for each of us. As long as God is, God is love.

Prayer Prompt:

What do you question about the future? In prayer, take time to praise God because He never changes, and the future belongs to Him.

....

....

....

....

....

....

....

....

....

....

....

....

....

....

....

....

Loving God, I praise You for Your constant nature. That forever fact about You brings me comfort, especially when my world is in flux. I love You, Father. Amen.

Jesus Is My Brother

*Both the one who makes people holy and those who
are made holy are of the same family. So Jesus is
not ashamed to call them brothers and sisters.*

HEBREWS 2:11 NIV

Imagine the headline: PRINCE WILLIAM, DUKE OF CAMBRIDGE, ANNOUNCES HEROIN ADDICT AS ADOPTED SIBLING AND COHEIR TO THE CROWN. A shockingly unbelievable story like this could only appear on a parody news site or a grocery stand tabloid.

But consider a headline of the *true* story of your salvation: JESUS CHRIST, THE KING OF HEAVEN'S ONLY SON AND HEIR, PROCLAIMS FILTHY, WRETCHED SINNER AS HIS BELOVED ADOPTED SISTER AND COHEIR TO THE KINGDOM. This one is even *more* unbelievable.

Hebrews tell us that, despite our imperfection, Jesus makes us holy. That's why He's not ashamed to call us His sisters. And not second-class sisters in name only. No, Christ Jesus is proud to share His inheritance with each of His siblings: salvation that provides eternal life in the Father's presence.

Don't get so comfortable in your salvation that you lose perspective on the awe factor of just how amazing your salvation is. Your today, tomorrow, and forever is secure—and glorious, not to mention totally awesome!

Prayer Prompt:

What does being a coheir with Jesus mean to you? Spend time in prayer with the Father who has adopted you into His family.

....

....

....

....

....

....

....

....

....

....

....

....

....

....

Jesus, I am proud and humbled to call You my brother. Thank You for claiming me as Your sister and making me holy. I don't deserve Your good gifts, but I am thankful for them. Amen.

Hidden Sins

He said to me, "Son of man, have you seen what the elders of Israel are doing in the darkness, each at the shrine of his own idol? They say, 'The Lord does not see us; the Lord has forsaken the land.' "
EZEKIEL 8:12 NIV

Time and again, God used Ezekiel's prophecies to tell the nation of Israel how furious He was with her idol worship. God's message for the leaders of Israel was clear: *"Stop worshipping idols or suffer the consequences."*

But idol worship continued—behind closed doors and in the dark. *If Ezekiel can't see it, he won't be able to tell the Lord.* Nice try, guys. Maybe they forgot that God is all-knowing (1 Chronicles 28:9) and always present (Jeremiah 23:23–24; Proverbs 15:3).

Turning off the lights to worship an idol seems like a ridiculous thing to do, but we are as guilty in trying to hide our own sin. Maybe we think we can get away with unseen sins like judging others, lust, envy, or pride. But God sees our hearts, and His Holy Spirit will convict us if we are tuned in to His promptings.

Your Father God isn't a cosmic cop just waiting for you to mess up. He loves you and He wants the best for you. So let light flood the recesses of your heart and mind; ask Him to help you destroy those hidden sins.

Prayer Prompt:

What do you struggle with in the dark? Ask God to bring light into your heart and clean out the dark deeds.

....

....

....

....

....

....

....

....

....

....

....

....

....

....

....

....

Lord God, examine me, purify my heart,
and renew Your Holy Spirit in me. Amen.

Let Love Prosper

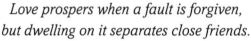

Love prospers when a fault is forgiven,
but dwelling on it separates close friends.
PROVERBS 17:9 NLT

. . . .

Forgive and forget. Sounds simple, right?

If only it *were* simple. But that would take short memories and humility instead of our elephant-like rememberers and out-of-control egos.

So how can you truly forgive and forget? First, realize that real, lasting, healing forgiveness is something that comes from God. Ask the Holy Spirit to help you get a handle on it. Acknowledge how difficult forgiveness is, and thank Him for forgiving your sins over and over again.

Next, understand the difference between *forgetting* and *choosing to not remember*. God doesn't ask you to develop amnesia; wrongs done to you will always be a part of your story. But when God forgives you, He banishes your wrongs from His thoughts, as He explains in Isaiah 43:25 (NLT): "I—yes, I alone—will blot out your sins for my own sake and will never think of them again." And the psalmist wrote that God "has removed our sins as far from us as the east is from the west" (Psalm 103:12 NLT). So as the forgiver, you must do the same for the forgivee.

God can and will use difficult points in a relationship to create fertile ground of forgiveness. As Proverbs 17:9 promises, love will then prosper and grow.

Prayer Prompt:

How hard is it for you to forgive someone? Pray for a forgiving spirit. You can't do it alone. God will help you.

....

....

....

....

....

....

....

....

....

....

....

....

....

....

....

....

Forgiving Father, You know how difficult it is for me to forgive sometimes. Help me create a fertile ground of pardon so that love can grow. Amen.

Solid Food

You are like babies who need milk and cannot eat solid food. For someone who lives on milk is still an infant and doesn't know how to do what is right. Solid food is for those who are mature, who through training have the skill to recognize the difference between right and wrong.

HEBREWS 5:12–14 NLT

· ·

It's a fun and messy milestone in a baby's development when she starts learning to eat solid food. And just like everything in an infant's life, trying new textures and tastes and using a spoon and a sippy cup take practice.

But with patience and encouragement from Mom and Dad, most developing children *do* move from milk or formula to rice cereal to mashed bananas to steak.

So when the writer of Hebrews chastises the church for remaining immature in its faith, it's a significant matter. To grow, the church needs someone to reteach its people the basics, feeding them the milk of God's Word. As they then put into practice what they learn, their capacity to understand more will grow. They'll gain the skill to tell right from wrong.

No matter where you are on the milk-to-solid-food spectrum, there's always room to grow. If you're comfortable with your bottle, you're missing out on the delicacies God offers as His banquet feast for His beloved children. What's holding you back?

Prayer Prompt:

Are you feasting on milk or meat? Ask God to give you an appetite for the solid food of His Word and Spirit.

Father, give me a hunger for You so my palate can mature and I can enjoy Your gifts and work more effectively for Your glory. Amen.

Just a Few

A truly wise person uses few words.
PROVERBS 17:27 NLT

. . . .

Women talk more than men: fact or fiction?

Despite your own opinion about this statement, researchers are divided on whether it's true and whether there's a biological reason one way or the other. Regardless of whether we're the chatty sort or generally quiet, scripture is clear: to be wise, talk less.

So why are few words better than a whole slew? Consider:

1. It's impossible to listen while talking. "Understand this, my dear brothers and sisters: You must all be quick to listen, slow to speak, and slow to get angry" (James 1:19 NLT).

2. Truly listening results in more thoughtful replies. "There is more hope for a fool than for someone who speaks without thinking" (Proverbs 29:20 NLT).

3. Speaking fewer words can give each one more importance, and you'll likely choose them more carefully. "Let everything you say be good and helpful, so that your words will be an encouragement to those who hear them" (Ephesians 4:29 NLT).

You know the difference between idle chatter and meaningful conversation. When you hear yourself talking just for talking's sake, take a breath and listen. Without the noise of your own voice, you may just hear God speak in a new and active way!

Prayer Prompt:

Are you a talker or listener? Ask God to give you wise words to speak and a listening heart to hear His voice.

God, teach me the discipline of listening and thinking before I speak. Give me the right words that are filled with Your truth. Amen.

Opinions: We've Got 'Em

An unfriendly person pursues selfish ends and against all sound judgment starts quarrels. Fools find no pleasure in understanding but delight in airing their own opinions.

PROVERBS 18:1–2 NIV

· ·

If you'd like to know someone's opinion about anything, hop over to her social media page, and odds are good you'll see what she thinks. Whether it's a post about what the government is doing right/wrong or a link to a news article or a pithy quote that supports/refutes a specific view, social media has given the masses a platform to opinionate for the world to see.

While it's not wrong to have an opinion that's grounded in God's truth, Proverbs 18:1–2 encourages us to set our own feelings aside to first care about the other person and put in the time and effort to understand him or her, asking God for wisdom in the situation (see James 1:5–6). That means seeing others through God's eyes—as deeply loved and highly valued people.

We should strive to first and foremost be known as women of love and understanding—not recognized for our knee-jerk reactions and loud opinions. When others know us as a listening ear, they'll be more likely to ask our opinions, opening the opportunity for us to share the love of Christ in every situation.

Prayer Prompt:

Why do you feel it's necessary to express your opinion? When you pray, ask God to give you an opinion that pleases Him.

....

....

....

....

....

....

....

....

....

....

....

....

....

....

....

....

....

Father, when my own ball of feeling and opinion wells up inside me, don't let it drown out the voice of the Holy Spirit. He is who I want to follow. Amen.

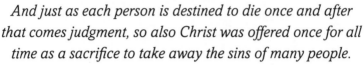

One and Done

And just as each person is destined to die once and after that comes judgment, so also Christ was offered once for all time as a sacrifice to take away the sins of many people.

HEBREWS 9:27–28 NLT

Before Adam and Eve disobeyed God's instruction, His creation was whole and perfect—poised to spend eternity in the presence of the Creator. But when sin entered the world in the Garden of Eden, death entered too. That mortal wound to the relationship between God and humans resulted in spiritual death that we tried to fix with the priest and sacrifice system in the Old Testament. But even a lifetime of blood sacrifice and ritual wasn't good enough to heal that relationship. Only Jesus dying on the cross could provide complete restoration.

Each of us will die physically, but Christ died on the cross, once for all (Hebrews 9:26), so we would not have to die spiritually. If we have accepted His gift of grace, He has forgiven our past sin; He has given us the Holy Spirit to help us deal with present sin; He stands for us in heaven as our High Priest (9:24); and He promises to return (9:28) and raise us to eternal life in God's presence where sin will be no more.

Prayer Prompt:

What does having Jesus as your High Priest mean to you? Spend
time talking with your High Priest, getting to know Him better.

....

....

....

....

....

....

....

....

....

....

....

....

....

....

....

....

Jesus, I am eagerly awaiting Your salvation.
Thank You for making the perfect way for me to
live with You in the Father's presence forever. Amen.

That New Covenant Smell

*The old system under the law of Moses was only a shadow,
a dim preview of the good things to come, not the good things
themselves. The sacrifices under that system were repeated
again and again, year after year, but they were never able to
provide perfect cleansing for those who came to worship.*

HEBREWS 10:1 NLT

. . . .

Sometimes it's good to make do with what we already have. Maybe it's not the newest, shiniest, or fanciest thing around, but it works well enough (mostly), and we can get by.

But when we're talking about the old covenant (priests and sacrifices and atonement and ceremonial washing and more) in contrast to the new covenant, there's no comparing the two. The writer of Hebrews describes the old way as "only a shadow, a dim preview of the good things to come." The heroes of the faith (mentioned in Hebrews 11) from the old covenant accepted and lived within the law and got a small taste of God's glory. But we who live under the new covenant can receive the perfect cleansing that Jesus' sacrifice on the cross gives us.

God offers you the best, the most perfect new life you can never hope to earn on your own. Don't make do with what you already have when it comes to your faith. Accept God's grace, His cleansing, and His new mercies every day (Lamentations 3:23).

Prayer Prompt:

Are you living on yesterday's experiences or the new mercies available each day? Ask God for a daily renewal of your spirit.

....

....

....

....

....

....

....

....

....

....

....

....

....

....

....

....

....

....

*New covenant God, thank You for making
a new way—the best way—Jesus. Amen.*

Patient Endurance

*Patient endurance is what you need now, so that
you will continue to do God's will. Then you
will receive all that he has promised.*
HEBREWS 10:36 NLT

. . . .

Patience is a word often associated with waiting—in a line, in a reception area, for a special day on the calendar, for a loved one's arrival. And when a mom instructs a child to be patient, she's probably asking her to be still and quiet while she waits.

Endurance is a word often used to describe what it takes to be a long-distance runner. It connotes grueling, unrelenting work toward a goal, coupled with a runner's confidence of completing that goal and the hope of a race well run.

Hebrews 10:36 urges us believers to practice *patient endurance* as we do God's will then wait to receive all that God has promised. To do so quietly while unrelentingly working toward our goal. We can do that by expecting God to move according to His timing. To anticipate receiving all He has promised as we do His will. That means to get busy, to endure, and endeavor to do God's work where we are, with the unique abilities and passions with which He's gifted us, using them to love God and others (Mark 12:30–31).

Prayer Prompt:

How do you patiently endure as you wait for God's promise? Ask God to keep you busy for the kingdom.

....

....

....

....

....

....

....

....

....

....

....

....

....

....

....

Father, I admit I struggle with patience. My head knows Your timing is perfect, but my selfish heart wants everything You've promised NOW. Give me good work to do as I strive toward the goal. Amen.

Forward Thinkers

All these people were still living by faith when they died.
They did not receive the things promised; they only saw
them and welcomed them from a distance, admitting
that they were foreigners and strangers on earth.

HEBREWS 11:13 NIV

Each family tree has its own unique story, but every family has a heritage passed down from one generation to the next.

The heritage of faith in God's family tree is a line that goes back to Creation. From Adam and Eve in the Garden through the single righteous family of Noah to Abraham and Sarah, Isaac and Jacob, Hebrews 11:13 tells us these individuals did not receive the promised salvation while on earth, but they never lost hope that God would provide a way for them to be with Him.

If you're going through a difficult time, God's promises may seem far away. Don't give up! Take courage from these heroes of faith who lived and died without seeing the reward of their belief on earth but who are now at home in God's presence. Ask God to show you what He has promised from afar—even a glimpse of what's to come can help you stand strong.

Prayer Prompt:

What can you do to keep God's promise alive in your heart? Pray for a renewal of that promise so you don't grow weary.

....

....

....

....

....

....

....

....

....

....

....

....

....

....

....

God, I know this place is not my home, and I'm trying to keep that in perspective as I grow more and more homesick to be with You. Thank You for the heritage of faith in Your family tree. I am blessed to be a part of it. Amen.

Something Better

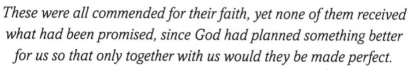

These were all commended for their faith, yet none of them received what had been promised, since God had planned something better for us so that only together with us would they be made perfect.
HEBREWS 11:39–40 NIV

. . . .

God created us for community. Jesus established His church to be individuals who make up one unit. And the apostle Paul described the church as a single body with many parts (1 Corinthians 12), each part dependent on the other parts to be whole. We often think about this passage in the context of our own church congregations or believers all over the planet, but it's bigger than that.

Hebrews 11:39–40 explains that God gives unity among believers throughout history. All of God's children—since day one of Creation—will be glorified together. Not only are we one in the body of Christ with living believers, but we are also one with all those who ever lived. It takes all of us along with Jesus to be perfect in Him.

Your faith stands on the shoulders of history. You are counted alongside the names of the Hebrews 11 faith hall of fame, the faithful of today, and the generations of believers to arrive before Christ's return.

Prayer Prompt:

How can you contribute to the body of Christ to create community? Ask God to give you a heart for others in His community.

....

....

....

....

....

....

....

....

....

....

....

....

....

....

....

....

*God, I am thankful to be a part of the body
of Christ. Give me a heart for Your community.
May I never take my role for granted. Amen.*

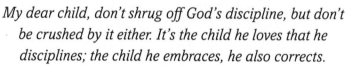

A Wake-Up Call

My dear child, don't shrug off God's discipline, but don't be crushed by it either. It's the child he loves that he disciplines; the child he embraces, he also corrects.

HEBREWS 12:5–6 MSG

. . . .

From the time a child is old enough to understand right and wrong, a loving parent will correct her wayward behavior. Although it's uncomfortable for parent and child alike, the cost of *not* disciplining is far greater than the parent doling out and the child enduring correction.

As adults, we probably don't receive the same kind of discipline from our parents or other authority figures on a regular basis. But no matter how old we are, God *does* discipline us when we're outside of His perfect plan for our lives.

Hebrews urges us to listen to God's correction, accept it, adjust, and understand that we're being corrected because He loves us and wants the best for us. Hebrews 12:11 (NLT) provides a dose of reality followed by a great promise: "No discipline is enjoyable while it is happening—it's painful! But afterward there will be a peaceful harvest of right living for those who are trained in this way."

Be willing to endure God's discipline, knowing a peaceful harvest of right living will follow. Remember, God's way is always the best way.

Prayer Prompt:

How do you feel about God's correction? When you pray, ask Him to show you His love through His correction.

....

....

....

....

....

....

....

....

....

....

....

....

....

....

....

....

Good Father, please help me understand that Your discipline is guiding me back to Your good and righteous path for my life. Despite my actions, that's the path I want to be on. Amen.

Life's a Garden

Work at living in peace with everyone, and work at living a holy life. . . . Watch out that no poisonous root of bitterness grows up to trouble you, corrupting many.
HEBREWS 12:14–15 NLT

. . . .

Gardeners learn it's easier to pull up small weeds before the roots have a chance to develop, so they're on constant watch for the beginnings of weeds to pull and destroy. It's hard work, but the rewards of a bountiful harvest are worth it.

Hebrews describes bitterness in a relationship as a "poisonous root"—a slow-growing weed. It starts out as nothing: a little annoyance or an unintentional slight. But if we're not on guard, a seed of bitterness can find a crack in our hearts, where it burrows in and sprouts.

If you find yourself in a state of annoyance with someone, if you're rolling your eyes in her presence, if you find yourself avoiding her, check your heart. Has a bitter root sprouted? Get out the gardening gloves and pull and dig to remove and destroy that root!

A right relationship with God leads to right relationships with others. Although we will not always feel loving toward all other believers, we must pursue peace as we become more like Jesus.

Prayer Prompt:

How can you keep bitterness from taking root in your heart? Ask God to help you do some weeding, and replace the bitterness with peace.

....

....

....

....

....

....

....

....

....

....

....

....

....

....

....

....

....

....

God, I know what it feels like when a bitter root has developed in my heart—and I choose peace! Show me where I need to dig. Amen.

Bring It On

So we say with confidence, "The Lord is my helper;
I will not be afraid. What can mere mortals do to me?"
HEBREWS 13:6 NIV

. . . .

The cares, worries, challenges, and frustrations of dealing with difficult people have an uncanny way of distracting us from the fact that if we're in God's family, we've *already* triumphed over every challenge someone can throw at us. We have nothing to fear. We're saved. We are victorious. God wins!

But life happens—twenty-four hours a day, seven days a week. Seasons of discouragement, setbacks, and disappointments shift our focus away from the truth of our situation. People fail us; some may even attack our faith. Instead of looking to the light, we turn around, distracted by the isolating darkness that sets fear in our hearts.

Before these times come (and they come for us all), arm yourself with this mighty reminder from Hebrews 13:6 (a.k.a. Psalm 118:6). Make it your heart's battle cry in the face of every difficult person: "God is my confidence! I will not fear because He is *already* helping me. Do your worst, world, because He is bigger!"

Believe it, sister. He's got your back—now live like it!

Prayer Prompt:

What is worrying you and pulling you down today? Ask the Father to be your helper and make you victorious in battle.

Father, I need Your help today. My spirit is beat up by the constant barrage of challenges from difficult people. Restore my spirit of power, love, and mental strength that You have promised me (2 Timothy 1:7).

A Prized Possession

He chose to give birth to us by giving us his true word.
And we, out of all creation, became his prized possession.
JAMES 1:18 NLT

Out of everything God created—the majestic expanse of sky, the most breathtaking mountain range, the bird with the most exotically beautiful plumage, the mysterious waters of the deep—James 1:18 tells us that we humans are His most prized possession.

When God conceived of Adam and Eve in the Garden of Eden, He already knew they would be different than the other living beings He'd designed. He created this man and woman in His own image (Genesis 1:27), beautifully complex and wondrously crafted. His relationship with the first humans was personal and intimate. God spent time with them in the Garden and had audible conversations with them. If only they hadn't messed everything up by sinning, causing a separation between God and all of humanity.

But before Creation, when God wrote His plan for us, He already knew the separation was coming. And He chose to send His true Word—His only Son, Jesus Christ, to make a way for Him to reclaim us and draw us into His presence for all eternity.

You are His prized possession, daughter of God! Claim that promise today and every day!

Prayer Prompt:

How does it feel to be a prized possession of God? Spend time with Him, and claim your position as His daughter.

....

....

....

....

....

....

....

....

....

....

....

....

....

....

....

....

....

....

Creator God, when I'm feeling down on myself,
keep reminding me what I mean to You. Amen.

Faith Plus Action

Now someone may argue, "Some people have faith; others have good deeds." But I say, "How can you show me your faith if you don't have good deeds? I will show you my faith by my good deeds."
JAMES 2:18 NLT

Imagine your first appointment with a dentist. After introducing herself and motioning to her diploma on the wall, she pulls out a tray of dental implements and tells you what each one does. Then she shakes your hand, wishes you well, and tells you to pay the receptionist on the way out.

If she never actually *did* any work on your teeth, is she really a dentist?

If we never display good works in our lives, are we really Christians?

While scripture clearly tells us that our good deeds cannot earn salvation (Ephesians 2:8–9), James tells us that true faith *always* results in a changed life and good deeds.

James uses Abraham to make his point: "Don't you remember that our ancestor Abraham was shown to be right with God by his actions when he offered his son Isaac on the altar? You see, his faith and his actions worked together. His actions made his faith complete" (James 2:21–22 NLT).

Is your faith resulting in actions? If you're not sure, find a trusted Christian friend who is busy doing God's work, and jump in!

Prayer Prompt:

What actions in your life point to your faith? Ask Jesus to show you how to have actions that make your faith complete.

Jesus, I want an action-packed faith that You can use to do big things. I will not be idle. Amen.

Extreme Transformation: Spiritual Edition

"Speak a prophetic message and say, 'This is what the Sovereign LORD says: Come, O breath, from the four winds! Breathe into these dead bodies so they may live again.'"
EZEKIEL 37:9 NLT

. . . .

Everyone loves a transformation—especially an *extreme* transformation. Pounds lost amount to a triple-digit number; a modest, dumpy house morphs into an immaculate model home; long, wavy hair becomes a perky straight bob.

Ezekiel's vision in chapter 37 illustrates an extreme transformation that held a promise for God's people yesterday and for us today. The dry bones are a picture of the Jews in captivity—scattered and spiritually dead. At the time of the vision, Ezekiel felt he *was* speaking to the dead as he preached to the exiles, because they rarely responded to his message. But those bones responded! And just as God brought life to the long-dead bones, He would bring life again to His spiritually dead people.

If you've been a Christian for a while, you've probably experienced some seasons of being spiritually alive and others on spiritual life support. If God can take long-dead, dried-up, crusty bones and transform them into living, breathing people, take hope in the fact that He *can* and *will* bring your faith back from the dead. Ask Him to start that extreme transformation *now*!

Prayer Prompt:

What dead bones are rattling around in your life? Tell God you're ready for Him to breathe new life into those bones.

....

....

....

....

....

....

....

....

....

....

....

....

....

....

....

....

....

....

....

God, I'm ready for a change. Breathe new life into me so I may live fully in You again! Amen.

Zip It

Watch your words and hold your tongue;
you'll save yourself a lot of grief.
PROVERBS 21:23 MSG

· ·

If ever there's a day to wear stretchy pants, it's on Thanksgiving. And if you're spending the holiday with family, you might think about packing a pair of boxing gloves too. We all love our families, but sometimes they bring out the worst in us.

No matter your Turkey Day scenario—immediate family or in-laws, functional or dysfunctional—it's likely there's some situation that you'll need to navigate carefully. The inevitable political debate. The conflicting social stances. The clashing worldviews. The dating or marriage advice. The array of child-rearing suggestions. The judgment of wearing stretchy pants to a family event.

If those moments of insanity pop up between turkey and pie, today might just be the day to adopt the advice of Proverbs 21:23: keep your mouth shut.

Need more convincing? Consider James 4:11 (NLT): "Don't speak evil against each other, dear brothers and sisters. If you criticize and judge each other, then you are criticizing and judging God's law. But your job is to obey the law, not to judge whether it applies to you."

If you're entering a volatile situation today, know that you aren't called to fix the problem. God will be glorified in the words you speak in love. Ask Him to guard your heart and tongue today.

Prayer Prompt:

Who pushes your buttons and makes you see red? Ask Jesus to give you a peaceful spirit in spite of the button pushers.

....

....

....

....

....

....

....

....

....

....

....

....

....

....

....

....

Father, today as we celebrate, give me the wisdom to know when to speak and when to stay quiet. Amen.

(Don't) Fake It Till You Make It

The wicked bluff their way through,
but the virtuous think before they act.

PROVERBS 21:29 NLT

. . . .

Do you know anyone who is really good at baloney? Not completely dissimilar to actual bologna, the lunch box sandwich meat made up of leftover scraps, verbal baloney is the made-up kind of nonsense that consists of half-truths and bluffs, often used to get the upper hand in a situation or to make the speaker seem smarter than someone else.

Proverbs 21:29 tells us it's the wicked who baloney their way through life, unprepared for the challenges that inevitably come. But the virtuous *think* before they *act*.

So on a practical level, how can we be more virtuous and less baloneyous? First, follow the wisdom of Proverbs. Take a breath. Think. Be transparent and admit when you *don't* have an answer or know what to do, and be willing to think and pray on it. Another way to stay on the virtuous track is to imprint God's Word on your heart and mind. Then if you're caught unprepared in a challenging situation or conversation, His truth is more likely to be on the tip of the tongue, ready to be offered in love.

Prayer Prompt:

Which is more important, speaking your mind or pleasing Jesus? Ask Him to show you when to speak and when to listen.

Jesus, I know I'm the kind of person who wants to always have an answer, who always knows what to do. But I also admit that isn't always the case. Give me patience to act and react virtuously in a way that honors You always.

Handpicked

God the Father knew you and chose you long ago, and his
Spirit has made you holy. As a result, you have obeyed him
and have been cleansed by the blood of Jesus Christ.

1 PETER 1:2 NLT

No matter how beautiful, accomplished, athletic, smart, capable, creative, or loving we might be, we've all experienced rejection: didn't get the job; didn't make the team; didn't receive the scholarship; didn't get asked to the dance; didn't get the leadership appointment; didn't get a second date; got cheated on; never received an invitation; didn't make first chair. . . .

Try as we might to pretend we don't care when we're not chosen, rejection hurts. A lot. Young or old, green or experienced, simple or sophisticated, rejection makes us question our worth and wonder why we even try.

Before Jesus came, only the nation of Israel could claim to be God's chosen people. But because of Christ, all believers—Jews and Gentiles—belong to God. Here's a beautiful truth in scripture, sister: When you were born, God had already chosen and accepted you. Your salvation and security rest in the free and merciful choice of your almighty God, and nothing can take away His love for those who believe in Him (Romans 8:38–39).

Prayer Prompt:

How do you handle rejection when it comes? As you pray, remember that God had plans for you long ago. Rejection isn't the end with God.

_Father, You chose me first, but I choose You now
and forever. Thank You for wanting me even
if others reject me. You hold my heart,
God. I trust You with it. Amen._

Get Me Off This Slip 'n' Slide

Don't slip back into your old ways of living to satisfy your own desires. You didn't know any better then. But now you must be holy in everything you do, just as God who chose you is holy.

1 Peter 1:14–15 NLT

Black ice is invisible. You don't even realize it's there until you're on your back, staring up at the sky, wondering what happened. Old temptations and pitfalls from your old life can make you lose your footing in the same way, tripping you up, pulling you back to your old ways of thinking and acting. The Christianese term for that is *backsliding*.

But once we're made new in Christ, we're to be holy like our heavenly Father. Holiness means being totally devoted to God, set aside for His special use and set apart from sin and its influence. Our priorities must be the same as His.

Sounds hard, right?

The truth is, you can't become holy on your own power. Don't use the excuse that you can't help slip-sliding back into sin. God gives you His Holy Spirit to help you overcome temptation. So call on God's power and Spirit to put you on stable footing. He is faithful and will deliver you every day!

Prayer Prompt:

What old desire rears its ugly head when you least expect it? Pray and ask God to empower you to keep you from backsliding into that place.

....

....

....

....

....

....

....

....

....

....

....

....

....

....

....

....

....

Father, I don't want to return to my old ways.
Give me the power to resist my evil desire.
Bring friends into my life who'll reach out
a hand to keep me from sliding. Amen.

Living Stones

*You are coming to Christ, who is the living cornerstone
of God's temple. He was rejected by people, but he was
chosen by God for great honor. And you are living stones
that God is building into his spiritual temple.*

1 PETER 2:4–5 NLT

Stonemasonry is more than simply stacking rocks. To become a master stonemason takes years of training to build beautiful, structurally sound walls that stand the test of time. A mason carefully chooses each stone for its shape, size, and composition, and he fits them as meticulously as pieces in a jigsaw puzzle.

Peter describes the church as a living, spiritual house, with Christ as the foundation, cornerstone, and the stonemason and each believer as a stone. This picture, just like Paul's description of the church as a body in Ephesians 4:15–16, emphasizes the importance of community. Just as one stone does not make a temple, one bone does not make a body. Peter and Paul agree: we need each other.

In our individualistic society, it is easy to forget our interdependence with other Christians. But when God calls us to a task, He is also calling others to work with us. If we work together, God can exponentially multiply our efforts.

So look for those people who are passionately pursuing God. Then join them.

Prayer Prompt:

If you're an introvert, how can you step out and be a part of community? Ask Jesus to bring people into your life that will draw you out.

....

....

....

....

....

....

....

....

....

....

....

....

....

....

....

....

Jesus, thank You for surrounding me with Your beautiful, living stones. Bring us together in unity to be set apart as God's holy temple. Amen.

Fit for a King

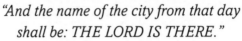

*"And the name of the city from that day
shall be: THE LORD IS THERE."*
EZEKIEL 48:35 NKJV

Jesus can be found throughout the scriptures if we look for Him. Jesus' title Emmanuel, "God with Us" (Matthew 1:23), coincides with the name given to the city in Ezekiel: "The Lord Is There." Just as Israel's restoration and healing foretold by Ezekiel would be accomplished through God's presence, we are also brought transformation through His dwelling with us.

When we call on Jesus' name for salvation, God's Spirit comes to make His home in us. Once there, He isn't content that we stay the way He found us. In *Mere Christianity*, C. S. Lewis compares God's work in us to a house being renovated: we know God plans to make a home out of our run-down mess—and assume it'll be a modest cottage with working plumbing and a sturdy roof. But then He keeps going, knocking down walls to add new floors and towers. Then we realize He's making a *mansion* out of us, a dwelling that reflects His beauty and truth, a palace fit for a king—Himself.

This Christmas, let Jesus' presence within you strengthen you for whatever "renovation" work He has under way. He has grander plans for you than you can ask or imagine (Ephesians 3:20); you can be certain He will be with you every step of the way.

Prayer Prompt:

In what ways can you allow God to renovate you? In prayer, surrender your life (house) to Him, and let the renovation begin.

....

....

....

....

....

....

....

....

....

....

....

....

....

....

....

....

....

....

....

....

Thank You, Emmanuel, for Your nearness.
I welcome Your work to make me more like You!

Revealer of Hidden Things

"Praise be to the name of God for ever and ever; wisdom and power are his. . . . He gives wisdom to the wise and knowledge to the discerning. He reveals deep and hidden things."

DANIEL 2:20–22 NIV

. . . .

After God revealed King Nebuchadnezzar's dream, saving the lives of Daniel, his friends, and the other wise men of the court, Daniel praised Him as the source of all wisdom.

God desires us to be wise people, and His scripture testifies to that. In Proverbs 23:15–16 (NIV), the father says he will be glad when his son's "lips speak what is right," showing knowledge of the truth. Jesus' disciple Peter instructs his readers to "always be prepared to give an answer to everyone who asks you to give the reason for the hope that you have" and to do so "with gentleness and respect" (1 Peter 3:15 NIV), signaling the need for relational wisdom.

No matter our IQ or EQ, we all have room to grow in wisdom. How do you "wise up," able to answer kings, family, and neighbors in all things gently and respectfully? By humbly and expectantly asking the revealer of hidden things: seeking Him through His Word and prayer, by His Holy Spirit's power. Whatever puzzler you may face today, God can and will reveal the wisdom you need going forward.

Prayer Prompt:

What puzzle are you trying to solve? As you pray, ask God for wisdom so you can see the pieces fit together.

....

....

....

....

....

....

....

....

....

....

....

....

....

....

....

....

....

....

....

Father, I open the eyes and ears of my heart expectantly to receive the wisdom You have for me today.

Hidden in the Background

She who is in Babylon, elect together with you,
greets you; and so does Mark my son.
1 PETER 5:13 NKJV

Wrapping up his letter, Peter adds this "hello" from Mark, a.k.a. John Mark. What isn't apparent here, though, is Mark's personal transformation.

Mark had accompanied Paul on one of his missionary journeys but had abandoned the work and gone back to Jerusalem (Acts 13:13). This led to Paul and Barnabas arguing so strongly over him that they split their missionary duo (Acts 15:38–39), Barnabas taking Mark with him. Though we don't see the growth process, Peter's words above and Paul's later comments show the change in Mark: "With Mark the cousin of Barnabas (about whom you received instructions: if he comes to you, welcome him). . . . These are my only fellow workers for the kingdom of God who are of the circumcision; they have proved to be a comfort to me" (Colossians 4:10–11). Paul went from refusing to work with Mark to his being "a comfort"!

Perhaps the phrase *God's work* makes you think of scripture's big miracles. But God labors quietly in the background too, transforming your day-to-day life, restoring relationships, and helping you serve in a God-pleasing way. Be encouraged: like Mark, no child of God is too far in the "background" to escape His notice and loving care.

Prayer Prompt:

What transformation would you like to see in your life? In prayer, express your wishes to Jesus and ask Him for change.

....

....

....

....

....

....

....

....

....

....

....

....

....

....

....

....

....

....

....

....

....

....

Jesus, thank You for Your transforming work in me and my brothers and sisters. I will rejoice in Your "hidden" work!

Watch Out for Pride!

*Now I, Nebuchadnezzar, praise and extol and honor the King
of heaven, all of whose works are truth, and His ways justice.
And those who walk in pride He is able to put down.*
DANIEL 4:37 NKJV

. . . .

Nebuchadnezzar, king of Babylon, had been sent a disturbing dream by God, which Daniel interpreted would be the king's fate—removal from the throne and being given "the heart of a beast" (Daniel 4:16 NKJV)—if he did not repent. The prophet urged Nebuchadnezzar to pursue righteousness, particularly through showing mercy to the poor, so that the king's prosperity would be lengthened (Daniel 4:27).

God desired that Nebuchadnezzar acknowledge that He is the Most High, the true originator of Babylon's prosperity. But when the unrepentant king pridefully took credit (Daniel 4:30), God instantly transformed his circumstances from high to low. Nebuchadnezzar ate grass and lived like a wild animal for seven years, until he learned humility and praised God.

The scriptures tell us that God disciplines those He loves. If God lavished such correction on Nebuchadnezzar, helping this pagan king change his ways so he would proclaim God's greatness, how much more should we, His children, expect His guiding hand in our lives? Let's be open to His correction and listen to His Word *before* pride makes us take a tumble.

Prayer Prompt:

What correction might you need? As you pray, ask God to show you any pride in your life that might need to be removed.

....

....

....

....

....

....

....

....

....

....

....

....

....

....

....

....

....

....

....

....

*Father, discipline hurts, but Yours is done in love,
with an intent to heal and restore. Root out
pride in my heart; let me boast only in You.*

Comfort Food

*My son, eat honey, for it is good, yes, the honey from the comb is
sweet to your taste; know that wisdom is thus for your soul; if you
find it, then there will be a future, and your hope will not be cut off.*
PROVERBS 24:13–14 NASB

. . . .

Think of your favorite sweet treat. It might be gooey chocolate brownies
that chase away the blues or a favorite coffee concoction that helps you
get going in the morning. Comfort foods delight not only our taste buds
but lift our spirits, reminding us of home, of better days, of the company
of friends.

The speaker here in Proverbs 24 instructs his son to nurture his heart
as well as his body with sweetness—with the taste of *wisdom*. Wisdom
nourishes and brightens the soul—it will guide a woman forward, giving
her confidence and a hopeful outlook on her future. For the woman who
savors wisdom in her heart is spending time with its author, her Savior
who has promised to care for her.

Find spiritual "comfort food" for both the trying days and the happy
ones: sing the truth in hymns; recite those verses whose savor provides
the pick-me-up you need. Fill your heart with your Savior's sweetness—
He will give you hope for the time to come.

Prayer Prompt:

What comfort food does your spirit need? In prayer, ask Jesus to fill your spirit with His spiritual comfort food.

....

....

....

....

....

....

....

....

....

....

....

....

....

....

....

....

....

....

Jesus, thank You for the comfort You've provided in Your Word. Help me to taste its sweetness, to be nourished by it, no matter what part I am reading.

How the Story Ends

"I kept looking in the night visions, and behold, with the clouds of heaven one like a Son of Man was coming. . . . And to Him was given dominion, glory and a kingdom, that all the peoples. . .might serve Him. His dominion is an everlasting dominion which will not pass away; and His kingdom is one which will not be destroyed."

DANIEL 7:13–14 NASB

. . . .

In the season of Advent, as we look back on Christ's incarnation and saving work, we can simultaneously look forward to when He will come again. In the future both Daniel and Peter (2 Peter 3) describe, Christ will return to cast down His enemies, restore the world, and reign forever in His kingdom that "will not be destroyed."

This truth gives us hope to go on amid personal- and planet-level suffering: washed clean by Christ, we anticipate His transforming our world from a sin-struck place to one of fullness and wholeness forever (2 Peter 3:13). Since we know how the story ends, let's work toward it, practicing "holy conduct and godliness," being "diligent to be found by Him in peace, spotless and blameless" (2 Peter 3:11, 14). We have nothing to lose for we know who ultimately wins.

Prayer Prompt:

What disturbs you about the world around you? As you pray, focus on Jesus and the promise of His coming, knowing He is able to keep you.

....

....

....

....

....

....

....

....

....

....

....

....

....

....

....

....

Jesus, I trust Your promise of completing the work You started in this world and in me. Help me not despair when the brokenness of this earth glares in and around me. Help me lift my gaze to You, the victorious, eternal King.

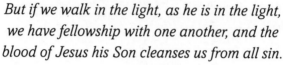

Back to Basics

But if we walk in the light, as he is in the light,
we have fellowship with one another, and the
blood of Jesus his Son cleanses us from all sin.

1 JOHN 1:7 ESV

. . . .

If you've ever played an instrument or sport, you know how crucial the basics are—scales, drills, and warm-ups form the bedrock of your skills. John also knew the importance of the basics. To combat false teaching plaguing the church, the apostle John wrote this first letter to reiterate the foundational truths about the gospel—the reality of Jesus' coming to earth and the signs of faith.

Where false teachers had been claiming "secret knowledge," available only to those who joined their group, John affirmed the foundational truths: "That which was from the beginning," "the message we have heard from him and proclaim to you" (1 John 1:1, 5)—nothing new, nothing requiring a special membership, just embracing God's merciful gift of forgiveness through His Son's sacrifice.

Working so hard to grow in our faith, sometimes we can forget our foundation—that all we are and have come from Jesus. Are there places in your faith walk that would benefit from your getting back to the basics? Ask Jesus to lead you there. No matter where you are, His grace and desire to see you thrive in Him remain the same.

Prayer Prompt:

What basic truths do you need to reaffirm in your life? As you pray, ask Jesus to strengthen you in those basic truths.

....

....

....

....

....

....

....

....

....

....

....

....

....

....

....

....

....

Dear Jesus, show me where I need Your strength
and grace to shore up my foundation.

Wordsmiths

*A word fitly spoken is like apples of gold in a
setting of silver. Like a gold ring or an ornament
of gold is a wise reprover to a listening ear.*
PROVERBS 25:11–12 ESV

. . . .

No matter your level of creativity, you have the opportunity to be an artist—with your words! The writer of Proverbs 25 compares "a word fitly spoken" with art of the highest craftsmanship: golden apples. Reminiscent of the pomegranates and lilies of the temple's bronze pillars (1 Kings 7:19–20), golden apples clasped by silver delight the eye and touch and display the artisan's imaginative skill. Just as an artist considers her audience members so her work will move them to a new understanding, hope, or appreciation, we can take similar care with our words, fine-tuning them before they reach others.

A rebuke—a word meant to guide another back into God's ways—received is also precious. It beautifies the listener's life like a sparkling "ornament" in her ear. While its reception affects its beauty, the one who gives the rebuke should be sure to fashion it lovingly and carefully.

Because our hearers likely carry our "works of art" with them for much longer than we assume, we should take our responsibility as "wordsmiths" seriously. Thankfully, the Spirit helps us develop this artistry of our tongues, teaching us as we abide in Jesus (1 John 2:27).

Prayer Prompt:

What are some ways you can use your words to bless others? In prayer, ask the Holy Spirit to give you words to encourage others.

....

....

....

....

....

....

....

....

....

....

....

....

....

....

....

....

....

....

*Holy Spirit, teach me to consider my words carefully,
even in the smallest matters, to show Your love to others.*

Like He Is

"And those who are wise shall shine like the brightness of the sky above; and those who turn many to righteousness, like the stars forever and ever."
DANIEL 12:3 ESV

Daniel and 1 John look toward the future—Daniel to the time when "everyone whose name shall be found written in the book" would be delivered (Daniel 12:1 ESV), John to our hope of being like Christ: "We know that when he appears we shall be like him, because we shall see him as he is" (1 John 3:2 ESV). We live in this expectation, that we will be complete when we see Jesus face-to-face (1 John 3:3).

But that hope issues a challenge: How can we be more like Christ now? Today's verse from Daniel offers an answer: by being wise and turning many to righteousness. After all, Jesus' main task in His work before the cross was loving others and sharing the good news of the kingdom—that God had restoration for all who knew their brokenness and came to Him.

Until our image bearing is restored to full brightness like dazzling stars, let's work as Jesus did, following God's good commands to love others and to share His good news, knowing Jesus will help us do both.

Prayer Prompt:

How can you be more like Christ? When you pray, ask Jesus to make you more like Him so you can influence others.

....

....

....

....

....

....

....

....

....

....

....

....

....

....

*Jesus, thank You for Your promise and the hope
I have of being like You. I want to lead others
to You—give me wisdom, opportunity, and
grace to live and share Your gospel well.*

Love Himself

*The L*ORD* said to me, "Go, show your love to your wife again,*
though she is loved by another man and is an adulteress.
*Love her as the L*ORD* loves the Israelites, though they turn*
to other gods and love the sacred raisin cakes."

HOSEA 3:1 NIV

The prophet Hosea offers a beautiful insight into God's love. In chapter 3, God instructs Hosea to go and buy back his adulterous wife who, like Israel with the Lord, had been seeking her good from others rather than her husband. Hosea would have been completely within his legal rights to divorce Gomer. But Hosea obeyed the Lord's command—his marriage a picture of the Lord taking Israel back and restoring her, faithful to His covenant promises despite her unfaithfulness.

God's Love came down to us in the incarnation, lived among humanity in poverty, and paid the redemption price to save His people. Christ beckons, welcomes us home from our wilderness wanderings, from the "adulteries"—little idolatries—we may not even realize we hold.

Let Love Himself call you away from the things that you are tempted to believe will fulfill you—success, family, other good goals—to find your fullness in Him.

Prayer Prompt:

Where are you looking for fulfillment in life? In prayer, confess anything that may cause you to stray, and ask Jesus for more of Him.

Jesus, where in my heart do I go looking for good from others besides You? Where in my holiday stress am I holding on to something more than You? Thank You that Your love can always reach me, but move me to confess when I feel my heart straying.

Knowing Him

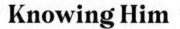

We know also that the Son of God has come and has given us understanding, so that we may know him who is true. And we are in him who is true by being in his Son Jesus Christ. He is the true God and eternal life.

1 JOHN 5:20 NIV

John highlights two things as important in our relationship with God: obedience to Him and knowledge of Him. The Lord's desire for relationship with His people—their love shown through heart-deep obedience—is seen in Hosea as well: The Lord said, "I desire mercy and not sacrifice, and the knowledge of God more than burnt offerings" (Hosea 6:6 NKJV). More than their possessions, God wanted Israel's affection and reverence. With Israel held back by sin, though, the relationship was stunted.

Relationships can't thrive without intentional effort. Humanly speaking, it would be like having a friend who gives presents on birthdays or holidays, but whom you'd hardly hear from otherwise. How can a friendship grow without time spent together or shared memories? It would quickly fade, even with pleasantries exchanged from time to time.

Jesus gave us the gift of access to the Father, of communing in spirit and in truth. Even in this busy month, aim to go deeper in your friendship with God, for knowing Him "who is true" gives you new life.

Prayer Prompt:

Are you intentionally spending time with Jesus or just coasting? Pray for a closer, deeper walk with Christ, living intentionally for Him.

....

....

....

....

....

....

....

....

....

....

....

....

....

....

....

....

....

....

....

*Jesus, my life may be busy, but my heart feels
its deep need of You and fellowship with You.
Please keep revealing Yourself to me.*

DAY 346

Looking to the Harvest

*Sow righteousness, reap love. It's time to till the
ready earth, it's time to dig in with GOD, until he
arrives with righteousness ripe for harvest.*
HOSEA 10:12 MSG

. . . .

In Hosea 10, Israel is compared to a "heifer" who "loved to thresh"
(v. 11 MSG)—to prepare harvested grain. But Israel had "plowed wicked
ways, [and] reaped a crop of evil" (v. 13 MSG) rather than righteousness.
Though Israel had been enjoying the harvest of good things, the nation
had been getting them through idolatry and alliances with other nations, not by trusting God. For this, the Lord would "put a yoke on her"
and make Israel "break up the ground" (v. 11 NIV). So God would turn
Israel back to Himself through toil, restoring her by teaching her again
to trust Him.

While we cannot cultivate righteousness in our own strength, we can
help God's growing work within us. Each of the actions we choose—like
adding or not adding fuel to the fire of gossip or fanning or not fanning
the flames of contention (Proverbs 26:20–21)—will either push us away
from or pull us toward God.

In the "field" of your heart today, with Christ's help, you can deter-
mine to do your best to plow in righteousness and sow the seeds of love
moment by moment, knowing God will bring in the harvest!

Prayer Prompt:

What are you sowing today? As you pray, ask God to help you plant seeds of righteousness and reap His love.

....

....

....

....

....

....

....

....

....

....

....

....

....

....

....

....

God, till the soil and pull the weeds so my heart can be good, productive ground where Your love grows bountifully.

More Than Just "Being Nice"

Better is open rebuke than hidden love. Wounds from a friend can be trusted, but an enemy multiplies kisses.

PROVERBS 27:5–6 NIV

. . . .

Thinking about confronting loved ones about sin can make our mouths go desert dry and send our heart rates into overdrive. For fear of ruining the relationship, we may find it easier to just "be nice" and say nothing.

But is it really "nice"? Proverbs 26:23–28's chilling discussion on hidden hate describes a person who covers up her malice toward another with "charming speech" and flattery and her hatred with lies. While we wouldn't consider our silence about another's sin as being intentionally malicious, refusing to speak the truth in love does leave a friend to her own devices, possibly to her harm.

On the other hand, the joke goes that "a good friend stabs you in the front." Think back to a time when someone spoke lovingly into your life. Though she had "wounded" you, were you refreshed by the pleasantness of your friend's "heartfelt advice" (Proverbs 27:9 NIV)? If so, it was because you *knew* she just wanted to see you flourish.

Loving confrontation can be scary, but it's necessary to spur each other on in our faith journey. How can you be open to correction or correcting in love this holiday season?

Prayer Prompt:

Who do you need to confront about their lifestyle? Ask the Lord to show you how to speak loving words to them.

....

....

....

....

....

....

....

....

....

....

....

....

....

....

....

....

Lord, when You prompt me to "wound" a friend with rebuke or counsel, help me do it out of love, with gentleness, rather than being tempted to stay quiet out of "niceness."

Mercy Will Be There

*But you, beloved, building yourselves up on your most holy faith,
praying in the Holy Spirit, keep yourselves in the love of God,
looking for the mercy of our Lord Jesus Christ unto eternal life.*
JUDE 20–21 NKJV

· ·

Do you have a lot on your mind today—worries about what's coming in the future? Take encouragement from Jude. In his letter, after his warnings to readers about apostate teachers in the church, Jude encouraged his readers to persevere in the faith despite their great trouble. He instructed them to follow this pattern: turning away from your "mere natural instincts" (v. 19 NIV), stop focusing on yourselves and look toward God, from whom comes your good; look for Christ's mercy actively and expectantly, for He will keep you eternally.

No matter the danger you see ahead or the worst-case scenarios that leave you trembling, Christ's mercy will be there. The one who promised is faithful. Ask yourself: In your starkest imaginings, how could God's mercy show up? Then look for it—*expect* it—to show up in your life, doing so in the Spirit, submerging yourself in God's love, enriching your faith. And trust Him to be merciful to you as you strive toward the good.

Prayer Prompt:

Who or what are you focusing on today that causes you worry? In prayer, take it to Jesus, and trust Him to show mercy.

....

....

....

....

....

....

....

....

....

....

....

....

....

....

....

....

Jesus, Your goodness and mercy will follow hard after me all the days of my life, for You are good and perfectly faithful—when fear hits, help me to be looking for how Your mercy will show up.

Apocalyptic Prophecy

Behold, He is coming with clouds, and every eye will see Him, even they who pierced Him. And all the tribes of the earth will mourn because of Him. Even so, Amen.

REVELATION 1:7 NKJV

In today's readings, both Joel and John (the author of Revelation) point to the "latter days," when God will judge the nations and then restore the world. Their apocalyptic books contain difficult passages with intricate, often violent imagery, raising questions about exactly when these things will happen. But the prophets, calling their audiences to repentance, didn't write only messages of terrible events but included encouraging promises as well. In today's readings, we're reminded there will be deliverance for those who call on the name of the Lord (Joel 2:32), deliverance that comes through Jesus who "loved us and washed us from our sins in His own blood" (Revelation 1:5 NKJV). Though the day of judgment will be terrifying, God's justice will right all wrongs, and He will preserve those who love Him, for God is a place of shelter for His people (Joel 3:14–16).

Though reading Revelation and the prophets may not be your go-to scriptures during the Christmas season, you can use them as a special time of reflection, taking the admonitions and the promises of the prophets to heart as you seek to hold fast to Christ, your true reward.

Prayer Prompt:

Do scriptures about end time judgment scare you? Pray and ask God for understanding as you read, knowing He will care for you.

....

....

....

....

....

....

....

....

....

....

....

....

....

....

....

....

....

....

....

....

Father, as I spend time with the prophets' messages from You, help me be open to what You want to teach me.

Love the Poor

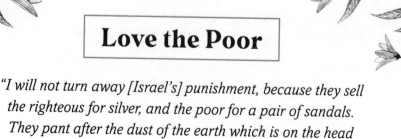

*"I will not turn away [Israel's] punishment, because they sell
the righteous for silver, and the poor for a pair of sandals.
They pant after the dust of the earth which is on the head
of the poor, and pervert the way of the humble."*

AMOS 2:6–7 NKJV

God's concern for the poor appears consistently in the minor prophets. Amos was sent to the northern kingdom, Israel, to address her disobedience. Among her sins, Israel had been gaining prosperity at the poor's expense. Incensed, God reminded Israel that all she had was from Him, starting with deliverance from her enemies (Amos 2:9–10). Though she still performed sacrifices, Israel's unkindness to the needy revealed that her worship was hollow (Amos 4:4–5). The people had become what Proverbs warns against: "Better is the poor who walks in his integrity than one perverse in his ways, though he be rich" (Proverbs 28:6 NKJV).

Revelation's message to the Ephesus church is as relevant for Amos's audience as it is for us: "Repent and do the *first works*" (Revelation 2:5 NKJV, emphasis added)—likely referring to the "greatest commandments," loving God with our whole being and our neighbors as ourselves.

Remember the poor, your hearts and hands open to their need, ready to defend them when unscrupulous policies or customs would seek to profit off them.

Prayer Prompt:

How can you be more compassionate to those less fortunate? Ask God to give you a heart to help others in need.

....

....

....

....

....

....

....

....

....

....

....

....

....

....

....

God, increasingly turn my heart to generosity;
all I have comes from You. Thank You for Jesus,
who became poor for all our sakes.

DAY 351

God Delights in Repentance

"Those whom I love, I reprove and discipline, so be zealous and repent. Behold, I stand at the door and knock. If anyone hears my voice and opens the door, I will come in to him and eat with him, and he with me."

Revelation 3:19–20 esv

The Laodicean church is famous for being "lukewarm"—neither on fire for God or totally cold. But what follows its rebuke is today's verse: God's promise that those He loves, He disciplines—He provides opportunity for repentance so that fellowship with Him can be restored.

Amos contains the same promise. Israel had committed "mighty sins": she afflicted the just, took bribes, and sent the needy away (Amos 5:12 nkjv). Tired of her empty religious festivals, God wanted to see justice "roll down like waters, and righteousness like an ever-flowing stream" (Amos 5:24 esv). But despite her sins and the discipline He'd already sent, God would heal Israel if she turned back to Him.

It's the same with us: we cannot go so far away from God that He will not hear our cry for forgiveness, our sincere return to Him and His ways. God keeps seeking us—knocking at the door of our hearts—and if we respond to His call, He will fellowship with us anew.

Prayer Prompt:

Do you consider your relationship with God hot, cold, or lukewarm? Pray honestly, knowing that God already knows and desires a closer walk with you.

....

....

....

....

....

....

....

....

....

....

....

....

....

....

....

....

Jesus, are You knocking on my heart today?
What doors have I kept shut from You?
Encourage me to open them and turn to back to You.

Sovereign in Earth and Heaven

The Lord GOD of hosts, he who touches the earth and it melts. . .and all of it rises like the Nile, and sinks again. . . who builds his upper chambers in the heavens and founds his vault upon the earth; who calls for the waters of the sea and pours them out. . .the LORD is his name.

AMOS 9:5–6 ESV

Amid Amos's message, he includes a description of God's power over the earth—His setting its foundations, the earth roiling at His touch, and the seas obeying all His commands.

Turning to Revelation 4 and 5, we get the awe-inspiring picture of the throne room of God in heaven. John saw not only the majesty of the throne encompassed by a rainbow and the sea of glass before it but also the four living creatures and the elders worshipping the one on the throne, He who is holy above all.

Heaven and earth testify to God's glory, and God is sovereign over them both. His gracious rule extends over you and *your* life as well. Where do you need to see God's awesome power, His grace, today? His hand is there, working where you cannot see; His love is already with you to hold you up. Praise God for His matchless grace!

Prayer Prompt:

What is your reaction when you are in God's presence? Ask Jesus to make you more aware of the awesomeness of God.

....

....

....

....

....

....

....

....

....

....

....

....

....

....

....

Jesus, Father, Holy Spirit, I long to grow in greater awe of Your power and love. Your holiness and glory are incomparable! Thank You for Your Word that paints pictures of them for me.

His Great Mercy

The LORD said, "You have had pity on the plant for which you have not labored, nor made it grow, which came up in a night and perished in a night. And should I not pity Nineveh, that great city, in which are more than one hundred and twenty thousand persons who cannot discern between their right hand and their left?"

JONAH 4:10–11 NKJV

. . . .

It's hard to watch enemies succeed, but even harder to desire their good—to show mercy. God's mercy is on display in the book of Jonah. When God sent the prophet (after a fishy delay) to preach to the famously cruel Assyrians in their capital city of Nineveh, Jonah actually *complained* about God's mercy toward them when they repented (Jonah 4:2); the prophet would've rather had Israel's longtime oppressors wiped off the map! But, teaching Jonah through the withered vine, God explained that His mercy extended to the Ninevites because of His great love for His whole creation.

One day we'll meet Ninevite believers in heaven; they may be before the throne now, saying: "Blessing and honor and glory and power be to Him who sits on the throne, and to the Lamb, forever and ever!" (Revelation 5:13 NKJV).

May you not be as reluctant as Jonah in sharing God's mercy with others, instead being eager to share His free grace with everyone, including your enemies.

Prayer Prompt:

Do you struggle to wish good for an enemy? Ask the Lord to give you a heart of love and grace toward them.

....

....

....

....

....

....

....

....

....

....

....

....

....

....

....

....

Lord, I am only Your child by grace. Soften my heart toward those to whom I struggle to show Your mercy.

Needed Rest

Nation will not take up sword against nation, nor will they train for war anymore. Everyone will sit under their own vine and under their own fig tree, and no one will make them afraid, for the LORD Almighty has spoken.

MICAH 4:3–4 NIV

Rest. That's something that there's just too little of around Christmas. The parties, presents, people—though enjoyable——can wear us out. You might read this peaceful vision of the Lord's future rule in Micah and heave a sigh, wishing this day were here.

Seemingly paradoxically, it is both here and not yet—we receive rest through Christ, for He has earned our righteousness through His death and resurrection; we don't have to hustle for worthiness (Hebrews 4:9–10). We enter His rest when we choose to trust Him—handing Him the things that deplete our energy, test our resilience, sap our hope. His shoulder is strong enough to carry it all (1 Peter 5:7).

Trust your Savior for the ability to work toward that day of perfect rest, intentionally setting aside space to receive nourishment from Him. Jesus will replenish your strength so you can follow in His footsteps, bringing in the kingdom by His will, seeking to share God's mercy with others so that they too can sigh in anticipation at the day of rest rather than tremble at the day of judgment.

Prayer Prompt:

What can you do to intentionally set aside time to receive strength from Jesus? In prayer, ask Him to direct your decisions during this busy season.

....

....

....

....

....

....

....

....

....

....

....

....

....

....

....

....

Jesus, thank You for Your sacrifice that secured my eternal rest. Strengthen me for Your mercy-sharing work.

Jesus Our Shepherd

"The Lamb on the Throne will shepherd them,
will lead them to spring waters of Life. And God
will wipe every last tear from their eyes."
REVELATION 7:17 MSG

. . . .

The image of the good shepherd was one of Jesus' favorite word pictures for Himself. How fitting that the news of His birth was first given to shepherds! This picture of Christ appears here in Revelation 7 in the promise given to those who had come through the tribulation, people from every tongue and tribe and nation. It also appears in Micah's prayer to the Lord: "Shepherd, O GOD, your people with your staff, your dear and precious flock" (Micah 7:14 MSG).

Using Jesus' names can direct your prayers in a new, powerful way. Consider how you can address Him as your Good Shepherd today, using Psalm 23's depiction to guide you:

Shepherd me, oh Jesus, for I am one of Your precious lambs. Lead
me to good pasture, where I can feed on Your Word and grow strong
in the faith. Show me anew Your springs of Living Water, that I may
be refreshed with You, for You are the Truth. Pull burrs from my coat
and thorns from my flesh; nurture me by Your hand. Protect me from
the wolves that would wound; show me Your strong staff is always
near. And, Lord Jesus, help me to be a willing sheep who hears only
Your voice calling amid the cacophony. Amen.

Prayer Prompt:

How do you address Jesus when you talk to Him? As you pray, call Him by name, knowing He recognizes your voice.

Jesus, my Good Shepherd, today I pray. . .

Encourage Your Appetite

*Where there is no vision [no redemptive revelation of God],
the people perish; but he who keeps the law [of God, which includes
that of man]—blessed (happy, fortunate, and enviable) is he.*
PROVERBS 29:18 AMPC

. . . .

When tough seasons come, being able to see the redemption in our situation (or trusting God to reveal it one day) can help us keep going. But what do we do when we're wrestling with the scriptures themselves?

In Revelation 10, an angel gives John a little scroll to eat, which is sweet at first but turns John's stomach sour afterward. Though the scroll's contents are not revealed, they may have to do with the final trumpet. Some commentators say John's eating of the little scroll is a picture of our reaction to God's Word: some things are hard to swallow—the devastation in Revelation, for instance. Yet what we know of God's character—His steadfast love and His promise to undo evil—is sweet.

Perhaps today you are feeling discouraged (a word to which *perish* in today's verse can also be translated), trying to see God's redemptive revelation in your scripture reading. But you need not be. Ask the Holy Spirit to reveal God's goodness to you, encouraging you as you wrestle with difficult passages. For God doesn't hide from those who have an appetite to know Him more.

Prayer Prompt:

What do you struggle with in your Bible reading? As you pray, ask the Holy Spirit to open your understanding and reveal God's truth to you.

....

....

....

....

....

....

....

....

....

....

....

....

....

....

....

Holy Spirit, You know where my heart is discouraged. Please sharpen my vision and my mouth, to see and taste God's goodness in His Word.

Humble Wrestling

Though the fig tree may not blossom, nor fruit be on the vines;
though the labor of the olive may fail, and the fields yield
no food; though the flock may be cut off from the fold,
and there be no herd in the stalls—yet I will rejoice in
the LORD, I will joy in the God of my salvation.
HABAKKUK 3:17–18 NKJV

. . . .

This verse taken alone out of Habakkuk makes the prophet sound like a believer who never wavers, even when all signs of prosperity vanish. But Habakkuk, like Job, spent nearly his whole book wrestling with God about the impending invasion of the Chaldeans, raised up to discipline Israel. Habakkuk argued, essentially, "Why let the wicked devour the righteous?" (Habakkuk 1:13).

But after asking his questions, rather than being indignant, Habakkuk waited earnestly for the Lord's correction (Habakkuk 2:1). And God told him more: the just shall live by faith (Habakkuk 2:4), and the true end of the "proud man" (Habakkuk 2:5–20). Habakkuk then responded to God in trustful, joyful praise (Habakkuk 3).

You can learn a lot from Habakkuk's and other faithful believers' "humble wrestling." God invites your questions, for they will help you trust Him more, which anchors your heart to dwell in joy in Him despite your outward circumstances (Philippians 4:11–13).

Prayer Prompt:

What are you wrestling with and questioning God about today? As you pray, accept that God is faithful and patient with us. Trust Him.

....

....

....

....

....

....

....

....

....

....

....

....

....

....

....

....

....

....

....

Father, thank You for Your patience with me. When I feel anger or disbelief, help me be honest with my questions and hurts and then humbly wait for Your answer.

We Know His Name

Who has ascended into heaven, or descended? Who has
gathered the wind in His fists? Who has bound the waters in a
garment? Who has established all the ends of the earth? What
is His name, and what is His Son's name, if you know?

PROVERBS 30:4 NKJV

. . . .

The only answer to Agur's beautifully vivid questions is *God*. But as we reflect on these queries today with Christ's birth in mind, we can give equally lovely answers using our knowledge of His names.

Who has descended? Emmanuel, God with Us, who came from heaven in a miraculous birth, born of a woman. Who bound the waters and held the wind? The Creator, who commanded the winds and the waves, "Peace, be still!" (Mark 4:39 NKJV). Who established the ends of the earth? Wisdom Himself, who was there when God laid the universe's foundations.

But He chose the name Son of Man. He, who was prophesied to come as a conqueror (and will rule with a rod of iron [Revelation 12:5]), first came in a humble state to save His people as the Lamb of God who takes away the sins of the world. What is His name? Jesus, which in Hebrew is *Yeshua*, meaning "to rescue, to deliver."

Prayer Prompt:

What are some of the questions you have for God? When you pray, acknowledge Him for who He is—Creator, Emmanuel, Redeemer.

....

....

....

....

....

....

....

....

....

....

....

....

....

....

Jesus, I praise Your holy name. Thank You for Your deliverance and Your closeness. Help me spread Your name far and wide so many others may know it and testify to Your saving work in their lives.

A House for Him

"Does anyone remember this house—this Temple—in its former splendor? How, in comparison, does it look to you now? It must seem like nothing at all! But now the LORD says: . . . Be strong, all you people still left in the land. And now get to work, for I am with you."
HAGGAI 2:3–4 NLT

. . . .

After the Israelites became so discouraged they stopped work on the temple in Jerusalem, Haggai urged them to continue the rebuilding project. Although the Lord first admonished them that they had been so focused on their own homes they had neglected His, He gave the people special encouragement: "My Spirit remains among you. . . . So do not be afraid" (Haggai 2:5 NLT).

Take this encouragement on as your own. As you remember King Jesus, born in a cattle stall, surrounded by animals, and greeted by the lowliest men in His culture, continue to work on the home you have for Him—your heart. Take courage and bolster your faith's foundations, inscribing scripture on your heart's walls, strengthening the pillars of grace and mercy. And don't be afraid: your transformation will be helped by the Spirit every step of the way (Colossians 1:9–10).

Prayer Prompt:

What work have you stopped because of discouragement? Take it to Jesus, asking for His Spirit to give you courage to finish the work.

....

....

....

....

....

....

....

....

....

....

....

....

....

....

....

....

*Jesus, thank You for coming to earth to save me
and for making Your dwelling within me. Keep
working in my heart, dear Savior; I want my
"home" for You to be pleasing and beautiful.*

Keeping On

"Do not despise these small beginnings, for the
LORD rejoices to see the work begin, to see
the plumb line in Zerubbabel's hand."
ZECHARIAH 4:10 NLT

. . . .

What adjectives come to mind when you think of God? Perhaps the words *great, marvelous, righteous, just, true,* and *holy* (see the saints' celebration song in Revelation 15:3–4 [NLT]). Or maybe the words *might* and *power* immediately flood your thoughts.

But, in Zechariah 4, we learn God's greatness, described by the words above, doesn't stop Him from delighting in small things. He rejoiced to see the Israelites' "small beginnings" as they recommenced work on the temple. Our loving Father delights in His children starting the work He gives, and He helps them persevere to the end, like those saints in Revelation who'd withstood tremendous persecution (Revelation 15:1–2).

Each of us has journeys we're either beginning, in the middle of, or ending. Let God's delight in "small beginnings" encourage you to persevere in His power—while doing justly, loving mercy, and walking in humility before Him (Micah 6:8). It's not up to you to complete the work—Revelation shows you that—but you're to "keep on keeping on."

And, sometimes, "keeping on" might just look like starting a "small beginning."

Prayer Prompt:

What small beginnings have you laid aside? When you pray, ask the Lord to give you the motivation to pick up those beginnings once again.

....

....

....

....

....

....

....

....

....

....

....

....

....

....

....

....

....

Lord God, You know what work I dread to begin (maybe New Year's resolutions) and what I need to pick up again. Bring Your "great and marvelous. . .works" (Revelation 15:3 NLT) to my mind so I'll trust You to help me finish what I begin.

DAY 361

Wisdom in Creation

"Four things on earth are small, yet they are extremely wise: Ants are creatures of little strength, yet they store up their food in the summer; hyraxes are creatures of little power, yet they make their home in the crags; locusts have no king, yet they advance together in ranks; a lizard can be caught with the hand, yet it is found in kings' palaces."
PROVERBS 30:24–28 NIV

. . . .

In today's proverb, we see how God equips creation for living and thriving, even down to its tiniest members. The ants are hardworking communicators, working together to gather supplies to feed the community in winter. Hyraxes, small rodents of the Middle East who live in rocky, shrubby areas, can eke out a living where many others can't. Banding together, locusts can devour a field, and despite its size, a lizard can make its way into the most unlikely places.

If God prepares the smallest of His creatures so they'll thrive in their habitats, how much more will He do so for you, His beloved child? Perhaps you wouldn't naturally put yourself in the same category as these small creatures, but the same loving Creator who cares for them will also provide for your living and thriving if you ask. As you should.

Prayer Prompt:

What are you worried about—provision, protection, peace? When you pray, acknowledge God's care for you and depend on Him in every situation.

....

....

....

....

....

....

....

....

....

....

....

....

....

....

....

Creator of all, help me be humble like these creatures, dependent on You for my needs and for the wisdom I require. Help me grow more in my talents and abilities and in my dependence on You.

Victory Awaits

"These will make war with the Lamb, and the Lamb will overcome them, for He is Lord of lords and King of kings; and those who are with Him are called, chosen, and faithful."
REVELATION 17:14 NKJV

· ·

Amid stark apocalyptic imagery, Revelation provides this comfort: no matter how long evil seems to prevail, Jesus will be victorious. And just as He will win at Armageddon, He can gain the victory over the things we struggle with in our lives.

But do we consistently bring our battles to Him? So often we look to other places for comfort and help instead of Christ—friends, favorite foods, vacations—all good and helpful things, but not sources of lasting peace. On a similar note, the prophet Zechariah warned the people that idols "comfort in vain," leaving the people wandering like sheep without a shepherd (Zechariah 10:2 NKJV). Because earthly comforts can only alleviate our problems temporarily, our focus needs to be on Christ, our true and everlasting good.

The Word promises that Christ will give you the victory over the sin that beats you down (1 Corinthians 15:57), that He works all things together for good for those who love Him (Romans 8:28). He, faithful and true, will lead you forward; you will hear His voice as a shepherd calls His sheep (Zechariah 10:6). You have His promise.

Prayer Prompt:

Where do you turn when the battle gets tough? Ask Jesus to remind you of His promises to take care of you and make you victorious.

....

....

....

....

....

....

....

....

....

....

....

....

....

....

....

....

....

Jesus, when I'm tempted to look elsewhere for comfort, please remind me and strengthen my heart with the promise of Your Word and Your victory.

Set Apart for Service

In that day "HOLINESS TO THE LORD" shall be engraved on the bells of the horses. The pots in the Lord's house shall be like the bowls before the altar.
ZECHARIAH 14:20 NKJV

This curious image comes at the end of the prophecies of Zechariah, tucked amid the description of God's future reign in Jerusalem, a time of peace when all the nations will come to worship Him there. These harness bells (engraved with the same phrase as on the golden plate on the high priest's turban, Exodus 28:36) and kitchen pots, ordinary, everyday objects, would be considered as holy as the objects used in serving in the temple! Where God dwells, *everything* could and would be used in worshipping Him.

Though the day Zechariah spoke of is still coming, you, as a child of God, are set apart now as "Holiness to the Lord." No matter your earthly vocations, you are a priest to God (1 Peter 2:9), a temple of His Spirit (1 Corinthians 3:16), and a vessel for His use (2 Corinthians 4:7–9). You can use every good gift you possess in His service.

Perhaps today you feel less than holy, worthy, or useful. . .but God can transform what is lowly to be of great use to Him, if only you are willing.

Prayer Prompt:

Are you feeling unworthy or useless today? Why? Ask God to mold you into a vessel that can be used by Him.

....

....

....

....

....

....

....

....

....

....

....

....

....

....

Dear Jesus, I want to be living and growing in holiness and in my worship. Change my perspective on what I consider ordinary occasions to be extraordinary opportunities to praise You.

Valuable Work in Progress

*A capable, intelligent, and virtuous woman—who is
he who can find her? She is far more precious than
jewels and her value is far above rubies or pearls.*

PROVERBS 31:10 AMPC

. . . .

The Proverbs 31 woman deservedly is the ideal: she is strong mentally, fiscally, physically, relationally, and spiritually. And she serves as an example for all women—married, unmarried, widowed, or divorced— as a force for good and for God's light in her community. Reading this chapter often gives us women a lot to reflect on—where we do well. . . and fall short.

But before you go wild setting New Year's resolutions, consider this: the Proverbs 31 woman, rather than a description of a literal person, can be considered a personification of all the wisdom from Proverbs. Rather than her ideal requiring you to be perfect in every way, she instead encourages you to develop her strengths through applying the scriptures to your life. For it's true: spending time with the author of wisdom with an open heart will change you to reflect Him more.

And, if you ever feel discouraged on this transformation journey, look back at how much you have grown in your faith already! You are God's valuable work in progress, designed to become stronger in faith and in wisdom so you can bless others.

Prayer Prompt:

Do you feel like a failure—for what reason? Ask Jesus to remind you of all He has accomplished in your life, then praise Him.

....

....

....

....

....

....

....

....

....

....

....

....

....

....

....

....

*Jesus, thank You for Your work! Give me strength
and discernment to apply Your Word to my life,
to become a strong woman of faith in Your kingdom.*

Healing in His Wings

*He who was seated on the throne said, "I am making
everything new!" Then he said, "Write this down,
for these words are trustworthy and true."*

REVELATION 21:5 NIV

You stand on the cusp of the New Year, Revelation closing with the beautiful hope of God making all things new. As you look toward a new calendar, new beginnings. . .perhaps you're excited, or maybe you sigh, dwelling on things that cannot be fixed by time's passage. Remember God's promise: He who will take away all tears and suffering says to you, "And let [her] who thirsts come. Whoever desires, let [her] take the water of life freely" (Revelation 22:17 NKJV). Whatever hope, wisdom, or provision you thirst for in the New Year—Christ can quench it, according to His will.

For the Word says, "But for you who revere my name, the sun of righteousness will rise with healing in its rays. And you will go out and frolic like well-fed calves" (Malachi 4:2 NIV). Trust Jesus to have nourishment, healing, and more waiting for you in this New Year. And in expectation of His goodness, leaning on Him alone, you can "rejoice in time to come" (Proverbs 31:25 NKJV).

Today, let this old year rest, and look forward to what your faithful and true one has for you.